What people have said about

Karna's Wheel

Karna's Wheel is compelling, multi-layered and beautifully written. Set in Scotland and India, it interweaves class and colonialism across the generations in a novel which is never less than highly entertaining.
Chris Given-Wilson, shortlisted for the Wolfson History Prize, 2017

This is top-class historical fiction with strongly realized characters and an emotional punch ... one of the most human and engrossing novels I've ever read ... human history at its finest – making us see the Raj not as a list of events but as a succession of relationships, decisions and human frailties ... I absolutely loved the evocative description and lyrical language in this novel and got swept up in the story so much that I didn't want to leave. I can't recommend this book highly enough – it's an intelligent, immersive and atmospheric read that draws you in and holds you tight until you've turned the final page.
On the Shelf Books; a bookblog for readers

Historical fiction at the cutti ng edge, a bravura performance of style and structure.
Gordon T Stewart, Professor Emeritus of History at Michigan State University.

Exquisitely writte n, quirky, remarkably well-paced and wonderfully readable, *Karna's Wheel* is touching, humorous, informative and pretty shocking. The research is faultless but never stands in the way of the telling of a good story. I hope this book gets to where it deserves to be – on the bestseller lists. Incredible work.
Robin Pilcher, novelist

A beautifully written historical novel that takes place in Scotland in 1999 and Calcutta, India from 1923- 46. What a story this is! So evocative, thrilling and quirky, I absolutely loved it. The history of the Raj and the jute trade, both in Scotland and India, make for fascinating reading. The secrets that come out of his research and writing were shocking and sad, but the ending was excellent, very satisfactory. I liked all the characters; Seamus in particular is appealing and got me chuckling quite a bit. A must read that deserves to be a big hit.
Hannelore Cheney, Reviewer at Sidney Memorial Library, New York

Karna's Wheel is ... such an immersive read ... The characters really bring this story alive ... Descriptions of the settings are so crisp and vivid, the language used evokes clear images of the periods, and no matter how vastly different Dundee and Calcutta are, they both felt so impressive, so detailed, so terrific. I have to say that after reading this, I really wanted to find out more about jute trading and the connections between Scotland and India. Don't you just love it when a book inspires you to start looking for knowledge?
Kate Noble, The Quiet Knitterer, book blog.

The writing was fluid, beautiful, but easy to read. The historical sections felt real and alive. I could so vividly picture everything described ... It is very fluid ... at its core, an extremely internal book ... very intriguing to read ... The story itself was terribly tragic but in some ways still oddly beautiful.
M.L.V Reviewer, Net Galley

Dazzling and inventive ... an enthralling journey into early twentieth century Calcutta and the dark corners of the Raj.
Andrew Duff, Author of *Sikkim; requiem for a Himalayan Kingdom*

A remarkable, multi-layered narrative that slowly unravels to reveal the truth behind life-changing secrets. Three stories intertwined (mythology, past and present time) aim to answer the most fundamental questions – who are we supposed to be and who can we become. A thoughtful reflection on colonialism and the importance of knowing where you are from. The rich, vivid descriptions – whether in contemporary St Andrews, early Twentieth century Dundee, colonial Calcutta or ancient India – and imaginative character depictions make this novel truly gripping. It ends with a poignant denouement that lingers with you. I can't recommend this book enough.
L.Ines, Goodreads

I think it [*Karna's Wheel*] is magnificent. The portrait of Stephen the elder is extremely touching, perhaps even potentially dangerous. What would happen if everyone started cutting off their armour? Seamus is hilarious ... leaped off the page.
Dr Simon Brodbeck, Cardiff University (Sanskrit)

Karna's Wheel is seriously good. Its combination of pacey page-turning story-telling, erudition and historical accuracy kept me engaged throughout. Bravo!
Tony Hastings, organizer of educational tours in India

Just the book to keep you entertained during the long, dark, cold nights ... *Karna's Wheel* is the literary equivalent of a Russian nesting doll; stories within stories that are revealed as the book moves forward, each one more decorative than the one before ... unique writing talent ... an almost lyrical style of narrative.
Emma Reekie, *The Dundee Courier*.

Karna's Wheel

Michael Tobert

Karna's Wheel

Published by Ormolu Publishing, Fife, Scotland.

ISBN: 9798324861797

Karna's Wheel was originally published (2018) in the USA and UK by Top Hat Books.

The rights of Michael Tobert as author have been asserted in accordance with the Copyright, Designs and Patents Act 1988.

Copyright © Michael Tobert 2018, 2024. All rights reserved.

The author's photo is by Caroline Trotter - www.carolinetrotter.co.uk

The cover of this new edition has been designed by the very talented Dan Forde - www.danforde.com

To Katerina, Miliana, Elenoa and Ralph

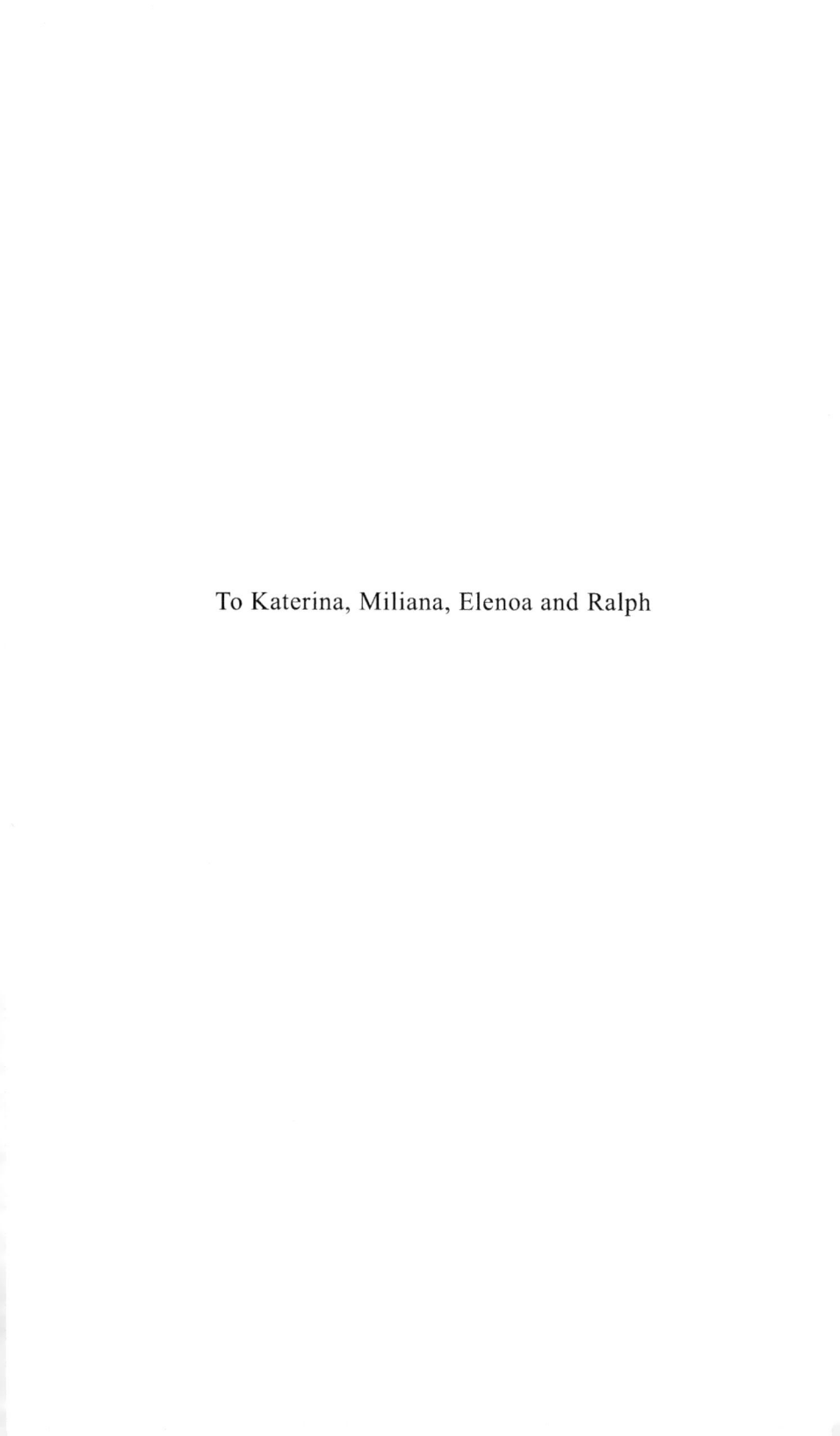

'Which one of us invented the other?'
Krishna to Vyāsa, author of the Mahabhárata.

1

A butterfly flapped its wings and I caught my toe on a cobblestone. Spinning left round the corner rather than straight on, and struggling for balance, I became aware of images: her nose pressed into the windowpane of that second-hand bookshop, her intense, almost child-like concentration, the shape of her legs between black ankle boots and short black coat. Just images, just mind photos, but also something more; some instinct deeper than desire which made me stand at Julia's side and follow her gaze through the bookshop window.

Aligning my sight with hers, I saw she was looking over the first row of books towards a worn copy of MacDonell's *Sanskrit-English Dictionary*. This was unexpected, not to say extraordinary, not only because she seemed to be studying the MacDonell, albeit at a distance, but that the bookseller should have put it in the window. Apart from me and our cadaverous (though most eminent) Professor Pilikian, no one in St Andrews had the least interest in the subject, certainly none of my students. I immediately realized that the bookseller, an otherwise astute individual, must have been moved by forces more powerful than he himself understood. I took this as a favourable portent.

A hazy image shimmered in the air in front of the MacDonell, the reflection of Julia and myself in the glass. We were standing apart, but not the distance of strangers, closer, in the same frame, as if some tenuous post-MacDonell connection now existed between us, a connection that reinforced a growing feeling within me that the universe, for once in its life, might be on my side.

'Excuse me,' I said, 'but are you interested in the Sanskrit dictionary?'

She turned towards me, her eyes fixed on mine, green and pale like spring leaves caught by frost. 'Me? That Sanskrit dictionary?' She pointed. I nodded. 'Erm, not really. I was looking in that general direction, it's true, and was vaguely aware of it, but I wouldn't say I was interested. In fact, I was thinking of something else altogether.'

'Oh...sorry to have disturbed you. I hope you don't mind. It's just that for a moment I thought I recognized the look.'

'The look?'

'The dead language look.'

'And what sort of look is that, exactly?'

'Open...reflective...far-sighted...broke.'

'Well, I'm certainly broke,' she said laughing. 'And, as it happens, I was thinking of something from an ancient language.'

'You were,' said I, much encouraged by the turn things had taken, 'what, if I may ask?'

'Something from ancient Icelandic, an old poem.'

'Really. I don't think I've ever heard ancient Icelandic. Could you recite a line or two?'

'*Gáttir allar, áðr gangi fram / um scoðaz scyli / um scygnaz scyli / þvíat óvíst er at vita, hvar óvinir / sitia á fleti fyrir.*' No preamble, her voice alive in melodious chant, her eyes almost closed. Then her lids lifted and I saw the dawn.

'That's lovely. What does it mean?'

'It means, "Before passing through a doorway, look carefully. There may be enemies on the other side."'

I laughed, both at the sentiment and at the way she seemed to suck the words before letting them go. 'You're not exactly Scottish, are you?' I said.

'No, not exactly.'

I waited.

'Born Provideniye. Left for the West. Now I am here.'

2

It seems so long ago—before my mother's funeral, before Detective Sergeant McCorquodale, before the first box was opened and my blood's secret came dripping out—that day when I first met Julia, when I ran back to my flat and looked up Provideniye, arctic cold, bedraggled and god-forsaken as it seemed to be.

And yet providence might never have had a chance, had not Séamus announced his discovery of a new pub on the outskirts of town. 'Rouse yourself, Stephen,' he exhorted. 'The stout they serve in there, it's good stuff alright, as fine as I ever drank.' Though I sincerely doubted there'd be the slightest discernible difference between this and most of the other stuff that had gone down the wee man's throat in the time I'd known him, I said I'd meet him there. So, I was walking out past St Salvator's and into the Big Quad with its old stone and its lecture theatres and there she was, Julia, her books under her arm, another girl with her and the pair of them all lit up. I've no idea what they were talking about but it was enough to have them both holding on to each other's arms and laughing with that infectious mixture of humour and goodwill which you hear in the laugh of young women and— improbable though it may sound—hyenas. Then they stopped suddenly, kissed on both cheeks, *goodbye goodbye,* and the other girl, glancing sharply at her watch, turned and left.

I moved closer casually, doing my best not to appear to sidle (hyena-like) but, rather, as if lost in my own thoughts. When I was almost upon her, I looked up and said, 'Oh. Hello. It's you.'

'It is,' she replied. Whether she had noticed my approach or not, I wasn't sure.

'You must be a student,' I suggested, 'you know, being here, in the Quad. With the students. Are you an undergraduate, a postgraduate or something else altogether?'

'I think I must be something else altogether,' she replied and a broad smile sent little wrinkle lines of pleasure wandering down her nose. 'I go to lectures which interest me.'

'And did this one?'

'The Songs of Odin are always interesting.'

'And always enemies on the other side of the door?'

'Sometimes. Not always.'

'Sometimes friends?'

'Sometimes.'

'That's a relief,' I said. 'Would you feel safe then in entering a coffee shop with me?'

'Relatively,' she replied laughing. I would have liked to link arms with her as we walked but thought better of it.

'Sanskrit?' she queried. 'Strange choice, isn't it? Why?'

A simple question but, as I would come to understand, the truth of intimate things is never simple. 'I can't say precisely but I was always drawn to it...family connections...my mother.'

'Your mother knows Sanskrit, does she?'

'That's the last thing she'd learn. Much too close to what she tries to forget.'

Julia looked at me as if noticing something she hadn't noticed before. 'Is she Scottish?'

'Half.'

'And her other half?'

'Indian.'

And then, because Julia widened her eyes expecting more—an appeal I couldn't resist—I added, 'She's spent her life bleaching out the dark stains on her genes.' My index finger made screw-turns into my temple.

Perhaps the indicators of insanity are universal because this signing seemed to mean something to her. Laughing, her eyes pointing skyward, she said, 'So your half-white mother is also half-mad?'

'Let's just say she has problems with reality.'

'Well, it's common enough. Not in Provideniye. When reality

is as harsh as it is there, you can't escape it. But, here, there are too many distractions, don't you think, too many ways of turning away from what's real.' She tapped her chest. 'You know, real on the inside, I mean.'

I said nothing. My mother and her distractions; that was a subject in itself, but not one I wanted to think about, not then, not with Julia.

'Where is your mother now?' she continued.

'She lives in Dundee...where I was born. Though I don't see her much now. Hardly ever really.' And then I added, I don't know why, the words I hoped were true. 'The fact is you and I have both escaped: you from Provideniye, me from Dundee.'

'Ah, the distant Dundee,' she said smiling.

'Escape is not a matter of mileage,' I replied, wondering as I spoke what precisely it was a matter of, and hoping she wouldn't ask.

'So you never go back?'

'I go back when I have to, that's all.'

'That's all?'

'More or less.'

She looked at me quietly, appraising me and, so I imagined, coming to her own conclusions. 'Mothers, eh,' she said, the brown-and-white straggles of her llama hair collar flicking the leather of my jacket as she rose to leave.

3

In a corner, a man with a moustache played the accordion. He stood up every so often and said *Sankeyoo*. I assumed he was Hungarian, like the owner, like the music, like the food; a foreigner making a living from what he knew best, clinging to his old familiar like any foreigner in a foreign place.

The restaurant was busy. Diners on the move brushed against each other, their apologetic hands on the arms of strangers. Crockery clacked. Conversation hung thick over the tables. I hoped Julia would like it.

I was sitting, waiting, just watching. I watched the owner and his son at their station by the kitchen door like two balding vultures, beaky and hunched, a lifetime and a half of carrying too many plates, also watching in case a crumb should fall. Which it did, the crumb, from a single table by the wall, a seeded roll to be precise, but was felt for and found by a man with loaf-thick glasses before the vultures could spread their wings. Gobbled down too. A hungry man in a restaurant. Or greedy. Or just the blind fear of things being taken away.

It was then, semi-vacant, disinterested, my eyes sweeping mindlessly over the heads of the diners, that I thought I saw her sitting in a dark corner with her back to me: my mother; the baggy blue cardigan, the leggings, the cigarette hanging out of her mouth, its smoke losing itself in the wisps of her lank piebald hair, white and black, striped, the product of age and inheritance and misuse. I shrank back.

Was it my mother? Could it be? Hardly likely since I'd seen her the day before and one visit normally kept us going for months. At least. She turned to stub out her cigarette. She raised her hand for the bill. No, not Kitty, some other woman, not like my mother at all, not from where I was sitting. I breathed out. Relief. God! I may even have laughed. Now she wouldn't come between me and

Julia, not today anyway.

Julia showed up soon after. She angled her cheek and waited for me to kiss her; which I did, first on one side, then the other, and then, because I thought it was the thing to do, on the first one again. She put the books she was carrying—a grammar, Hrafnkel's saga, and something else I couldn't make out—on the floor. Looking round, she said, 'An accordion in St Andrews, that's nice. Sorry I'm late, I asked the lecturer a question about Hrafnkel's mother.'

I cast about in the dim distant. 'I don't remember Hrafnkel having a mother.'

'Most people have mothers,' she replied, eyes wide, offering me the joke. 'Even half-good, half-bad heroes like Hrafnkel have mothers... So, how is yours?'

'I survived,' I replied.

'That's good.'

'It was just lunch. We got through it. My uncle, my father's brother, was there, thank Christ. We were both on our best behaviour.'

'You all talked about the weather?'

'More or less...' I hesitated, a flash of green, her *don't fob me off*, that look. 'Though there was something strange going on.'

'Strange? In what way?'

'With the phone.'

Julia waited.

'The first time, it rang for God knows how long, I mean ages, ring, ring, on and on. The second time it rang even longer, as if whoever was on the other end knew that someone was in.'

'So what did she do?'

'Nothing. She did nothing. You'd think from looking at her she hadn't heard it. And when it stopped, all she said was, "More custard, Stephen?"'

'And what did you say?'

'I said, "Yes please."'

Julia laughed. 'No. About the ringing phone?'

'What could I have said?'

'You could have said, "Mother, please answer the phone before it drives me crazy and I kill somebody."'

'You think that would have made any difference?'

'So, what are you telling me? That you all just sat there, little spoons in hand, eating custard. Wow, Stephen, impressive. So British.'

'If Kitty could only hear you,' I told her. 'God, she'd lap it up. So British! For her, that would be the highest compliment in the book.'

'She'd think *British* was a big compliment?' She paused trying to make sense of it and then said, 'Your mother...when will I meet her?'

'Soon,' I murmured, wondering how to get out of it.

Just then, a powerful, brown-skinned man with long black hair and a leather jacket barely managing to stretch across his shoulders got up from a table in a corner. I hadn't noticed him earlier, perhaps he'd been looking away, though once he moved I was sure he'd been there for a while. He made his way towards the door, but when he reached our table, he stopped. He pulled up a chair and sat down, leaning his elbows on its back. 'Smith?' he said. 'Stephen Smith?'

'Yes.'

He looked at me slowly, without blinking. His eyes seemed to weigh him down like time, or death. 'Tell your mother,' he sighed, the reluctant messenger, 'that we wish to avoid unpleasantness, if at all possible.' He paused. 'Of course, if we can't, we can't,' and here he seemed to gather into his unblinking eyes the inevitable cruelty of a world about which he knew too much. 'Just business, you understand,' he said, 'so, please, tell your mother to be a good girl.' He looked at Julia. 'Sorry to disturb. Enjoy your dinner.'

4

One day, in the early afternoon, Julia knocked at the door of my flat.

It was opened by Séamus, who was dressed in pointed shoes, a green jacket struggling to find its way around his barrel chest, and a yellow cap of the sort men used to wear to bed a hundred and fifty years earlier. Séamus, at four foot eleven inches tall—an inch or two shorter than Napoleon—was not a man to do things by halves.

The opening of the door was followed by a moment of silence which I put down to the fact that Julia was clocking Séamus for the first time. Then I heard her say, 'I have come to see Stephen Smith. Is he here?'

His reply came up rumbling and deep. 'Are you from the electricity?'

'Me? Electricity? No,' replied Julia.

'Environmental Health?'

'No.'

'Benefits?'

'Benefits? No.'

'Are you an evil spirit?'

There was a pause. 'Do I look like an evil spirit?'

'Well now, come to think of it, you do not.'

This was followed by more silence in which I imagined Séamus pinching his ear between his thumb and forefinger and staring at the girl as if in search of revelation. After a while, I heard him say, 'Are you here for potatoes, then?'

Nothing from Julia. At least, nothing I could make out.

'Well, is it a book? It must be that. What else can it be?'

'A book it is,' replied Julia. 'At last, that is the truth of it,' and something about the way she said it made me sit up: I could have sworn she was trying on an Irish accent. Was she taking the piss?

Or were the pair of them, in the two seconds they'd known each other, in on some private game of their own? It must have been that because the next thing I heard was the sound of Séamus's boot heels beating in pleasure on the stone landing outside the flat. No doubt he was also giving her one of his little winks, or tapping the side of his nose, or being Séamus, both at once. And she? Was she bending down to reward him with a kiss?

 I couldn't let that carry on. 'Who is it?' I called out.

 ''Tis a beautiful woman.'

 I appeared. 'Julia,' I said, summoning a note of surprise.

 Séamus bowed to Julia and kissed her hand. It's the kind of thing he does. Then he went on his way, an unwhistled whistle seeming to hang in the air behind him: and with Julia's eyes on him. I couldn't help noticing that.

 A fragment of an ancient Upanishad came to me and, thinking it might retrieve the situation, I let it out.

 '*A person of the size of a thumb*
Stands in the middle of yourself,
He is Lord of what has been and what is to be:
Don't shrink away!'

 Before she could respond, I kissed her, took her by the arm and said, 'You don't want to listen to everything Séamus tells you.'

 'But didn't you just tell me not to shrink away?'

 'Did I? I suppose I did. Well, yes, don't shrink away but don't take any notice either. Anyway, look,' I said, changing the subject, 'come in.'

 I rinsed a couple of glasses and filled them with wine. The afternoon sun streamed through the window and filled the space between us with particles of sun dust.

 'I hoped you might lend me a book,' she said.

 'Well, I have plenty of those,' I said pointing at the books piled up against the walls of my room. Which one?'

 'You choose. Something good.'

 'Good for what? Good for laughing or good for crying?'

She considered the alternatives. 'Today laughter, but tomorrow who knows? Don't forget where I come from.'

'Never,' I promised. We clinked our glasses. 'Here's to a thousand years of misery.'

Julia laughed. 'Only a thousand?'

'Julia...is that a common name in Provideniye?'

'Julia is my Western name. It's a small concession.'

'Do you make many concessions?'

'Me? What do you think?'

I leaned forward to inspect her. At close range, her eyes didn't seem—not in any nuance of reflection that I could detect—to be interested in concessions. Nor her eyebrows which lifted slightly with amused questions of their own; nor her upturned nose; nor her lips, soft, coral pink and apart, with their hint, no more, of a willingness to yield. She was so self-contained, so entire in herself, that I wondered then, and not for the first time, what she could possibly want from me.

'Not many concessions that I can see,' I said, slipping down onto the carpet. I put a cushion under my head.

Bending over, she drew the tips of her fingers through my hair and touched them to her nose. 'Coconut oil?'

'My mother hates it.'

Neither of us spoke for a while after that, and then I reached up for the back of her arm, pulling softly. I didn't know if she'd let me bring her to the floor. I didn't think she would. I wondered even if I should try. But she did. She laid her head on my chest.

'Tell me what you like about Sanskrit,' she murmured. 'Let me in on your secrets.'

'I like its stories, I suppose; very nuanced, very open to interpretation. That's what most of Sanskrit is; stories: the Ramáyana, the Mahabhárata, especially the Mahabhárata, the greatest epic of them all. But you like old stories too, don't you; *Before passing through a doorway, look carefully...remember?*'

'Yes, I like stories: old, new, any kind. Tell me one please,

Stephen, will you?'

'Okay,' I ventured, 'if you want me to,' and no sooner were the words out of my mouth than I found all my stories gone clean out of my head. I searched but found only fragments, phrases, nothing that came to me whole. So I went through the motions and hoped that one sentence would lead to another. 'Once upon a time, a girl, let's call her Julia, wearing only a simple...'

Julia sat up sharply. 'In Provideniye, the telling of stories is not a trivial matter.'

'Trivial? No, well...I was hoping that as I went along it might turn into something good.'

'No story with a beginning like that ever turned into something good, not here, and certainly not in Provideniye. There the storyteller always pauses before he starts. He gathers himself. He looks into his heart and digs for what lies within, because only by doing this can he hope to win the prize.'

'There are prizes for stories?' I asked.

'There are.'

'What sort of prizes? An extra mouthful of food?'

'Sometimes.'

'A seat closer to the fire?'

'Perhaps.'

'Are there other prizes?'

'Of course there are other prizes. What do you think? That Provideniye is like St Andrews? No, it is a desolate land, beautiful but desolate, where no one comes to visit, where there are no distractions, no televisions or fancy restaurants, only polar bears hunting outside our meagre cabins of wood and tin. It should not surprise you then, Stephen, that in such a place women find special ways to reward their menfolk through the endless shivering hours.'

'They have special ways of rewarding their menfolk?'

'They do. So, Stephen, tell me the story that comes from your heart and, who knows'—did I imagine it, her index finger tiptoeing up her tights, whispering its promises, playing with the hem of her short cotton skirt?—'maybe, if you are worthy, I will reveal the secrets of the women of Provideniye.'

I became aware, then, of the breath catching in my throat which, for the sake of the bigger prize, I did my best to ignore.

'Can the story be true or false, fact or fiction?'

'True, false, fact, fiction...anything at all.'

'Must it be my own, or could it have been told before?'

'Everything has been told before. But to win a prize in Provideniye, you must give birth to your story as if you are its first mother.'

'Okay,' I said. I gathered myself, I concentrated, I asked myself the question she wanted me to ask: what is the story that comes from my heart? And with the question came the answer: Karna. I laughed at the obviousness of it. Karna's story had been mine from the beginning. No story was better than his. 'Then I shall let India's most magnificent, yet most derided, hero speak for me. In his own words.'

'Mmm...sounds like good,' said Julia, poking fun at herself or at me, I couldn't be sure. Her head wriggled down, making itself comfortable just above my navel. 'I am not sleeping you know,' she said.

Anticipating prizes, or at least hopeful, I cleared my throat. *Acchh*. This was to buy time while I considered *voice*: epic or contemporary? There was a lot riding on it.

* * *

'I, Karna, have spoken to my mother for the first time. And for the last. I made her promise to suckle me bare-breasted on the battlefield after I am killed. That'll teach her.

'But all that comes later; the battlefield, the promises, hers and mine. First I have to be born.

'I have been accused of many things—I don't intend to lower

myself by repeating tittle-tattle—but no one has ever accused me of being ordinary. I was not ordinary even on the day I was born. Well, look at my father for a start. But that, again, is to get ahead. First up—if we're considering how I came to be—is Kuntī. She's in her father's house greeting an unexpected guest, a holy man: holy but filthy, stained loincloth, twigs sticking out of his hair, mud caked all over. Kuntī approaches him with a smile. She bows so low that her hair falls forward and causes the bell on the silver bracelet round her ankle to tinkle as if shaken by a breeze. When she straightens, she offers him a tasty sweetmeat.

'That's how it started.

'The holy man, unused to the attention of young women, doesn't know what to make of it or, perhaps, makes more of it than he should. He laughs. His fingers reach out. He presses the sweet thing to his mouth. Then he beckons Kuntī closer, puts his calloused lips to her ear and whispers into it a secret, a mantra: any God she wishes for, she has only to say the words and he will appear.

'My mother is curious. When alone, she thinks, *Any of the gods, all I have to do is ask*, and before she can help herself, Surya, God of the Sun, slips into her mind and the mantra from her tongue.

'The Sun God appears, as only the Sun God can, splendid, bathed in honey, irresistible. "O beautiful black-eyed maiden," he declares, "tell me your desires."

'Seeing Surya standing before her, Kuntī swoons. "Forgive me," she begs. "I was given this mantra and I only wanted to see if it worked. It was a whim, nothing but girlish meddling. I didn't wish to drag you all this way…"

'"No trouble," he says. "When I have a beautiful woman in my arms, I can forgive her anything."

'My mother is frightened. She is young. She knows nothing of men, let alone of gods. *In his arms? What can he mean?* She steps away, raising her hands to cover her breasts.

'"Beautiful girl," says Surya, his voice of molten gold, "I have travelled so far"—he points lazily at the heavens—"I must be... rewarded."

'Kuntī looks away, a blush of modesty (or is it desire?) on her cheeks. "No, no, it is not possible, it cannot be."

'"Ah, but it can, and so easily. Come." He takes her tenderly by the chin and turns her towards such sights of burning passion as only a god can put into a woman's mind and as only a woman can imagine. And when the show is over, when Surya's fingers touch lightly the cloth that covers her, she does not resist.

'...And I, Karṇa, am the result, conceived and delivered on that same day. Kuntī swelled and pushed me out, remaining nonetheless—so it was reported—a virgin throughout.

'I was unusual, even then. I did not mewl in amniotic stew like other babies. Not me. I emerged in armour, fully coated. Not only armour (cuirass, cuisse, cubitiere): also earrings, dazzling lights of amṛta. Amṛta, the deathless, impenetrable substance of the heavens. I was, in other words, invulnerable.

'Not a bad sort of baby for a mother to have, so you might have thought. Yet, on my first day, the Sun disappeared from my mother's life, and I from hers. I was kicked out by convention; a baby but no husband, what would people say? And love didn't enter into it.

'She put me in a small boat and floated me on the river, the earrings on my little ears flashing in the night.

'Do I remember the moment when I was cast out? Do I recall how I yearned for my mother's breast? Do I smell the faeces that clung to me when I was found? No. I remember nothing. I feel nothing. What I tell you now is what I have been told.

'I would have been in that boat until I starved had not a charioteer and his wife pulled me from the water and taken me to their mud hut where we lived the three of us, with their other sons. As for Kuntī, my mother whom I never knew, she married Pandu, the king, and lived in a palace. She provided the kingdom with heirs. They were the Pandavas, the sons of Pandu, though Pandu could not have sons of his own. They were, like me, God begotten, mantra born.

'Remember their names, these brothers of mine: Yudhiṣṭhira, the pure, the wise, sprung from Dharma himself; Bhīma, the mighty, who could hurl elephants across a battlefield, whose father Vayu the Wind fertilized Kuntī with his breath; and Arjuna of celestial accomplishment, sired by Indra, the thunderer. They haunted my dreams all of them, but especially Arjuna, whom I was born to kill.

'Kill or be killed. Him or me.'

* * *

I couldn't help myself. Every questioning part of my body—my forehead, eyebrows, cheeks, lips, hands—strained for an answer.

'How did I do?'

'You did okay,' she said.

'Okay? How okay? Good okay, or bad okay? Would my story win a prize in Provideniye?'

'Look,' she said, 'in Provideniye, you would have been kicked out of the hut by now, and, by morning, chewed to your bones by bears. But that is Provideniye. Since coming to the West, I have learned to accept less exacting standards. Let's just say'—and here she started to undo the waist button on my jeans—'that for an opening, and remember please that the stories of Provideniye continue for weeks, sometimes months, in one case three years (though that was an exception: the storyteller was fishing on an ice floc when it broke loose); for an opening it was not all bad... we'll have to see, of course, how it develops...' The zip was now on its way down.

'Does that mean,' I asked, raising myself off the floor to ease the passage of my trousers, 'that you might share with me one tiny secret from the women of the land of ice and snow?' Unconsciously, as I was speaking, I found the fingers of both my hands taking from their holes the buttons of her blouse.

'Secrets,' she replied casting my trousers aside, 'are difficult things. Not precise. Not always the same for the one who tells as for the one who receives. They make demands. They may cause you to ask yourself, "Am I worthy?"'

At which, as if to illustrate the point, she removed her bra, and watched me follow the lines of her magnificent form with my eyes.

While my field of vision was now filled completely by the sublime upward undulation of her breasts yet, at the same time, through some other means of perception, I was aware of her eyes gazing into mine. Without observing them in direct line of sight, or indeed at all, I could see in them the presence of questions, unspecific and unstated, waiting to be asked.

My fingers had by this time reached up to touch with their tips the points of her nipples, but there, perhaps because of her eyes upon me or because of other thoughts entering my mind, they remained, in intimate contact but somehow arrested. The sensations of her nipples received through the ends of my fingers, and of the soft lines of her breasts both real and processed in my imagination, together with my awareness of her hands now reaching across the small hairs of my stomach, were at variance with her fixed concentration on my face and, taken together with whatever else my mind chose to add to my imaginings, were enough to transfix me, to hold me motionless, to let me neither move on nor fall back.

I don't know how long I remained in that state of vibrant paralysis, but sometime after I shook from top to bottom, like a dog that's swallowed rat poison. The muscles in my chest and shoulders, as well as in my thighs, made sharp twitching movements: spasms they were really, one after the other, and entirely involuntary. I can't explain it, unless it was the result of suspension, of the natural flow being baulked: or of awe, of wonder, of moving too close to the sun.

I have no idea what she thought but, rolling me over onto her, and applying gentle pressure with her hands, she was able to soothe me until my juddering stopped. I lay with her for a while, gathering myself and, when I opened my eyes, was conscious of shafts of sunlight dappling her face. Her lips were parted and the sun, entering between them, flashed, revealing what appeared to me in that moment as a suddenly illumined cave from which radiated a warmth I had never felt before and an invitation whose glow I could not resist.

5

Stephen Ahimsa McLeod Smith, D.Phil. Oxon (to give me my full title). McLeod was my grandfather who was also called Stephen, and Ahimsa was my mother's aberrant acknowledgement of where she came from: a momentary lapse which I had to cart around with me all those years I was growing up. A-hiṁsā: non-hurting or injuring, much advocated by Gandhi. When they found out about that at school, they were surprisingly generous. 'Ahimsa?' they said, making sure they'd got it right, and then beat me to a pulp no more than two or three times.

Smith was my father, and it's his suit I'm climbing into. I don't mind wearing it, in memory of. He'd barely married my mother when he died. Natural causes: he didn't commit suicide or anything like that, as far as I know. The suit's okay, a little worn but it fits. I thought it was the only thing I'd inherit and then I discovered my grandfather had left these old wooden boxes with their strange drawings on the outside and who knows what within. Typical of my mother not to tell me about them: just another in her long line of secrets; big secrets, small secrets, who knows what secrets. When I was young, I used to ask her the obvious questions about her father, about her mother, about India, but I soon learned that, where I lived, mum was the word. Always and forever.

My uncle brought the boxes round yesterday. 'Pleased to get rid of them,' he said. 'Makes a bit of space in the attic.' I asked him what they were and he just shrugged and said, 'Your grandfather's life apparently. Courtesy of Angus. "You can give them to him when I'm dead. Dead. Not before." Those were Kitty's instructions. Too close to the bone, I suppose, you know Kitty.'

I put on black socks and shoes. A quick buff of the leather, a last fiddle with the tie, and that's me. Ready for the off. Ready to pay my last respects. I decide, while I'm waiting, to conjure a fond memory, something to focus a little mourning on. My mind doesn't focus, not on her anyway: on everything else but, and most particularly on what I have to look forward to today; the arrival of the car, the miasma of solemnity, the marsh gas of affected grief, mine as well as theirs, the whole bogus processional. And while all this is going round, I suddenly see myself playing in the closey again, running up and down the stone stairs, ducking under the lines of washing on the green at the back. Then I'm in her flat, our flat as it once was; the drab old carpet with its clusters of faded cherries; that smell of cleaning fluid, her housework binge of the morning after, her obsessive, ritualistic vacuuming which removed all traces, everything that got in its way, whatever its right to exist; the lead piping, the candlestick, regiments of horsemen; they were all sucked up past her dead-to-the-world eyes into that great mother sow of a hoover bag from which there was no escape.

The doorbell rings. The car is waiting. My uncle nods and says, 'Come along.' He makes a show of helping me in and sits looking at me, as if suggesting, by feats of self-delusion I can hardly imagine, that in his ripe, ruddy face I might find comfort. My aunt, in black, with a veil hanging down from her hat, damps her cheeks with a handkerchief.

The car pulls away. I stretch my hand absent-mindedly across my chest and remember a note I almost left for Julia. I take it out of my jacket pocket.

The car hiccups as it passes over cobbles. The tyres hum.

'What's that you've got there?' asks my uncle.

'A note.'

'Oh. Condolences, I suppose. People are kind at a time like this.'

'Mmm.' I wonder if she knows. Probably not...and who would tell her? I wanted to tell her myself. I almost did, it was on the tip of my tongue: 'Julia, my mother's dead, come with me to the funeral.' I couldn't get the words out. I tried, but they wouldn't come. Old habits. The words hung and the moment passed. Old habits rooted in old fears: that my mother would cost me one way or another, that I'd be tainted by association, that I'd have to look in Julia's eyes and imagine what she saw.

We stare in silence out of the windows as the car crawls along. Ten miles per hour in the town. People stand and watch, their interests personal, peripheral: 'Who…? Anyone I…? Is that…?' At the zebra crossing on South Street, a drunk with a half-empty bottle weaves across in front of us.

'That's claret, see that,' says my uncle turning round, 'drunk on claret at ten thirty. One of your students?'

I peer out as the man disappears into a crowd. 'I never see them from the back.'

We turn right. Bell Street. A car stops to let us go ahead. Then Greyfriars Gardens, left into North Street and, picking up speed, on and out of town. Leafless trees, winter sun. 'It's a beautiful day,' I announce, loosening my arm by flicking it downwards. My aunt sniffs. Under her veil, a handkerchief inches up and dabs the end of her nose.

'Never pleasant, these journeys,' remarks my uncle. 'How are you feeling? Holding up?'

I provide reassurance in the form of a restrained smile. An object, oblong and yielding, shifts in my trouser pocket as the car bounces over a bump in the road.

We reach the Tay Bridge. Flat water below. Do the carriages of the dead pay the toll like everybody else? And what about the mourners? How would they know, who was a mourner and who wasn't? Am I?

The driver winds down a window. Bells. The hollow sound of a half-remembered delusion tolling for itself. The car slows, a phone rings. A workman in blue overalls reaches into his pocket, puts it to his ear and says, 'No me, eh nivir, it wisna…' to which my mother from the coffin in front replies, 'It was you, wasn't it, Stephen?' She digs into her purse for a coin and hands it to me. 'Here, you pay,' she says in that voice of hers which could almost have been Scottish but for the undertow of something not quite right, something made up. Pride in there somewhere. Endeavour, determination...fear. The man in the restaurant holds out his hand, takes the money. From the north. Pathan. Second generation. The window closes.

Traffic lights. The Nethergate. Debenhams. A shopping centre on the site of old slums. Up the Lochee Road, a modern third-rate hotel, tall concrete crumbling multis, old stone tenements like the one we lived in, second-hand car yards, and Cox's stack, the big chimney, a million and one polychrome bricks, a monument now as it was then and silent as it has been for fifty years. We pass a newsagent, windows boarded, its door open. An Asian man in a turban watches with the same curiosity as those on the other side of the river. The car stops.

My uncle steps down and holds out a hand for his wife. He shepherds us forward. We edge past a huge limp-eared hound, whimpering and fawning under its chain.

'See that. Beaten. You can always tell. Disgraceful,' says my uncle. 'I can't abide cruelty to animals myself. Good dog.'

The crematorium is single-storey and concrete, mock medieval shields on the whitewashed wall, empty except for a handful of people sitting separately to the side and the back. 'The usual scroungers,' whispers my uncle confidentially as he removes from the fold-away wooden chairs the white sheets marked *reserved*.

The coffin is wheeled in to the accompaniment of an organ making a determined attempt at a raga. How my mother would have hated it: reminding her of where she came from even when she was dead. My mother, the chee-chee, half British and the other half air-brushed out. And me? I'm drawn to that other half, to the cradle. In a previous life, who knows?

My uncle steps forward, red-faced, dewlapped, serious.

'Thank you all for coming.' He regards the empty chairs with no indication of irony. After a short interval, his lips resume. 'Just a few words, Kitty was never one for sermonizing...'

It's morning, we are walking together, somewhere, anywhere,

not Dundee, she and I with him, he whose splendour was like the newly risen sun, *bālārka-samatejasam*, and in me is his frustration, his desperate sword-swinging need to cut himself free.

'...always a sad occasion, particularly when...'

There are trees. I am young, six, seven, ten. Was she how I found out about him? Seems unlikely. Probably added in later, one memory layered onto another.

'...she had a difficult life, with all its ups and downs, but what life doesn't have them? Perhaps Kitty had more than her share, who can say, but she was a brave woman, a good wife, a good mother to Stephen, and a friend to all of us.' My uncle searches the room for confirmation. 'And such a sudden end, so unexpected...into the furnace, burn everything, leave no trace behind, that's what she would have wanted.' I notice his eyes on me. Then he sits down.

The bearers at the back come forward and roll the coffin towards an opening in the wall. The organ starts up. My mother disappears behind curtains where the incinerator waits. A man in a raincoat crosses himself. I suppose I'll be sent the ashes. By post? And whose will they be anyway? Last week's business will have left its own residue. A dozen strangers in a jar marked 'Mother'.

Outside, the hound has turned nasty, growling and slavering. My aunt holds tight to my arm. A sort of instinct leads my free hand into my trouser pocket where I find something squashed and wrapped (a honey-coated breakfast bar). I lob it towards the beast and observe his great eyes following its flight, his back legs positioning themselves for the catch, his tongue lolling to the side, his cavernous mouth agape. I ferry my aunt past. She turns to watch the bar go down, then pats my wrist. The wrapper has disappeared with the rest of it.

At the hotel, it is sherry, an appropriate send-off: *a small glass of sherry*, her favourite euphemism. And also little things to eat. I fill a plate with prawn vol-au-vents, asparagus tips and some sort of mushroom spread on small squares of brown bread. Hardly have I got the first half-dozen mouthfuls down, than the man in the raincoat comes up to me and shakes my hand. 'McIntosh,' he announces. 'I knew your mother. A startling, splendid woman. A great loss, I just wanted to say.'

'Thank you,' I reply.

6

I am at the window. The boxes of my grandfather, passed on, post-mortem, by my uncle, are on the floor behind me. I gaze out at the rain. An image, blurred by water on the glass, of a dark man—darker than I normally think of myself—gazes back, hands in pockets. And beyond, in the lane, a woman with an umbrella stuck against her face like a wet cloth, pushes on into the wind as best she can.

My mother told me almost nothing other than that my grandfather, Stephen McLeod, was a Scotsman who lived in Calcutta, the city where she was born. Once, in an unguarded moment, she revealed that he was sometimes called Doig. 'Why Doig?' She didn't know. 'Why Calcutta?' She wasn't sure. 'What was Calcutta like?' No reply. Dead eyes. Leave me alone.

What was I to do then but make my grandfather up as I hoped he might be? Bookish, gentle eyes, a pipe, someone to visit my half-sleeping dreams when I was alone, or at night, or after my mother had disappeared into that other world of hers. And sometimes, I let him bring his wife with him, my grandmother. She was an Indian princess as well as a ravishing beauty, black-haired, black-bodied, black as night.

My grandfather flickered like a chimera in my world of make-believe, but in the fire behind the flames lurked my mother. She was his daughter, so her shadow was over him however much I might wish it otherwise. And I was her son; him, her, me: a midden of an inheritance into which, even now, I wasn't sure how far I wanted to dig.

A loose shutter bangs. The rain in strips stretched by wind strikes the old stone of which this town is built. It hits like spittle and slips reluctantly downwards, clinging on as best it can, as if preferring the struggle to a soft slide and a flat pavement. Water drums harder against the windowpane, its rhythms more insistent.

Perhaps the wind has changed direction. The reflection of the dark man who stared back at me is broken up, pierced by a thousand arrow points, obscured by refraction.

I turn towards my grandfather's boxes, which are all made of wood and all except one decorated with leaves, the tendrils of plants, the faces of animals peering out, and of birds, machines, blood and entrails, fantastic castles underground with turrets as breathing holes, the empty casings of bodies: fluid shapes describable or not, merging into each other like hallucinations. They form a dense canopy along the four sides and on the lid, although here each has a small number in the top right corner, neatly drawn in black ink and followed by a dot. As if an archivist or librarian has been at work.

The first box is clamped around its corners with a dark metal. The lid is hinged with four screws countersunk. The space is lined with zinc, its contents neatly folded and packed.

I remove drawings, papers, notebooks, letters and newspaper cuttings, placing them on the floor in the shape of a fan, with myself kneeling at the point where all lines diverge. I am on the edge of a shimmering lake, and in that mirror, in that instant, I see my own reflection. I will shortly see the warts on his nose. All will be revealed. Kill or cure.

I call out in a voice I hardly recognize. 'Julia, come here, I have a grandfather.'

She doesn't come. She calls back, 'Good. Congratulations. But not a mother.'

'But the funeral would have meant nothing to you,' I reply. 'You didn't know her.'

'I know you.'

'Which means you're entitled to my history?'

'I am not talking about your history, Stephen.'

7

My grandfather looks down from the heights of Dundee Law. In one hand he holds a stub of soft pencil, in the other a slice of dusty bread. Below him, the shimmering Tay, shafts of evening sunlight and, hidden in a corner, S. McLeod, the signature of the artist as a young man.

I also am sitting, cross-legged, straight-backed. I breathe as easily as I can through a nostril that is blocked on the left side high up. I allow my lids to rest. I observe the writing on my inner wall, I watch the words as they form and disappear. My mind empties...empties, that is, apart from a voice behind my right ear, and a thought that speeds through like a swallow in pursuit of a flying insect...a March fly perhaps, a sawfly, a ladybird, a mosquito. Not that you see many mosquitoes round here. I shake my head. Once more, I am watching. I am aware. A car is revving its engine. Far away, a child blurts out its tears and a wood pigeon sings in a tree, *coo-cooo cooo*. My mind is thoughtless...except, fuck it, leaves are blowing across, they're fluttering like whispers and they feel like chaff on the impenetrable edge of what I want and don't want to know. I draw breath and begin again. I follow the movement of my ribcage and am riven by an awareness of things in flux, a sort of sadness. Try as I do to hold it back, this sadness spreads like ink through blotting paper and forces me to my feet.

But there it is: my grandfather's hand sticking out of his unmarked grave, his leavings like half-rotted fingers beckoning me from where she left him to fester: the discarded dead. Too late now to close the lid and pretend. I will fashion his story from what he's left me. My inheritance. Why shouldn't I? He deserves a life. Innocent until proven otherwise.

Well then—*tap tap tap tap tap*—the river Tay is stretched out before him, Perth upriver to the west, the pillowy hills of Fife in the foreground, the open sea at his elbow. My grandfather is a skinny youth of fifteen (thereabouts, that's how he's drawn himself), with a ragged sweater and frayed grey trousers rolled up at the bottoms. A pair of too-large hobnail boots have toppled over beside him. He is bent over a sheet of paper. Down below, within the lead-shaded walls of Dundee harbour, a ship is docking. In the foreground, little stick men (with smudges for heads) are unloading. The little men have hooks where they should have hands. The hooks are grabbing bales of golden straw, and out of one peer the eyes and twitching whiskers of a mouse. Its hair is standing on end, terror is cut into its face, and into the faces of other mice knocking each other across the harbour stones in their blind panic, dropping dead, jumping to a quick end in the sea, or finding a sanctuary of sorts in the calf length boot of a fat woman with an enormous hat, who screams.

Bales of jute, that was the cargo—as any Dundee schoolboy will tell you. It's what made Dundee the place it was. Baleful bales, thrashed, wound, woven and dragged like debt into the hovels of the labouring poor to be sewn into bags—because Dundee was once the epicentre of jute, once Juteopolis, the beating heart of the humble gunny, the world's universal wrapper of grain, wool, ores, nitrates, salt, everything from chickens to chicken feed. It was once big business, jute: big money, big profits, the only show in town.

I see my grandfather put down his pencil, scratch his armpit through a hole in his sweater, and bite off a mouthful of dusty bread. The dust doesn't bother him, even though it will make him cough, like pepper. *Ecchh.* He wipes a finger under his nose, flicks it and chews slowly. Bread and dust are swallowed without a second thought. Why? Because Dundee is a city of dust—dust is in the Dens Road, the Hilltown, the Overgate, in the smoke of a hundred and twenty-one factory chimneys, on cobblestones, slate pavements, in the lungs of every tenement and household of my grandfather's winded town, and on the daily bread. Dust is layered on the heads of pints of beer, heard in the wheezing of babies and old men squeezed like sardines in their cots, and gathered up in clouds. When the clouds burst in Juteopolis, it rains dust.

Tap tap tap tap tap.

Up on Dundee Law, my grandfather's mother sits behind him, watching as he concentrates, smiling as he bites his bottom lip. Something about the way he hunches his back as he draws makes her think to herself, 'Aye son, the fehster yi're oot o this shit hole thi beh'ir, but whar ti eh, whar ti?' She looks out to sea and imagines other worlds. It is the time of the Great War. Enemy submarines are at sea. On land, in France, the troops are digging in, miles upon miles of trenches, millions upon millions of sandbags, made of jute, made in Dundee. The day is drawing to a close.

'See this, son,' my great-grandmother calls out and reaches into the loose folds of her dress as a magician might delve into his hat. Her audience of one has looked up and is now held by the promise of something so magical that no one could possibly guess it. With a flourish, she produces a round wrapped object. 'Yi ken whut eh hay fir yer tea?' she says, folding back the cloth with great care. She reveals an egg. She raises it up. 'Jennie gie it me. Yi ken Jennie? Shis thi nikst frame ti me. Ir man's fay Fife. Eh bet yi kid fair gay an egg, eh son.' A fierce pride camps above her eyes. Pleasure in her son's pleasure laughs on her lips.

'Ull keep haud o this,' she says as he reaches for it, 'wi dinna wanna gay an drap it.'

A low sun stretches out across the creased waters of the Tay. The harbour still bustles and a forest of chimneys, Dundee's round-the-clock exhaust pipes, belch collectively. Nearer home, women are gathering.

'Wi'll gay'n see whut thi wee skunnir his ti say fir hiself,' she says. 'A meenit, nay mair.'

Maggie and Stephen pack up his sketch and move closer. They arrive at the fringes of a crowd outside the Logie Works, Dundee's aptly named Coffin Mill. The crowd is listening and also heckling. It is a political gathering, addressed by Dundee's Member of Parliament, a Liberal, the about-to-be-sacked First Lord of the Admiralty, twenty-five years before his pomp.

'Dundee sandbags,' growls the not-yet-so-famous MP, 'the buttress of the nation, like a cushion,' he says smiling a fat smile, 'like a punch bag that soaks up the best the Hun can throw at us. One million sandbags a day. Some number, you should be proud, you should be...'

'Eh dinna ken whut wi shid be'—heckling from somewhere in the crowd—'but eh day ken whut wi is, mister hey an meyty. Whut wi is, is stairvin. D'yi ken oor wages, yi and yir pals? D'yi ken it's is wiyfees that days thi wairk, while oor bairns stairve. Thirs nay wummin here whut doesna ken o a bairn, oor ain mair'n likely, wha's deed afore ee's groon inti breeks.'

The not-yet-so-famous MP enjoys the cut and thrust.

'Times, madam, are indeed hard. But what can be done? Do you want your wages added to the price of those very sandbags that keep your men safe? I think not. Your Indian brothers toiling in tiny plots in hot, humid, steamy Mymensingh, Dhaka, Faridpur and Tippera do not charge more because the Empire is threatened. The mills on the banks of the far-off Hooghly, the Samnughar, Titaghur, Naihati, the Hastings mill at Serampore, the Irvine jute factory, the Wellington and Champdany mills do not charge more. If Calcutta holds its hand in time of war, should not Dundee do the same? Yet I know that it will, and with good spirit. Your men, the men of the Black Watch, will fight the better in the knowledge that it is behind the sandbags of their own women that they shelter.'

The incipient bulldog shakes his jowls and looks sternly at the crowd.

'Aye, Mr Churchill, it's aw fine fir yi ti blether aboot whut oor men shid day, and whut we shid day, but yi're no oot thair, and yi're no heer. Yi dinna ken, di yi? The wummin o Dundee hay worked the mills and stairved fir it lang afore this war. An it'll nay be different when it's all by. Yi spend yer time doon in London, kid yi nay ha a word o twa wi yir pal, Mister Asquith?'

'May I remind you my good woman, that there is a war on. The Prime Minister does not have time to devote himself to the particular case of Dundee, much though I am sure he would like to.'

Mr Churchill smiles and lets slip a remark to the aide standing by his elbow. The remark is spoken softly, not more than a whisper, but a breath of wind wafts it into the crowd. There is a stirring like a hive of bees prodded with a stick. The women think they have heard. Perhaps they have. It wouldn't be the first time Churchill has declared himself on that subject, the subject of women. Churchill holds his ground. A mistake, yes, injudicious yes, but not fatal. His feet move apart. He takes his stance.

'Krehs hiself Winston Churchill,' shouts one from the back. 'WC mair leek. Weel, it's time, long awa, thit yon WC lost hees seat. A cludgee wi nay seat, thit's whut wi wan.'

'Ay, a duffie wi naywhar ti drap hees behoochie.' Laughter swells among the crowd.

'Reenge em oot,' shouts one.

'Flush em doon,' shouts another.

Mr Churchill smiles. It is the smile of one who eats three meals a day. He waits for the clamour to subside. 'I will of course bow to the wishes of my constituency. I have been sent to Westminster by them. I will be removed by them, if that is their desire. But not, ladies, by you. The representatives of the people of this country have not yet seen fit to award the vote to women. The time for this has not yet come, if indeed it ever will. The vote has to be earned...'

There is uproar in the crowd. Working women, rent payers, the wives of men who do not work or pay rent, make it clear to him who precisely has earned what.

'My good ladies, please,' says Churchill holding up the same hands that will one day give the victory salute, 'the right course, if I may offer this advice, and I do so humbly, is for women to be women first and suffragists second...'

Silence.

My great-grandmother's hand touches the contents of her pocket and her fingers close on an object that is hard. Without knowing, she unwraps it. It comes out of her dress and in that same movement finds itself in the air, heading with slow-motion predictability, a perfect parabola, for the egg-like face of Humpty Dumpty, MP. It lands precisely, dead centre, between the left and right eye of Mr Churchill. It sticks as if waiting for direction. The shell separates and falls, leaving behind a glaucous yellow trail that drips, divides left and right on the bridge of that pugnacious nose and alights on the puffy delta of cheeks. Churchill glares at his assailants. He is not afraid. He is not discomposed. He dabs his face with a silk polka-dot handkerchief, spits out such remarks as are consistent with dignity and injured wit (they go unnoticed) and slips away. There is nothing for Mr Churchill in Dundee now that darkness has set in.

The crowd breaks up. It is happy, triumphant. Some of the mill girls, leaving, nod at my great-grandmother, some cheer, some put hands on her arm (the throwing arm) and rub it gently, some wipe their eyes. The small victories of the impotent are always sentimental.

8

The grandfather of my imagination disappears like old film scorched by the flame of dates and details. There's no arguing against the holes in a fifteen-year-old's ragged sweater, his boots, his chiselled pencil, the egg on Churchill's nose; no pleading for the life of a figment, even if he will be missed. Now, the first box gapes. Its four screws stare wide-eyed, its drawings, papers, notebooks, letters and press-cuttings hold their positions, fanned out on the floor, yielding, impatient to yield more. How it sucks me in; how it spits me out.

I hear Julia. The sound of a bag being thrown over her shoulder, the turn of the lock, the banging shut. She's teaching this morning. Her footsteps clack for a moment on the concrete outside. They descend the stairs and are gone. I imagine her walking. A beret perched on top. Her collar turned up. Bright lipstick.

No 'Goodbye'.

I kneel forward, my elbows bearing my weight, and become conscious of a dull ache at the base of my spine. I come up on my hands. I breathe, I relax. After a while the ache eases and I make an attempt to go back to the papers. Immediately dots, little points of light, buzz in my head. I put my legs on a chair, lie back and try to watch with detachment the waves in my mind.

Séamus is cleaning his teeth. Water in the sink, gargle, spit, wipe. He opens the bathroom door, catching it against his toe twice, and making it rattle like distant thunder, *drrrm, drrrm.* Muttering to himself, he comes in. He doesn't knock or anything. He says, 'So, I hear you're writing his history now.' I open my eyes and look up. Perhaps it's the angle, but for a moment I think I'm staring at a squat, heavy-legged figurine, a hearth god from a diminutive past with a towel round his waist. I manage a cursory acknowledgement.

'Hmm,' he murmurs, and the next thing I know he's down on

the carpet on his hands and knees. He picks up a newspaper cutting and starts to read. He drops it to pick up another, holding it close to his face and screwing up his eyes. Then he's done with that and onto something else. Doesn't say a word.

I swing my legs over and get myself onto the chair. I watch him scrambling over my inheritance, seeing what he can make of it. And from it to me, I don't doubt, in one short leap. With my inner eye, I also watch my emotions. The secret is not to get attached, not to identify; to let the snags of unease rumble and tug without interference; to let it all come, to let it all go. It comes, it multiplies, it takes me over. I begin to sweat.

'Feck it,' Séamus says finally, 'but that is sad, all that work for not even the price of a square meal and that only once in a blue moon, what sort of life is it I ask you, and then the way she goes, his poor mother, just taken for no good reason. That is no life at all if you ask me. It is a poor downtrodden lot of relatives that you have behind you Stephen, so it is.'

Séamus, born in the bog himself as I've always understood, glows with what might be taken for sympathy. This doesn't last long. He pauses. Suddenly, he wraps his chunky arms around his chest as if for the first time aware that his upper half is completely naked apart from two clumps of red hair sprouting from his nipples. Attempting a smile of studied neutrality, he asks, 'And how do you think you'll get all this down? I mean in what form will you?'

'I don't follow,' I reply.

'Well, as a factual narrative of the sort you might find in one of your textbooks, or as fiction and, if so, in your own sweet voice or in his, or are you going to do it as notes to yourself to be read in your old age when you've no more than a threadbare blanket over your shoulders and not a tooth left in your head?'

'I don't know. I haven't thought about it.'

'Well, perhaps you should.'

'Should I?'

'I think so, and perhaps I might also suggest this to you now Stephen; that we work on it together. From the little I've seen, it could be commercial.'

'Commercial?'

'Yes, commercial you eejit, you know, money, that old sweet thing neither of us has any of.'

I should mention here that Séamus sees himself as a writer. He's about as much a writer as I am. Okay, he's had one script accepted, a half-hour film for children's TV called the *Ant and the Beetle*, or the *Locust and the Swallow*, or the *Aardvark and the Zygote*; I can never remember. He's told me a million times but it doesn't stick. I may have blotted it out.

'So, you think we could make money from it?' I say, to humour him.

'I don't see why the blazes not. There's all those sad things in Dundee and then, by the look of it, for reasons I don't fully comprehend as yet, off he goes to Calcutta, which place will, in all probability, be sadder still. I'd have to see the other boxes of course, what takes place precisely but, yes, I can sniff the folding stuff all right: a great tragedy, love, betrayal—bound to be both of those—and death to be sure; what else do you need, and it all leads up to the great inspiring conclusion, which is you boyo, the heir, the star, the one and only Stephen Ahimsa McLeod Smith.'

'Ha, ha,' I say.

'No, look at it this way, Stephen, to put all the aforementioned together into a story with some reasonable prospects of the sort I've half a chance of showing to the woman who helped me with the TV people the last time isn't going to be easy, not at all, the precise opposite in fact.'

'You might be right.'

'I am, Stephen, I am, and that's why, though you've no awareness of your great good fortune at all, the hand of fate is even now reaching down and touching your cheek—which the sight of a razor wouldn't do any harm to by the way. No, the hand of fate itself is offering your undeserving self the key that will unlock all doors.'

'The key that will unlock all doors?'

'Me, Stephen. I'd like to help you put this story together.'

His face is suddenly purposeful, his eyes quiet, his ledge-shaped eyebrows no longer entirely comic. He wants this. My ache returns. I think of something, anything, to put him off.

'But how can you and I work together?' I ask. 'I mean, won't the whole thing end up as unreadable if we have two different writing styles? And what about trust? The reader, if there ever is a reader, will just be starting to feel that the author knows what he's talking about, when he'll become conscious of a second voice behind the first, and wonder if this is the voice of the author he trusts or if it's the other one. Or maybe he likes the second one more than the first, but can't believe it because he hasn't heard it long enough for confidence to have built up. Or has he been hearing it all the time but been thinking it was the first voice, when in fact it wasn't? When you look at it like this, Séamus, it's a minefield, you have to agree. And besides,' (here comes the clincher) 'I don't want my grandfather turning into some lost soul of an Irishman. When I see him on the page, I don't want—best to be frank, Séamus—to think of you.'

Séamus pauses, his fingers clutching a lock of hair in a studied simulacrum of thought. 'No,' he replies finally, 'frank is good, frank is what we need. I'm glad you've levelled with me. Don't you concern yourself, boyo. I'll model my writing on your own fine words. That'll kill both those old birds with the same stone. Your grandfather will be as you would have made him, God help the poor bastard.'

Not knowing immediately how to rebut this, I gather up his remarks and rephrase them as a sturdy ultimatum. 'That would have to be the condition: that you make me, and of course any strangers who happen to stumble upon the text, feel that I've written it all myself. Otherwise, quite apart from the fact that the whole concoction will fall apart, I'll think you're stealing him from me. It's a funny thing to say, I know Séamus, but I believe it's the truth. He's my grandfather, he left me the boxes, I don't want to feel I've handed him over to a stranger.'

'Don't you go troubling yourself now,' he says. 'I am a writer who finds money hard to come by, which means that I will willingly accept even the contortion of my own immaculately conceived prose. I'll write as if I was you. You won't be able to tell yours and mine apart, except that you may be pleasantly surprised at how very fine and skilful you have become all of a sudden.'

'Well,' I say, (what else can I say?) 'fair enough'—and, before I can drag them back, the words I already regret tumble off my tongue into the air between us—'you write the Dundee section. If it's any good, we'll see.' I mean, what harm can it do?

Séamus gets to his feet. He beams. 'You know what, Stephen,' he says, 'you'll look back and thank your stars for the day you first met Séamus McGillicuddy.'

At this most improbable of sentiments, I nod helplessly.

9

It is the early morning dark, 4:30 a.m. The shriek of unseen gulls; curlews, kittiwakes, fulmars. Now (longshot) the gulls come into view, wheeling over a piece of dead meat in the Tay Estuary that might be (we can't precisely make it out) a dead seal. The camera tracks back up river, pauses above a steamship asleep in the harbour, and enters the town. Factories, chimney stacks and tawdry stone tenements are seen dimly.

Maggie is rinsing her face in the sink. She's in a hurry and anxious.

MAGGIE: Yi a thit bed, Mary?

No reply from the other room, the lodgers' room. We follow Maggie in, and see the white face of Mary nestled between the unshaven chin and left shoulder of a man the worse for drink. Mary's mother is in an armchair, and four children are lying like four baby mice in a matchbox, two heads at each end, asleep in the hurley.

MAGGIE (*bending down and breathing into the girl's ear*): C'mon yi, time to be awa.

The street outside is empty, lit only by a half moon: yet factory engines beat in the background and the working day is about to begin. Maggie steps out of the tenement and suddenly the street begins to fill with women, some running, some pulling their jackets around them, some lighting pipes, some, like Maggie herself, taking a pinch of snuff. From other tenements come other women, and soon all merge into one, like a herd of cattle off to market, clopping over the stone pavements and the cobbles, lowing with last night's news. At the factory, the foreman looks at the hands of the large, gold-plated mill clock, while the women file past punching their time cards. At 5:30 a.m. exactly we see him reach for an iron key and lock the gates.

Inside the mill are rows of machines, brick pillars, cables overhead, and dust everywhere. Maggie checks a bank of bobbins. She bends over to see that the slivers of jute pass freely through to the flyer which is moving up and down, up and down, twisting and winding. As she bends, she holds her side. She looks around but nobody has noticed. She wipes her brow. A clock on the wall tells us it is 6:21 a.m. Maggie steps over a child who is crawling on the floor picking away at the jute strands stuck to the bottom of a machine.

The shot widens to show other machines, machines for the carding, the drawing, the roving, the winding, the beaming. We see women and young girls hard at work. An overseer, one of the few men in the place, parades up and down. Young boys shift the full bobbins from the frames and replace them with empty ones. All is activity and noise and clatter and dust. Seven thousand spindles are turning and humming. Seven thousand flyers are going up and down, up and down. Engines are grunting, boys are yelling, women are talking in sign language, dust is flying and the morning is passing.

In a distant corner of the mill, wisps of smoke rise from a single over-oiled roll of jute while, elsewhere, Mr James Irvine, oldest son of Mr James Irvine, owner, completes his tour of inspection.

IRVINE (*in public school English, looking down from his six feet and thirteen beef-fed stone at the measly five foot and nine feisty stone of the foreman, Traill*): Time spent in reconnaissance, Traill, is never wasted, as my father always says.

TRAILL: So it is, sir. (*He tugs at a forelock that has been tugged once too often and now exists only in Traill's imagination, where it stands sprightly and erect, its pristine, and indeed much improved, self.*)

IRVINE: Indeed. (*He pauses, bemused.*) Well, I'd better be off. (*He looks at his watch.*) Breakfast.

Irvine leaves, and as he disappears we notice again the smoking roll of jute. The smoke is now seen to contain a thin flame. The flame crackles, licks at the dust in the air. Particles burst into light, leap upwards, and pop.

TRAILL (*running in, shouting urgently*): Sweep thi flair. It'll burn itsel oot.

REEKIE (*an equally diminutive, receded and long-serving foreman, also running, though from a different direction*): Thi Fire Brigade, Mister Traill, wulla...?

TRAILL (*gathering his breath*): Nay need son. Days mair harm than guid, wahtir aw oor thi place. Keep thi bobbins gayin roond, thi flames wullna touch em.

A puff of burning fibre dust, a multi-particled candy floss of combustible elements, is suspended on the draught from an open window. It floats. It climbs, up, up, towards the timber ceiling, exploding as it goes like a basket of tracer shells, and falls short, falls down, comes to rest, still popping, on an overhead beam. A silent hole forms amid the noise, confusion, barking of instructions, sweeping, brushing, fetching and carrying; a pure hole of silence. Traill looks up. Reekie looks up. Five mill girls look up, their mouths open. There is no background, no sound of any kind; we are in a timeless moment of nothing, a vacuum, empty except for the pressure of breath held. Towards the end of this timeless moment, towards the beginning of another, when the sides of this hole of silence are about to crumble into a noisy exhalation of relief, thank gods and a broad smile, when the uplookers' eyes are about to turn towards the comfort of each other; a layer of dust, lying along the beam like a quick fuse, catches. A flame races right to left and torched dust balls jump sideways, fall to the floor and set fire to loose strands of jute which we notice for the first time lying as if asleep beside every spinning frame.

TRAILL (*composed*): Keep sweepin. Dinna panic.

A splinter of beam, a sizzling fragment, exits the confusion. It leaves through a half-open window. It glides down the street, twenty feet no more, and enters a warehouse where a year's supply of raw simmering jute is waiting its turn. The camera stays outside. A moment passes. A minute. Five. Nothing. Then a sudden explosion. The warehouse goes up, the walls burst out; it has become an inferno, warehouse and now the mill itself united in flame.

Maggie jostles with the rest of them at the mill door, which is still locked.

Stephen kicks a football in the back green behind the tenement with Dougie and a couple of other boys. He runs towards a makeshift goal of two sweaters, the ball is in the air, he dives and heads it in. He lies on the grass looking up, his face lit by smiles. Dougie and the others jump on top of him. They wrestle happily together and laugh.

At the mill, Traill is fighting the fire with a water hose. Reekie reaches into Traill's pocket and pulls out a key. He runs to the door, opens it and the girls leave in an orderly fashion. It is only when they are outside that they see the warehouse, the fire licking its fingers, the pavement turning pink. Some cross themselves, some curse, all run.

We follow Maggie escaping, moving as quickly as she can back to the tenement, looking behind every now and again at the fire which is advancing behind her up the hill. She sees Stephen who has come down to meet her and runs to him, throwing her arms round him in relief.

MAGGIE: Wull gay haim, maybe the fire wullna git thit far.

STEPHEN: Aye, it wull aken.

The two of them climb the tenement stairs, Stephen helping his mother. Maggie looks in on the lodgers. The children are asleep in the hurley. The grandmother is still in an armchair, but her eyes are open and staring dumbly out. There is no sign of the unshaven man, nor of Mary.

MAGGIE (*to the grandmother*): The mill's gayin up. Yi'd beh'ir git oot o here. J'a wan mi ti gie yi a hond?

GRANDMOTHER (*says nothing, continues to stare*)

MAGGIE (*goes over and shakes her*): A fire, nan, time ti git oot.

A bitter black smoke is gusting up the hill, blown on a freshening wind. Only when it clears can a golden-red fan of flames be seen.

Maggie stands, smelling the air.

MAGGIE (*to the woman, a sharper edge of urgency now in her voice*): Awa noo.

The woman gets to her feet. Stephen lifts out two of the children and Maggie the other two. They move, with a child on each arm, bent-backed and furtive, through the rising smoke.

MAGGIE: Owir there. (*She points up the hill*).

A window lifts out of its frame and belly-flops to the ground while, elsewhere, other windows are blowing out and splintering and projecting themselves into the acrid air. Shards of glass, flittering like hungry horseshoe bats on a sultry evening, dive erratically in and out of the black swirling smoke; and elsewhere again, the pointed head and shoulders of a small church bow towards the flames that gnaw on its midriff; and a man with a broom is standing on a roof sweeping off the embers as they fall, until a gable crashes down and takes the broom-man with it, still sweeping his way towards the life beyond.

They hurry up the hill. Maggie, panting under the weight of the children, struggles to keep pace. In the background, the crack of timbers, the whoosh and gust of wind and flames, and then a sudden bang, like a bomb exploding. What feels like silence follows. Maggie stops to catch her breath. She puts the children down behind her. She straightens herself. The children cry. She looks down the hill at the flames, and a smile spreads across her face. We anticipate a line of gallows humour for which the working women of Dundee are renowned, perhaps a coarse reflection on the world she has had to endure, but as it turns out the separating of her lips is her final act. A piece of sharp glass penetrates between her eyes. Maggie collapses. The camera lingers above her prone form.

The scene is lost in smoke. When it clears, it is the following morning. All that is left of the tenement and its surrounds is smouldering rubble and a single wall, unsupported on either side, without a stanchion or a buttress or a helping hand. Just stone piled on stone, one layer deep, five stories high. It stands alone in the middle of carnage, watched over by a small crowd. Then for no obvious reason—there being no more reason why it should fall than stand—it collapses like a giant elephant that has been shot in the head. It sags to its knees and topples forward. Dust rises in great clouds around it. Stephen is in the foreground watching. There are no tears in his eyes. He stares in silence at the rising dust.

10

I put Séamus's script where I found it, on my desk, and am about to get up and go back to my bedroom, about to lie beside the naked body of Julia, when Séamus comes in. It's too well timed to be accidental; he's been listening out, his pointy ears pricked for a change in the wind.

He sits down, his elbows on his knees, his chin cupped in the palms of both hands. He looks at me closely from beneath the hairy outcrops that shade his eyes. 'So, you've read it then.' These are his first words.

'Séamus, it's eight o'clock in the morning. Yes, I've read it. Now I want to go back to bed.'

He straightens. 'Is it not the pig's whiskers?'

'It's a film script.'

'It is not a film script,' says Séamus by way of rebuttal. 'It may have elements of the film script in it, it may be on its way to becoming the film script that both my agent and Hollywood herself will desire, but just now it is not a film script. It is a primitive tadpole of a film script only.'

'Is that so,' I say.

'It is,' he replies.

'I liked it nevertheless,' I tell him magnanimously. The wholeheartedness of my declaration shocks me into a heightened state of alertness. I continue. 'It is true that I wasn't expecting to have to read your stuff as if sitting in the cinema and peering around the neck of the six-foot-eight person in front so to speak, but even so I could imagine what you had in mind. It was well done.'

This remark seems to please him. 'A plentiful imagination, that's your man. The ability to see a thing that is not there, as if it is. What is greater than imagination? Is it not, after all, what separates us from the animals?' He pauses in contemplation of something known only to himself—it comes to me (unlikely though a successful guess in these circumstances may be) that he's wondering whether a tadpole can look at a frog and put two and two together, a question I have wondered about myself—and then, with a shake of his head, he brings his attention back to matters in hand. 'Imagination; the lights dimming, the shriek of gulls wheeling over a dead seal beached on a sandbank, and then we're on our way backwards into that poor benighted city of yours, Dundee. That's how I'd start her off anyway but, of course, the director may have things to say on that.'

'Ah yes, the director.'

'And was not every trace of Séamus McGillicuddy removed? Did you believe for one moment that the typescript was anything other than the product of the literary genius of Dr Stephen Smith, and a Stephen Smith on the top of his game at that? The bit I liked especially was that of the man on the roof sweeping his way to the life beyond: wasn't that you, just down to a T?'

'I suppose I might have said that, or something like it.'

'So then Stephen, we're partners.' He holds out his hand, spits on the palm and offers it to me.

'Maybe, I don't know, I need to sleep on it.'

Séamus removes his hand, affronted.

'What in the name of Jaysus is there to sleep on?' he asks.

'What is there to sleep on?' I repeat. Nothing much apart from whether I want him to be the one who digs up the ground I come from and passes what he finds around Hollywood. I don't say that; I say, 'Well nothing apart from whether I see this as a film.'

'So, what do you see it as, then?'

'I just mean I might want to write it up myself.'

Séamus is quiet. He is thinking, his face parallel to the floor. 'Okay, fair enough,' he says finally. He stands up and makes as if to leave the room.

'Come back,' I call. (God, I'm a soft touch.) 'I don't mean we can't work on it together. It's just…'

'Just what now? That you think you can do it on your own, is that the thing of it? Or is it that you want it done, and the more help the better, but at the same time, deep inside yourself Stephen, you don't want it done at all?' He pauses thoughtfully. 'Is it a secret you are not telling me?'

Two penetrating eyes reinforce the question.

'No,' I say, 'it's not that, not really, I do want it done, though perhaps I am a little anxious about how it will turn out. It's...' Christ, how did Séamus drag me into this, '...personal. That's what it is, if I'm honest, personal. He is my grandfather. Before you say anything, I know he oughtn't matter in the slightest. He's dead, my mother's dead, what difference does it make? My little guy couldn't care less'—I tap my chest and lay my thumb on it—'but yet, don't ask me why, I feel as if he does matter. The fact is'—what am I doing? disclosures, at eight o'clock in the morning—'the fact is I suppose I've built him up a bit over the years, you know the way kids do. I wanted him to be something; to be better than her anyway. That's all. I just wanted him to be more than she was and, even now, I'm surprised to find that I still do.'

'That's an honest thing to say,' he says.

'Séamus, look, my grandfather has been dead all these years, buried so deep by my mother he might as well not have existed at all. Now I can give him his life back, and I want to. It's just that the more life I breathe into him, the more I breathe into her. She was a strange woman. There was no truth or openness in her, nothing to get hold of when I was cold or lonely or not knowing where to turn. But she came through him didn't she, so something must have made her what she was, some big terrible thing...rape, murder, incest? I've no idea what, but it has to be there, and I'm not sure I want to find it. Secrets—you want to know them but then again, at the same time, you don't.'

Séamus's body language doesn't suggest much in the way of sensitive appreciation. He just sits there looking pleased with himself and rubbing his hands together. 'Rape, murder, incest,' he says finally when he realizes I've finished. 'Holy God, boyo, wouldn't that be just the ticket. You know what that trinity means, don't you; it means bums on seats; it means you need me.' He is now beside himself with excitement, bouncing up and down like a little beach ball. 'Look,' he declares emphatically, 'don't you worry yourself about what you'll find. You'll find what you'll find, I'm sure of that. The thing is this: we'll work on him together, all the research and stuff, and you'll have the final say-so as to what goes in and what doesn't. I can't say fairer than that, now can I?'

'No, I suppose you can't,' I reply limply.

'Then when it's all done, you'll have yourself a real living, breathing grandfather, a man to be proud of I'm sure, a man who'll tap you fondly on the head and tuck you up in bed when you lay your hairy face on the pillow at night and, even more important than all that, we may even come out of it a shilling or two to the good. So, Stephen, what do you say?'

He looks at me with earnestness and conviction written all over his ridiculous face and, once more, sticks out his hand with the spit on it. Before I know what I'm doing, I find my own clasped in his, being pumped up and down, palm to palm, for better or worse, for richer or poorer.

11

Julia is still asleep as I climb into bed. I hold her for a moment but she rolls away. The bed goes cold in that spot where her body was. I shiver. A tremor passes through me like a stab of ice inserted and withdrawn in one quick movement. I move across so my stomach is against her back, my legs brushing hers. I raise myself on my forearm and whisper into the curls on the back of her neck, touching them with my lips, touching her skin, something, anything, to get her attention. 'I love you.'

Does she hear? Does she not? She does not reply.

I lie on my back, watching the columns of silence marching past. I am adrift, weightless, floating on cold currents. No tears, just a feeling that I will cry like a baby if I let myself start.

I get up, a glint of a headache above my eyes, dress myself and go to my 'office' at the university, which is no more than a small room I share with Charlie Mulgrew, a post-doc. He isn't in. It's early for Charlie.

I sit at my desk, my half-written paper on Karṇa in front of me. Karṇa means 'ear'. His mother's other sons have better names: Yudhiṣṭhira, 'pillar of battle'; Bhīma, 'strong'; Arjuna, 'silvery'. But Karṇa is 'ear'. It's what you drag kids along by. No name for a hero.

Yet it's by his ears that I know him, his ears with their earrings of amṛta, his bright lights shining in the lonely darkness of his first betrayal, his ears where the arrows struck. *Sa karṇam karṇinā karne...vivyādha—Karṇa pierced in the ear by the ear-shaped arrowhead (karṇin).* How subtly it is inserted, the idea of Karṇa pierced by Karṇa, Karṇa destroyed by himself. But then, what other fate is possible if you're born invulnerable?

Charlie comes in, nods once and begins to write. I listen to his pen scratching out its Chinese hieroglyphs. It scratches like nails on a cliff face. His pen, this imaginary cliff face, the Ear's ear-arrowed ear, Julia, the idea of love: they all bob together like boats in a harbour, touching sides, moving apart, rocking on the water of my mind, going nowhere.

When I get back to the flat, Julia is still in bed, the sheet draped over the scarp of her hip. Her eyes are open, apparently looking out, but unfocused. She is untouchable, like a painting in a museum, for admiration only.

Presently, I ask, 'Shall I continue the story of Karṇa? Chapter two?'

'Sure,' she says, sleepily raising herself onto her elbows.

'Are you? Really?'

'Yes, really. I'm beginning to think it's only by listening to your stories, Stephen, that I'll get to know anything about you. So tell me chapter two, but make it good, make me love you.'

How I would like to, how I wish I could, but at that moment what swirls in my stomach is the realisation that making Julia love me is more than I can do, further than I can stretch, beyond me utterly.

She beckons me into bed. I begin. I tell her what it was like growing up as the son of a charioteer in a mud hut on the fringes of the royal court, what it was like watching my brothers being taught the arts of war while I, who was better than them all, was taught nothing. I tell her of the great tournament held so that my brothers could demonstrate their prowess and how I appeared, unannounced and splendid, to outdo them all. How then Arjuna challenged me and how I readied myself to kill him.

'I like the story,' she says, 'especially when you enter the great arena, tall and straight as a cliff, lit up by earrings as bright as the sun.'

'Genes,' I say.

'And I like Duryodhana, your friend who also wants Arjuna out of the way. His mother planting him in a pot and him coming out braying like an ass, that was good too. Not the best start in life though, I wouldn't think, being born in a pot. I bet he sucked his thumb.'

I am aware of an erection growing. Karṇa: root meaning, *meat*. Latin, caro/carnis, flesh. English, carnal. Also *horn*. Latin, cornu. *The fleshy bit that sticks out*. I wonder if Julia notices. I carry on.

'I am at the centre of the arena, one knee bent, bow in hand, poised, ready to kill Arjuna or be killed by him, when I hear that voice which cuts me off at the knees, which takes the breath from my body and the blood from between my legs: "Tell us the names of your father and mother," demands the announcer, "and of the royal line of which you are an ornament. For only those of equal degree may fight with Arjuna."'

How much I tell her then of my shame to come, I can't be sure. Words swirl in my head, I know that, and take form or do not: words about how, from somewhere in the tournament crowd, there emerges an old man, perspiring and trembling, his loincloth loose and slipping, a charioteer, my father. 'What can I do but put aside my bow and bend down, while onto my unworthy head my father weeps. He embraces me. He calls me his son. So that I am revealed for what I am, a low caste cur not worthy to lick the butter placed before the sacrificial fire, not worthy to fight Arjun.

'In that moment, my worst, only Duryodhana comes to my defence. He rises up like an enraged buffalo out of a clump of lotus flowers and, snorting, poses the one great question, the only one that can save me. "Tell me, oh great Princes, who can be sure of the lineage of heroes? Who knows where a great river rises? Was not Drona himself, that foremost wielder of weapons, born in a water jar? Was not Kripa, of the race of Gotama, sprung from a clump of heath? Look at Karṇa. Behold his auspicious markings, the divine armour of his body, his earrings. See how he shines with the radiance of the sun. How can a tiger like this be born of a she-deer? How?"'

I stop. I wait. I prepare myself to tell Julia of the battle postponed and the battles to come, but Julia makes no sound. I listen closely and hear the breath drawing into her nostrils and leaving, murmuring its secrets as it goes. I fear for the prize. It will be withheld. She will weigh me and find me wanting. Karṇa on the butcher's block. Where else?

12

Séamus's eyebrows, like the antennae of the potato beetle but with a greater sense of grievance, poke forward as he delivers his first utterance of the morning: 'For eight long years, not a jot or tittle at all.' In the silence that follows, I do my best to give the impression of benign curiosity: my cheekbones and forehead widen in anticipation, my lips gap apart. Finally, he continues. 'After the fire and the death of his poor dear mother, your grandfather is silent as the grave. Then, when the eight years of nothing is up, he leaves us less than a whole lot: a few old cuttings torn from the newspapers, a notebook of his sketches, some of them no more than doodles they are, there's a photograph, and then there's the stuff about the steamships.'

'So?' I say, hiding a certain, not unexpected, disappointment.

'So? You ask, so? I'll tell you so, boyo, so you should be pleased you have me slaving away for you, that's so, putting at your disposal my ability to fashion the truth out of the slightest of those little hints.'

'Why? What have you done? Made it all up?'

Séamus manifests profound shock. 'Nothing is made up, not a thing. I don't know, Stephen, but sometimes I worry about you. No, I have plugged the gaping holes in his history, that's what I've done. I have taken the materials he has seen fit to let us have and, from them, derived the essential elements of his message. Your grandfather was an artist, and to understand the artist, you have to see the world as he does. Those misfortunes, pieces of bad luck, things which other men shrug off and forget, the artist absorbs into himself. He searches out meaning even when none seems to be there. He interprets the small stuff around him and the clues he leaves are never less than signposts to a larger truth. To the artist, two and two always make five; and all I've done is add the additional one that he hasn't left behind. As he himself would have wanted me to.' Séamus is fired up, his little eyes shining like the devil's.

'I see,' I say. I don't see, but hey. Well, I can see he's away with the fairies. I continue: 'Still, before we slip into the nether world of Irish mathematics, I think I should judge for myself on the basis of such hard evidence as he chose to leave me. He is my grandfather.'

'Very well,' Séamus says huffily, 'not that it'll help you at all. It will not. And don't think you can understand his external world, the world in which he walks and talks, until you have first looked at his other world'—here he pauses as if significantly—'within.' He illustrates this by poking his two index fingers into the sides of his eyeballs: to which act of self-mutilation, the rest of his face reacts appropriately; it reminds me of one of those puff-cheeked gargoyle monkeys, where the water comes off the church roof and pours out through its gaping mouth. Of course he's no idea he's making these faces. That's his problem; completely unaware. I just watch. I don't want to encourage him. Eventually, when he observes my total lack of interest, he disappears and, coming back with a file, chucks it in front of me.

The press cuttings are all about Irvine's: layoffs, skylight windows broken, machines sabotaged. There's a report of a minor assault on an overseer (bruised ribs, two fingers broken). I thumb through yellowed fragments of the *Advertiser*: a long walk-out, twenty-seven weeks…yada yada…workers start to trickle back, hardship, malnutrition, a twenty percent wage cut forced on the hapless strikers at the end of August 1923, workforce slashed. That's more or less it, apart from a notice that WC has lost his seat. Dundee goes to pot, and Churchill gets the kick up the behoochie he's been asking for. That's the gist of it.

The photograph is interesting though; a thin man, withdrawn, eyes that look in. A sudden understanding comes to me.

'He's got red hair,' I blurt out.

Séamus looks over my shoulder at the black and white. 'Is that so, indeed?'

'He has. I can feel it.'

'Red hair, the colour of a fox's brush. But not sleek. Unruly. Windswept. Like bracken in autumn.'

'Will it fall in place when the wind drops?' I ask.

'That is the question, certainly,' he says.

We look at each other in silence. Oh God...so this is what partnership means.

'I've filled in the dark years, the strikes, the sabotage and started him out for Calcutta.' Séamus, sitting on a chair, his legs swinging happily below him, points at a pile of paper. 'And, by the way, I've taken out all the Dundee lingo stuff, except on those occasions when I think it has to be in there. We don't want the audience demanding their money back because they can't understand the half of what they're hearing.'

* * *

It is murky black, out of focus. Once more the shriek of unseen gulls. Behind the sound of gulls are other sounds we can't precisely identify; perhaps they include glass breaking, perhaps voices raised, perhaps men running and being chased. The scene clarifies and we see across the Tay to snow on the distant hills of Fife. A stiff easterly is blowing. The top of the waves are cream white, ghostly in the light of the moon.

A cobbled lane. A puddle. Reflected in its surface is the aspen image of a ship tied up and slumbering dockside. Two men stand motionless beside a lamppost. After a few moments a sailor, previously unnoticed, takes a half pace forward. The two men move towards him. They whisper, as if in secret negotiation. One of them whistles softly. Stephen emerges. He is of medium height, spare. He has grown a beard. He looks to left and right and gazes, almost contemplatively, into the dark shadows that lurk in every doorway. Then, throwing back his shoulders, he walks up to the sailor and shakes his hand. We see that Stephen's eyes are deep, his features gaunt: a man used to making do with not much.

SAILOR: Thomson.

STEPHEN: Doig.

The sailor points and Stephen, now Doig, carrying no more than a small bag, steps across onto the adjacent deck. He pauses, looks round for a moment at his native Dundee, spits into the water, and is gone.

High seas, high winds, the ship tossing. There are no signs of passengers on this passenger ship. It is no weather to be on deck.

Tangiers now looms off the starboard bow. Forgetting earlier miseries, everybody savours the bright sea sunlight. All are dressed for high summer: the men in white suits, the women in long-waisted frocks of foulard and georgette. Some are in deck chairs, some looking over the rail.

A young British gentleman points at three camels trotting splayfooted along the retreating shore, their riders sitting on top like colourful laundry, apparently legless.

BRITISH GENTLEMAN (*disdainfully*): Behold the noble savage.

UNATTACHED AND OVERWEIGHT YOUNG SINGLE LADY (*enthusiastically*): Oh, yes, how exciting. Magnificent. So moody, don't you think?

BRITISH GENTLEMAN (*turning towards her. We see now that he is James Irvine Junior*): Moody! Pah!

In the ship's engine room, two Indian men are stoking the engines. Stephen, covered in black dust, stands behind observing. The scene reminds him of another, among the clank and whir of machines, amid dust flying and brown air, in which a mill girl, regarded minutely by an overseer standing behind, is tending a spinning frame. The overseer looks to his left and right, and then stepping forward, presses against her, catching her between himself and the machine.

OVERSEER (*soothingly*): No, no, Aileen, the breast plate. Looser, lassie. You've got to free it. It needs to lie much easier than this.

He fingers a piece of the spinning frame that looks like the teat of a bottle. As he straightens, he fondles her chest. She is unwilling. She struggles. Stephen is working his way down a line of machines, making adjustments here and there. The overseer steps back.

OVERSEER (*softly, to the girl*): Have it your own way. (*He picks up some yarn, shouting in a loud mill voice.*) It's not good enough, hen, not at all, not nearly. I've told you before. If you want to keep your job at Irvine's, you've got to give me something better than this. (*He holds up a spool, unwinding it with disdain.*)

AILEEN: Aye sir, sorry sir, but...

James Irvine Jr lies back on a moiré bedspread staring at a cut glass chandelier from Venice. A whisky and soda rests on a table by his bedside. There is a knock at his cabin door.

STEWARD: Stromboli, sir, you may like to take a look.

IRVINE: May I? Why? I'm about to go to bed.

STEWARD: As you wish sir, but many gentlemen who pass through like to see Stromboli.

IRVINE: Oh, very well.

He puts on his dressing gown and takes the night air. There she is: the Stromboli volcano rising straight from the sea, flames and lava decorating the darkness like a roman candle on a November night in Scotland; except that here the air is warm as bathwater. Irvine rests his forearms on the ship's guardrail and gazes out in apparent contemplation of its rosy mysteries. He returns to his cabin.

The fire of the volcano reddens the glass of a lower porthole, and licks, as if burning, the flickering image of a man looking through. The face, red-black and greased, striped in the reflection of the erupting Stromboli, is Stephen's.

Valetta, Malta. The Union Jack flies on all public buildings and on many houses. Irvine strolls around the narrow streets, takes breakfast, lunch and tea in sundry street-side cafés and restaurants. Other passengers (female) purchase hats and embroidered lace.

At a dinner table in Valetta's finest hotel, Irvine sits opposite a young woman from second class. She has on a tea gown of imitation crêpe de Chine that has been worn many times, and a panama hat bought locally at crippling expense. We understand immediately that she is both beautiful and poor.

IRVINE: More wine?

YOUNG WOMAN FROM SECOND CLASS: Oh yes, why not, you're only young once. (*She hiccups.*)

IRVINE: Of course you are. (*They clink glasses and drink.*) A pity your intended can't be here. An assistant superintendent of police in Rangoon, you say. Well, well.

YOUNG WOMAN: Yes, we met two years ago, he was a friend of my cousin Lily and we've been writing ever since, exchanging letters I think they call it. Then he, you know, popped the question. Which came as quite a shock really.

IRVINE: Did it? A beautiful girl like you? You must have dozens of admirers.

YOUNG WOMAN (*tittering*): Oh you.

IRVINE: Such a long way to go still. (*He sighs*). A man, a certain kind of man, can get very lonely on long journeys like this, very down on himself. Of course, if he's a gentleman, he'll never show it, but sometimes, when he meets someone special, he yearns to unburden himself. (*He sighs again and looks her in the eye.*) Do you have the slightest idea what I'm talking about? I suppose not. I can't imagine a beautiful girl like you knows what it is to feel alone.

YOUNG WOMAN: Please James, may I call you James? If there's anything you need to tell me, at any time, you know I'm here, if I can be of some comfort...

IRVINE: Ah, you are so kind. (*He looks thoughtfully into his glass. He raises it.*) To you, my dear delightful...and what should I call you?

—Here I respond to Séamus's constant salaciousness with a scribble in the margin. The scribble draws attention to the connection between the writings of the author and the leanings of his mind. 'You dirty little lech,' are my precise words—

The ship reaches Port Said, the bustling entrance to the Suez canal and gateway to the Orient. The harbour is alive with the hoot of tugs and the bandied exclamations of traders and mendicants. Small bumboats, almost capsizing under the weight of what they have to sell, mob the steamer. Ropes are thrown up, baskets of souvenirs are raised like flags.

NATIVE SALESMAN (*calling from halfway up the side of the ship*): No obligation, My Honour, looking only.

IRVINE (*leaning over the rail, watching*): No thank you very much. (*While pretending to nothing more than a lack of interest in the goods being offered, he adds under his breath*): Bugger off you little wog.

An ancient, half-naked gully-gully man has made it up to the deck. He is tattooed and has feathers around his head and upper arms. He is performing tricks before a crowd of passengers. He stretches out an arm, rotates it so that all can see it hides nothing, and turning to the gentleman who is standing behind him—it is Irvine, still leaning over the deck abusing the native salesman—pulls from his waistcoat pocket a newborn chick. The crowd laughs. Irvine, realising his pocket has been touched, straightens with red-faced outrage. The crowd laughs louder. From Irvine's ear, the gully-gully man now produces an egg. Irvine stomps away.

The gully-gully man shakes the egg to see what if anything might be inside. He holds it to the light. He waggles his arms like wings, he listens to the egg, he cups it in his hands and rubs. He opens his hands to reveal a second newborn chick. He takes a knife and with a sudden slash removes the newborn's head. The passengers gasp. He puts the chick down on deck, and it runs away, its head magically restored. The passengers clap and some give money. To these he bows and smiles and shows a mouth containing no teeth at all.

Irvine walks along the waterfront, shields himself against flies and the importuning of children, declines the insistent offers of pimps who compete with each other in offering the homespun charms of virginal sisters and finds his way to the department store of Simon Artz. He makes the ritual purchase that is required of anyone going East who wishes to look the part: a khaki-coloured polo topee, a Bombay Bowler. It sits on his head like a Christmas pudding and makes him smile.

Witnessed by three camels and a motionless Arab, two funnels seem to be moving through the desert. The camera moves closer. We see the side of the ship and the thin water of the Suez canal.

Ismalia. Sunset. To the accompaniment of a bugle sounding the last post, a Union Jack is being lowered. Again we see the ship from land. Irvine is standing at the rail wearing his topee, with his hand around the shapely waist of the young woman from second class. Directly below him, (two levels below), another hand, that of a working man, wipes a porthole. It discovers that the obstruction (the sand) is on the outside. It gives up the attempt, and drops downwards as if exhausted.

The ship reaches the Red Sea. Irvine reclines in a deck chair, his collar unbuttoned. He struggles with his breath. Sweat pours from his cheeks. The sea smoulders under the sun. That night, in his cabin, Irvine tosses and turns, alone. A cabin steward enters bearing whisky and cold flannels.

—There's a note from Séamus. 'I'm not going to be including every stopover, the likes of Colombo, Madras and all those places. I think it's important to maintain the forward momentum of the thing, and there's also the shooting costs to consider. We'll just pick her up as she comes down the Hooghly.'

The shooting costs! Of course, how could I forget: our immediate problem. Should I worry about the wee man? Is the frayed rope on which he balances about to snap?—

Irvine is leaning on the side rail of the ship. He is restless. Across the Hooghly is tedious flat landscape, low scrub jungle, mud huts, huts covered in reeds, and bungalows with lawns and flower beds. Poking above, are the chimneys of mills. Irvine looks down at the brown wallowing water, swatting.

IRVINE: Bloody mosquitoes.

Oil tanks at Budge-Budge appear and pass away. The Royal Botanical Gardens, Prinsep's Ghat, Fort William with its lofty aerials, the ridiculous Pepper-box memorial to those who died defending the Empire in the Gwalior campaign of 1843; all come and go as the ship moves slowly up river. Steamers with passengers en route from one city landing to another, tugs and small boats buzz under the sun. Great jute flats lie like dead whales midstream. Irvine checks the time from the clock tower of the Kidderpore docks. We hear the ship sigh like a man settling himself into an armchair after a hard day. It signals, with a quiet belch, Outram Ghat, the end of the line.

Irvine steps ashore and is met by Kinnes.

KINNES: I'm the general manager of Irvine's, sir. Kinnes.

IRVINE: Are you? First stop, Firpos, I think, don't you? Firpos is Calcutta, that's what my father always says.

KINNES: It certainly is, sir.

At Firpos, comforted by crystal chandeliers, Himalayan-white tablecloths and a palm court quartet playing discretely, Irvine and his general manager take tea. Plates of sandwiches and cakes rest silently between them and no words are exchanged.

It is night and desolate on the ship. All have left. Stephen, with a single bag over his shoulder, walks down the gangway.

13

Chewing a chili papadum dipped in fiery pickle, I conjure up my grandfather. For five weeks, he has been confined below decks. Now he takes his first breath of Calcutta. He is not surprised that it is hot, or that it is drippingly humid—he has lived long enough in the engine room—but he doesn't expect this assault on his senses, this strange cloying chorus of life and spices which dance and droop in the night air. He breathes again, wondering at the sweated traces and sweet pungency which has become the air itself, which hits him, saturates him and forces on him its own unyielding truth; that this is not Dundee. Or, if this city is, as he knows it to be, a haven for Scotsmen, and for Dundonians in particular, then there are things in it beyond the control of those who have come and taken over.

He clings to an address in his pocket. It is all that stands between him and the alarming night. Where does the address take him? I turn the page of one of his notebooks: a dried leaf drops out and powders into dust, leaving nothing behind but an outline, its ribs and spine. I shut my eyes.

My grandfather looks about him, left, right, straight on, and finds only silence, the dim light of a streetlamp, grey harbour buildings, brown bodies wrapped in blankets huddled together on the quayside, asleep or dead. He shivers in spite of the heat, and sets off towards what he hopes is the centre of the city. On a road paved with stone, he follows tram rails until he sees a half-naked Indian squatting by the curb. The man has no teeth, but smiles anyway. My grandfather squats beside him. Perhaps he is grateful for the smile, even though he suspects that the man would smile at anybody. He produces his piece of paper and reads it aloud. The man, still smiling but now also nodding his head, points a bony finger. Strand Road. My grandfather finds a coin and hands it over. The man bows from the waist, his palms together, his smiling and his nodding stopped.

My grandfather arrives at his destination, whether circuitously or not he doesn't say. No doubt there are negotiations (how many nights, how much), to which he puts up no resistance. He is directed to his room, he opens the door and what he sees is less than he hopes for, as much as he expects. It no longer matters. He is at journey's end, exhausted, empty. He collapses onto stained sheets. With a twitch of his foot, he kicks off one of his boots. His breathing slows. His mop of red hair flops listlessly across a mottled grey-white pillow and the muscles in his face soften. For a moment he looks young, younger than his twenty-three years. His body sleeps and whatever memories, fond or not, he may have carried from Dundee sleep with him.

When he wakes next morning, his first day in India, he recognizes nothing. Where am I? How did I get here? Slowly it comes back to him: I am in Calcutta; last night I took a room at the Sailor's Home; I have a little money in my pocket. He drifts back to sleep. He ignores the nervous drumming in his stomach and dreams instead the everyday dream of the Dundee mill hand; of a paradise where even ordinary men sip coconut water and dance in the sunshine around a swimming pool. It is a reassuring dream; that there is a comfortable world within this other world, a world within his grasp, a better world than the one he has left. At least in his dreams.

Séamus has invited me to the game. He has tickets. Dundee United's ground, Tannadice, is so close to the tenement where I grew up, I didn't know if I wanted to go. When I put this to Séamus, all he said was, 'Jaysus, Stephen, if it isn't one thing, it's another.' No understanding of the sensitivities of others, that's his problem. He then added, as if the decision was as good as made, 'Besides, should we not both sit on the top of Dundee Law before the start of the thing to give thanks for your grandfather's last happy memory before his dear mother passed away.' I asked him, 'Do you remember the times you were happy, or are they wiped out by the ones you'd rather forget?' 'Gob, but you're the miserable sod,' he said, providing as an afterthought, 'not that it matters at all since I'm doing your grandfather's remembering for him.'

St Andrews is looking good today: the old piled stones of the cathedral back-lit by thin sunlight; the composed houses attempting a smile; café tables on the pavement where the diligent and the couldn't-care-less read and chatter in overcoats; modern and medieval at the same time, on the up, confident of its place in the approaching millennium. Séamus and I walk to the bus station not saying much. I feel the cobbles under my feet. The bus is waiting. We get in. I haven't been back to Dundee since the funeral. Séamus rubs his hands. 'I have high hopes for the game today,' he confides.

The bus rattles out of town. A man sitting upright in front of us, stiff as a lamppost, (an ex-gym teacher? a retired major?) twists his neck to look out of the window. He presents in profile an immaculate moustache. It is a prompt. On cue, I mouth the word, *Briggs*, who is also the owner of a moustache, a giant handlebar. He stands erect in a pencil sketch, caressing its curves with his right hand while scratching his arse with his left, Indian style. In the background, the desk of the Superintendent of the Sailor's Home where my grandfather spent his first night. In the foreground, a pile of steaming shit, which Briggs pokes disdainfully with his toe. He appears to be lecturing my grandfather. A single word, *Prospects!* is captured in a speech bubble.

My grandfather could draw. I think so anyway. Take, in supporting evidence, his self-portrait standing under a colonnade outside a gentleman's tailor and outfitter, *Mitchells of Park Street*, adjusting the jacket across his shoulders and giving both its lapels a tug downwards. We can't see his face, but the jaunty set of his back and head suggests a man pleased with his new clothes, perhaps a man who is finding his feet in his new country. He is looking down on traffic: the engines, the horses, the men pulling rickshaws, the beasts of burden. They are plying backwards and forwards towing enormous loads; but my grandfather doesn't care what they're carrying. What he sees (what we see) are the muscles in the neck of a horse, the tensioned bicep of a rickshaw wallah, the groan of an engine in the open bonnet of a car whose passengers are invisible.

The bus crosses the Tay Bridge and pulls into the depot. Séamus and I walk to the Law Hill. We look down on the harbour as my grandfather once did, and across the river to Fife. Séamus says, 'Why don't you frame that first picture of his? I believe it would mean a lot to you.'

We go over to the game, stopping off on the way. The streets slip past like neglected history: Upper Constitution, Adelaide Place, Jamaica Street, Wellington Square. How familiar they are, but I wonder what I would think if I was seeing them for the first time, as my grandfather saw Calcutta on that first day of his exile. I hear his footsteps, like my own, on foreign pavements scratched into a notebook: Middleton Street, Harrington Street, Theatre Road; large houses in their own grounds, trees in blossom, the sun glinting through leaves, a gentle breeze blowing from the river. (Perhaps my grandfather thought on this, his first morning, that the rumours of paradise were true.) He goes to the Maidan, watches boys playing cricket, sees the statues of Empire, Ochterlony, Outram, Napier, Ripon, Kitchener. He has a sketch of them, all in a line, all looking the same, down their noses. He passes great stone buildings standing aloof.

Out in the murderous sun of midday, he sweats, blush pink. He thinks about taking a glass of water in the Imperial Hotel but he's not sure if they'll let him in. He turns instead to the Indian Museum. It is cool inside, peaceful. He sits in front of a red stone monument in which are carved stories from the life of Buddha before the Buddha was born. A group of Indian men crowd round him. 'They were poor and wanted to look at what I was looking at. They smelt terrible.'

Séamus says, 'Here's your ticket,' and hands it over. 'It's round the other side, the George Fox Stand. The seats should be okay.'

I look at it and notice the word *complimentary*. How has Séamus come by complimentary tickets? Who gets them? Perhaps there's some time-honoured tradition in the club whereby all adult males under five feet get in free.

I watch the milling crowd. Too much time spent among bare walls and lino floors, too much booze, fags, drugs etched into the creases of drawn faces and thinning hair. But not without humour, a sort of edgy, urgent humour and today made softer by hope. Today the crowd thinks it might win. The game flows in gentle waves, back and forward, forward and back, one end to the other. Then the ball is hit long to the left, the Hearts' winger crosses and it's in the net. The crowd yells abuse at the full back. Séamus yells with the best of them.

A stumpy pot-bellied man in front of us has hair growing horizontally out of his ears, and ears growing straight out of his bald head. When United score the equalizer, a curling left-footed shot from a free kick, the crowd goes berserk, they chant, 'Charlie, Charlie,' and the little man with the hairy stick-out ears turns round with a look of such joy in his eyes that my heart melts. Séamus laughs and dances around with him and, by the end, the two of them are like lost brothers reunited.

We walk back through the post-match litter of a big game and the swell of a crowd pleased with the draw. Dens Road. I turn around half expecting to see my mother standing on the corner, a spent cigarette lounging on her lip, just ash hanging on.

Even though I may never have known my grandfather, I feel his heartbeat more than I ever felt hers. I follow his paper trail of phrases around his new city: the stone buildings (a Dundee grander by far), the ordered clip of carts and tradesmen, a Chinaman mending shoes, carcasses of beef hanging in the sun larded by flies. He is still the tourist, watching from a distance, taking notes.

Now he changes direction, or perhaps continues in the wrong direction, it doesn't matter. He moves north: his first day, how can he know better? India clouds over: 'once more that smell of sick,' 'vultures,' 'wild dogs in packs.' Do the dogs pass him on this side of the street or the other? Do they sniff his legs or slink away expecting the boot?

His world closes in. The sky is endless no longer, but pieced into squares of brick and bright cloths hanging down to dry. Underfoot, no longer stone, but rubble, earth, the peelings and rotted scraps of the inedible. He smells the smoke of cooking fires, he hears men arguing and babies screaming like seagulls, he sees young women looking shyly down from out of high windows, exchanging glances. Now, he is no longer the watcher. Watched. Shouts echo in the dark between twisted walls and back alleys. A twisted smile in a doorway. A stranger's voice, a stranger's language.

'Hey, Rickshaw. The Sailor's Home, fast.'

White India and brown India, and my undreamt mother piebald.

14

When we're home, after the match, Séamus goes to my room. He says, 'You've opened it, the second box. About time.' He gets down on his knees and pores over the notebooks, my presence forgotten.

'Where did you get the tickets from?' I ask.

I don't think he hears. He shows no sign of it anyway. 'Séamus, those tickets, how come they were complimentary?'

He looks up. 'The tickets? Oh, a friend of mine gets them. It is a mystery to me how he manages it.'

Séamus returns to investigating the contents of the box, while I open a beer and drink alone, sunk in a chair, considering him and the ceiling with equal dispassion.

After, I don't know, half an hour, he pokes his head up and exclaims, 'Gob, but he's gone back to the jute, he's gone back to Irvine's. Sure, that's the saddest thing so it is, to go halfway round the world and finish back where you started.'

'Not sad at all, Séamus,' I say. '*Heroic* would be a better word.'

'Heroic, my granny,' he grunts, downcast, the cloak of a troubled man lying palpable upon his shoulders. I give him time to disclose the true nature of his burden. It is not long in coming. 'What's your man done but take up the softest of all the options available? Jute! Irvine's! What sort of a film script is there in a thing as easy as that?'

'Your reaction, Séamus,' I tell him patiently, 'is based on a gross, although understandable, misunderstanding.'

'I hope it is so, indeed, because I admit at this moment to an overwhelming strong sense of disappointment, or perhaps to a loss of faith. I believe your grandfather has let me down.'

'There you couldn't be more wrong, Séamus. He has done the complete opposite of letting you down. Let me open your eyes for you and your faith in him will be restored.'

'Go ahead then, open my eyes,' grumbles Séamus, palely contemplating the unravelling tufts in the carpet beneath him.

'Very well,' I begin, 'remind me, please, of the circumstances of my grandfather's sudden departure from Dundee.'

'He was up to his neck in the strike, was he not? He made an assault on an overseer. He crossed the thin line between the legal and the not.'

'Yes, I believe he did all those things. Then answer me this, how did that make him feel?'

'How did he feel? Let me see now...' Séamus searching within, feeds his thinking frenzy with a brutal attack on his earlobe. He pincers it between thumb and forefinger, and squeezes it until bloodless. It is not a comfortable sight. Eventually he says, 'I don't think he felt good, punching that overseer and all.'

'Why not?'

'Because, at heart, he was a decent man, was he not?'

'Good, Séamus, good. There isn't a scrap of hard evidence to support the conclusion but, yes, I think so. Now let me put two further questions to you, and a third which we'll come to in a moment.'

'Continue, you have my full attention.'

'Question one: why did he escape Dundee only to go to Calcutta, when he could have gone to Bombay, Madras, Sidney Australia or indeed Timbuktu for that matter?'

Séamus considers. 'That's the right question all right, Stevo,' he says.

I hurry on. 'Because nowhere was more like Dundee. Calcutta was the only other jute city of consequence on the planet and it was run by exactly the same people, the Irvines and their ilk. What does that tell you?'

'So, I don't know. What the devil does it tell me?'

'That he didn't want to escape. It was not escape he had in mind.'

'Not escape? Hmm. And the second question?'

'Why did he go to Irvine's, which was the one company that could have rumbled him and sent him back to face the music, when he could have tried for a job in another mill, or indeed in no mill at all?'

'That's another question that needs to be thought about,' says Séamus.

'For the same reason that he chose Calcutta. He wasn't interested in putting his past behind him. He wanted to return to Go, collect his £200, try the board again. Which brings me to the third question. Why does a man who's been given a second chance choose to duplicate the situation that caused him such grief before?'

I watch Séamus turning things over in his head. 'So he can do better next time around?' he asks. 'Is that it? So he can get his spanner around a few little details he believes need fixing. Inside himself, I mean. Is that it Stephen, is that what you're getting at?'

'Yes,' I reply, 'exactly that.'

Séamus is now with me, eager, excited, on the edge of his seat. 'Jays, but I'd like to think you're right, Stephen. His battle with himself! Sure that's the thing alright. Gob, yes, Hollywood can't get enough of that, the hero's journey into himself, the constant self-doubt that drags him to the bottom, the almost certain guarantee that the bottom is where he'll stay, and then he meets a little man by the roadside and the little man helps him and he comes through, teaching those bookies a lesson in the process and, as sure as night follows day, he wins the girl and, together, they ride off into the light of a declining sunset. Yes, yes, Stephen, brilliant, thank you. I like it, yes.'

'What little man?' I ask calmly, hoping by my tone to encourage him back from la-la land. 'And what girl? I haven't come across anything about a girl.'

'There'll be a girl. There's always a girl.'

15

Observed from a distance, a ferry working slowly across a wide river, a paddle dipping into flat water. It is a rhythmical movement, in and out, hardly a splash or ripple. As the camera moves closer, we see a black boatman, stick-thin, wearing only a dhoti. A European man in a white jacket is seated. The water is the colour of hot orange grilling under the sun.

The European is shading his eyes and looking forward from beneath his fingers. Buildings in white lie like vast yawning dogs along the approaching bank. Steam vaporizes through a towering steel stack into the simmering atmosphere. The steady drawl of turbines reaches him across the water.

STEPHEN (*astonished by the unexpected scale of what he sees*): Jesus Christ.

Two jetties poke out into the water. Around them, barges with Irvine and Company on the sides bring in raw jute and take away finished. *Irvine and Company* is etched on a triumphal arch under which jute and its operatives pass to and from.

Houses and bungalows in the European style are to the left of the white industrial buildings. Their names are Rose Villa, Moniefieth, Wee Hame, and behind them and between are a swimming pool, three tennis courts and gardens. The gardens are manicured and abundant with parakeets, bougainvillea, pink hibiscus, jasmine, the rare blue plumbago, gul mohur and an ancient Banyan tree.

Stephen steps off the ferry. He is clean-shaven. He brushes his hair into order and watches, with his hands in his pockets, as a small engine leaves the jetty pulling empty open-sided wagons. He steps on and, a minute later, off, trotting forward as his momentum takes him through the arched entrance of the mill. A soused blanket of heat and the vastness of what lies before him, bring him to a halt.

STEPHEN: Bloody hell.

In front of him are banks upon rows upon lines of machines, massive cast iron columns, a huge vaulted brick roof that contains the urgent metallic chatter of a million spindles like a mausoleum contains the whispers of the dead.

STEPHEN (*to himself*): This is it, then.

He sniffs the dust. Its familiarity makes him smile. Brown sweating women with jute in their hair feed roving machines. Brown men, also sweating, stand by frames, beams, looms. Pink and red men from Dundee, with shirts plastered to their chests, walk up and down.

ANGUS (*one of the pink and red men*): Stephen?

Stephen peers into the haze of jute dust and sodden air.

ANGUS: Is that you Stephen? Good God. Don't tell me you don't...

STEPHEN (*laughing*): Angie, yer wee shite. So you got out as well.

ANGUS: I don't know if I got out or got in. Anyway I'm here. Aye, but you're looking gey spree.

STEPHEN: You like it? My first and last investment. (*Stephen puts his thumbs in his lapels and preens.*) I need work.

ANGUS: Here? Are you mad?

STEPHEN: I'm not using my name. I've taken my mother's. Doig. Stephen McLeod is dead, may he rest in peace. (*He makes the sign of the cross.*) In the name of the mother, and the son, and all the spirits, holy or not, that will come to haunt me. (*Angus laughs.*) Without confessing a bloody thing Angus, I intend to stand at the altar of God, or in this place at any rate.

ANGUS (*his two outstretched fingers moving down and across*): Blessings be upon you. (*He pauses thoughtfully.*) Who knows you? By sight?

STEPHEN: Who does know me?

ANGUS (*thinking*): Most of them have been out here since the war. You might be in luck. And since they sent Jim Lyle home...

STEPHEN: Jim Lyle? That shite of a tenter from Dens Road?

Why, what did he do?

ANGUS: He killed one of the weavers.

STEPHEN (*taken aback*): And was sent home?

ANGUS: Returned to Dundee for his own protection. The judge decided that the weaver's fatal injury was caused by falling off the cart which took him away. Lyle was given a fifty rupee fine for rendering the man incapable of walking to the hospital on his own two feet.

STEPHEN: So that's how it is. (*He mouths an old favourite of the Dundee mill girls*): 'O dear me, the warld is ill-divided. Them that works the most are aye wi least provided...' (*Angus hums along.*)

ANGUS (*reflectively*): Ah, Stephen, the old songs. (*He is serious now.*) If you're sure this is the place for you, go to Clive Street. In that jacket, they might even take you on.

Clive Street, the mercantile heart of Calcutta, home of the money men, the men who make decisions, not of Empire, but of profit: buy, sell, cut back, expand, invest. Clive Street is lined with cars: Bentleys, Buicks, Auburns, Jaguars and Fords, though there are also horse-drawn gharries with native grooms in attendance. A traffic policeman, upright and smartly dressed in white, stands in the middle of the road.

It is morning. Office workers hurry to their desks behind the street's severe stone facades. We could be in the financial districts of London, Paris or another of the old world's merchant cities of the 1920s, except that the loins of these native clerks are secured by baggy cotton dhotis. Shirt tails dangle. Here and there a babu walks at a more leisurely pace, wearing a long white jacket with a fountain pen in his top front pocket.

Also making their way down Clive Street, and sharing the pavement, are Brahmani cattle which, earlier, were grazing on the Maidan. They proceed with apparent purpose in Indian file behind two rosy English secretaries from the Home Counties, who are sauntering slowly, arm in arm, engrossed in their conversation and unaware of what is gaining on them from the rear. The lead cow, finding itself within chewing range of the girls' skirts, takes a bite. The girls turn round and shriek, first one then the other. Both run off, their arms flapping. The cows continue on ruminatively and pass the main entrance of the offices of Irvine and Company, as Stephen mounts the stone steps that lead in.

Stephen is wearing white trousers, white shirt, tussah jacket and a topee. His posture appears stiff, his face expressionless, almost imperial. He removes his topee. His hair lies flat against his scalp. It has been groomed carefully and combed with oil so that it is now darker, hardly red at all. He crosses a marble floor. On the front page of a discarded newspaper, the *Amrita Bazar Patrika*, we read part of the headline: 'Investors Delighted. Another record...' Stephen climbs a staircase and is directed to a thick panelled door. He knocks.

STEPHEN: Doig, sir.

The door is now half open. From outside the room, we see a large desk. A fan whirs overhead, but out of sight. An old man, bent and sheltering beneath a tangle of white eyebrow, comes slowly into view. He invites Stephen to sit down. We see also the face of a younger man, his son, James Irvine Junior, who remains seated looking sternly at the applicant. Stephen sits. We see his right shoulder and a section of the door.

STEPHEN (*his voice only just audible against the sound of the fan*): I was told that after what happened to Lyle, there might be a vacancy.

IRVINE SENIOR: Ah, Lyle, a sad business.

IRVINE JUNIOR: Ah yes, Lyle, which is why we have to be careful. The right sort of man is difficult to find. The right sort is not usually blown in by the wind.

At that moment, the door, propelled by the draught of the fan, swings forward and hangs without entirely closing. The door, a dark and sombre veneer, now fills most of the screen except for a small crack of light that creeps through the opening. Voices are heard speaking behind it, but muffled. Occasionally a word or two can be made out.

STEPHEN/IRVINE JUNIOR: Harris Academy (*muffled sound*)...engine room (*muffled sound, the squeak of a chair*)... tennis? tennis? (*more muffling*)...the Hilltown, sir.

The door swings open once more.

STEPHEN: My mother. At Dens Road.

IRVINE SENIOR: How is your mother?

STEPHEN: She died, sir, in the fire of 1915.

IRVINE SENIOR (*leaning forward*): The fire yes, terrible business. You had a close shave then yourself James, remember. (*Irvine Jr says nothing.*) A dreadful matter for you, Doig, losing a mother like that. (*He pauses.*) Look here, for our mills we need young men, young Scots men, men who are reliable, who get the job done, who can look after themselves. We'll talk and let you know, but I think, your mother being...

IRVINE JUNIOR: Are you reliable, Doig? Can we count on you?

STEPHEN: Yes, sir. Thank you, sir.

IRVINE SENIOR: This is a great opportunity for you, Doig. Do you know, in my father's day, all up and down the Hooghly there was nothing but scrub jungle or a rice paddy if you were lucky. But, now, there are palaces wherever you look, palaces of industry, work for hundreds of thousands, shelter, water, light, all that the native man wants. Such is the company you join, Doig. Such is your responsibility. Much will be expected.

* * *

A Brahmin once asked a hunter, 'Why, when the killing of animals is loathsome, do you kill?' To which the hunter replied, 'A man must make the most of the work allotted to him.'

'And why was this work allotted to you?'

'Because of the evil I did in an earlier life.'

Séamus jumps into the back of my head, stamping his foot and shaking his fists like a deranged director whose lead has just walked out on him after six months of filming. 'Evil in another life, my granny,' he shouts. 'Your grandfather is the heroic man, Stephen. He returns to the jute in order to face down his demons, was it not yourself who convinced me?'

16

When the bell of my flat rings at four o'clock in the afternoon, I don't expect a policeman to be standing outside.

'Sorry to disturb you, sir,' he says. 'Detective Sergeant McCorquodale, it's about your mother.' Detective Sergeant McCorquodale is an enormous lighthouse of a man with the untroubled skin of a baby and not a trace of facial hair; a sort of man-boy who's overdosed on growth hormones.

'My mother is dead.'

'Yes, we know. But there are a few things to clear up if you don't mind. May I come in?'

I invite him to step past. 'What kind of things?'

He perches on the end of the sofa with the cup of tea I've given him invisible inside his fist. 'We have discovered £100,000 in her account.'

This is a shock. One hundred thousand pounds. My mother. It hardly seems possible. 'Are you sure? How do you know?'

'We found her building society passbook.'

'You did, where?'

'I'm afraid I'm not at liberty to divulge, sir. Let's just say in the line of duty.'

'In the line of duty?' I repeat, readjusting the emphasis to form a question.

'Can you offer an explanation for all that money?'

'Me? No, I can't, we haven't lived together for years, how would I know? Do you know how much money your mother has?'

'I am an orphan, sir,' he says, 'have been for a long time, in fact all my life.'

It seems a curious remark. I wonder whether apparently offhand intimacies of this kind are now encouraged in the CID. I don't know how to respond. Then I find myself saying, 'I am an orphan too, I suppose. Funny, I've never thought of it like that before.'

'No, well, those who've had the benefit of parents don't as a rule, so I find.'

'No, perhaps not.'

McCorquodale straightens. 'We'd like to exhume your mother's body. Do you have any objections?'

I consider this. Before I can speak, McCorquodale says, 'Dig her up, that's what I meant.'

'I know, sergeant.'

'Once the spirit has flown, sir, what is left, really?' He waggles his head from side to side, a gesture of such meaninglessness that it conjures up surprisingly well the state of bodily affairs after the departure of the immortal Self. For a moment, I find myself wondering about my mother, about her next reincarnation; princess or pooch, ant or aardvark, the great totting up of suffering endured against suffering inflicted, the rising or falling on the ladder of life. But, when it comes down to it, how little I know about her personal balance sheet. £100,000. And that man at the funeral, McIntosh, what does he have to add?

And who does the accounting anyway?

McCorquodale's voice. 'So, your mother, can we dig her up then?'

'Yes, I don't have any objection, except she was cremated you know. There are only her ashes. They won't tell you much will they, especially when you consider contamination? I mean, there must be a residue from the last person who went through.'

McCorquodale sighs. 'We never advise cremation. From a police point of view, it is tantamount to the wilful destruction of evidence.'

'Evidence of what? You don't think, you don't suspect that she didn't die naturally, that somebody might have'—the man in the restaurant, the Pathan, I am looking into his eyes—'She was a sick woman, she'd had problems with her lungs for years.'

'We have a duty to make sure, sir, that's all.'

'Are there things you're not telling me sergeant? Why should you believe she didn't die of natural causes?'

'We don't believe or disbelieve at this stage. We're just trying to eliminate possibilities. About the £100,000? Was your mother a wealthy woman?'

'My mother? No, not at all, she had a bit of a pension I think when my father died all those years ago, but I don't know how long that lasted. We never had much money when I was growing up, but we had enough for food and clothes, and for books. I always had books. She believed in books, I'll say that for her.'

'She sounds like a good mother.'

I nod noncommittally. Christ, if I told him about my mother, where would that end up? Those red eyes that wouldn't open beyond a slit at ten o'clock in the morning. The absent presence.

'So, how do you explain the £100,000?' The dogged McCorquodale.

'Sergeant look, I don't know, I'd like to help, but I can't. Perhaps she won it. At the races.'

'Hmm. May I ask, sir, were there people coming to the flat, people you didn't recognize? Strangers?' He spits the word out like a bad taste.

'I haven't lived with my mother for years, as I told you.'

'When you did?'

'I don't know, I don't remember anyone, no one who comes to mind.' Fatal words, to prod the sleeping monster. Suddenly a man is pressing something into my mother's hand. The man stares at me and I look away. None of my business.

'You may or may not be aware, sir, but the tenement in which she lived has, in the past, been connected with drugs.'

'There are drugs in many of them, aren't there, sergeant?'

'Yes, in some, but when a woman without apparent means dies suddenly and is later found to possess £100,000, we have to ask questions.'

'She wasn't an addict, if that's what you think. I'd know that.

She drank, that was her vice.'

'No, not an addict, addicts don't usually have cash. We were wondering about the other side of that coin.' McCorquodale turns his head, taking a sudden interest in the wall.

'You're saying what? That my mother was a dealer? You have evidence, I hope, for an allegation like that.'

'Now calm down, sir, we're not saying she was, and we are not making allegations. We are just looking at possibilities.' McCorquodale stands up. 'Well, thank you, sir. If you remember anything, anything at all, please get in touch.' He hands me a card. 'Oh, by the way,' he says, 'I nearly forgot to ask. Would you mind if we searched your mother's flat?'

'No. Go ahead.'

He closes the door behind him but the ghosts remain on the inside. My breath is coming in bursts. I groan, 'For God's sake, you're dead. Leave me in peace, leave me alone.'

17

A table in the corner. Julia has on that startling lipstick I bought for her: *Forest Rose*. Her mouth is a beacon. When she speaks, it's a flickering fire lit on chalk-white skin. She is speaking now. 'That man with the warning for your mother, do you remember how wide his shoulders were? How can a man have shoulders that wide?'

'Probably a requirement of the job.'

'Why have you never told me about him, Stephen? Why was he threatening your mother? What had she done?' She looks at me straight on and, I can't help it, I turn away. 'What did she do, your mother? Do you know?'

I pour a glass of wine. Do I know? Do I? Really? Beyond reasonable doubt? And if it's true what the police suspect, can I tell Julia? How will she see me after that, my mother dealing drugs? And, anyway, why should I let myself be saddled with Kitty's crimes and misdemeanours, like some donkey labouring under her dead weight.

She thinks I haven't heard. She asks again, 'Who was he, that man with the message?'

I play through, in my head, a small lie. It'll do. 'I don't know. I really don't. He was probably a loan shark. My mother was always borrowing money, paying off one loan with another. It must have caught up with her.'

Julia pauses, seemingly balanced between belief in the truth of what I've told her and an equal measure of disbelief: an equilibrium I don't want to upset. I watch her lost in her own thoughts. 'So, it was time to pay up, was it?' she says.

'Something like that, probably. But, as I say, it's a bit of a mystery.'

'Ah, a mystery. Another mystery. There are so many mysteries in your family, so many unanswered questions, your mother, your grandfather, and you too, Stephen. It must be in the blood. You think your secrets keep you safe, don't you, that if you don't tell, you can't get hurt. But I get hurt when you don't tell, because I don't know what you feel, that is if you feel anything at all. Did you feel anything when your mother died? Or was it so unimportant you didn't think to tell me? A man comes up to you with a message for her but you don't know what it's about, or you know but you don't say. I don't know what to believe anymore, I don't know what's real and what isn't. Karṇa is now more real to me than you are.'

She looks at me while she condemns me, she looks at me out of a place so rooted within her that I feel as if I could pass along the channel she's opened up and touch her deep within: a moment of strange, unsettling beauty, a terrible prelude to what is to come. 'It makes me sad, Stephen,' she continues. 'When I am with you, what I feel the most are the things you hide from me. You probably hide them from yourself, I imagine you do, but it all seems to come out of a dark place, that cold place in the middle of you, which is not a place to live in, not for me anyway. I can forgive Karṇa for wearing his armour in bed; he was born with it. But you, Stephen, I cannot forgive.'

I cast around, I deflect. 'I'm sorry I've been preoccupied lately. With my grandfather. Séamus and I, we're working on him together.'

'I know. I've seen you.'

'He's become important to me. You talk about my mother and my secrets but I feel they all start with him. If I can discover what happened to him, maybe I can understand my mother and perhaps come out of my cold place. I want to, that's all I can say. I want to try. I am sorry if that hurts you.'

'This is good, Stephen, good. I don't want you to choose between your grandfather and me. I am not asking you that. You have already chosen. And you should find out all you can about him. It will help you. But it won't help me. I have tried to understand your reasons for shutting me out and, sometimes, I think I do, but it's not enough. I can't live with a man who keeps all the things that matter to him a secret, I just can't; a man who can't even find it within himself to tell me when his mother is dead.'

With this, she stands up. 'Goodbye, Stephen,' she says. She might have been crying then, but she turns and leaves so quickly I can't be sure.

18

That old hole within me—I know it well—my cold place, which I thought Julia had warmed for me, is back now with its gas and sharp aching stabs, the way fear, aloneness, nothing to cling onto, gets into you when you're young but you can't say what it is because you haven't learnt the labels. And even if you had, what would you do?

And what will I do?

I'll get on with the business of life until it goes away. What else? I will follow old trails, pursue the continuities.

I make it to the Rook which is a down-and-out sort of a place to which no one goes except sad bastards like me. Well, some shabby chin-up specimens too who spend months on end in there getting sadder and more miserable by the hour. The whole place is a monument to misery. The carpet on the floor is drenched in misery: it's riven by sad old threadbare runnels that smile inanely like gap-toothed, sad old men who've lived for a hundred and forty years and learned nothing.

The barman, who must have been picked specially to make the residents feel young, takes five hours to pour me a pint. I move it to a corner table. Heads follow me and watch as I sit down. I look one old bastard in the eye. He nods and turns back to his drink.

The pub door opens and slams shut. Séamus is inside, greeted by a yellowing arcade of denture and drool, the ancients' gapping mouths. I can't blame them for taking an interest. Séamus is wearing some ludicrous get-up, Afghan would be my guess: a flowing caftan of many colours; looks as if it's been specially designed for an effete tribal who's been cut off at the knees. I told him I'd be at the Rook. 'The Rook?' he said. 'Yes, the bloody Rook,' I repeated: so he comes like this. Still, there is no threat, nothing I can't handle if the geriatrics get nasty.

'Over here, Séamus,' I call. He comes over. I get up, wade

through yards of native hostility, order him a pint, and myself another. The purity of the silence around me is interrupted only by the *slurrup* of pouring beer clouding the insides of our glasses. I take the drinks over. The moment for sharing misery has arrived.

'A bloody fool is what you are,' he announces as his head lifts out of his beverage.

'Me?' I reply. I can't raise the energy to exchange insults.

'Your sensitive reactions to the needs of others, if such elusive birds can be said to exist at all, are on the brink of extinction. Or worse. That's all I'll say.' He pauses in his dispensation of good cheer to take another draught. 'As to the question of heart, Stephen,' he adds, sighing and slapping his chest with his free hand, 'a woman would have to be nibbled near to death by frostbite before she'd think of warming her hands on yours.' A further swill goes down. 'And if you'd like me to be frank...' (here he engages me eyeball to eyeball so I can say sure, go on, why not—which I do of course) '...you're not exactly the sort of fella a woman, if she's taking the long view of things, would want to cuddle up to, now are you?'

I remain unoffended. 'But if it was because I didn't take her with me to the funeral,' I say mildly, 'why did she wait so long? She could have gone as soon as she found out.'

'*Ppa.*' Froth flies off his top lip. 'It is not the funeral. Well it is not just the funeral, though that is a good enough reason in itself, right enough. What it is at bottom is you. It's the fundamental nature of you, boyo, that's the problem.' He accompanies these words with an interrogatory raising of the skin across his forehead, the sort of encouraging gesture a teacher offers his least-promising student.

'The fundamental nature of me, whatever that may be, is a big subject,' I reply.

'So it is indeed.' He pauses reflectively as if about to say more. He doesn't. He looks at his watch instead. 'Jays, is that the time?' he declares, bringing his words of comfort to an abrupt halt. 'We'll need another of these.' He nods at the barman who begins his long journey towards the pump handle, glass in hand. Suddenly I have to be alone. 'Must go,' I say, 'work, you know.' Draining what's left of my pint I run out, leaving him in command of his convivial surroundings, his opening remarks to the man closest almost audible as I pass through the door.

Karṇa is waiting for me in my office. How he ached for Draupadī, how cruelly she rejected him. *Nāhaṃ varayāmi sūtam. The son of a charioteer is not good enough for me.* And instead she chose his half-brothers, Arjuna and the rest of them. She became their communal wife, used by them all, their whore. And whose fault was it? Kuntī's of course. She was his mother. If she hadn't held on to her secret, Draupadī would have known him for who he was: Karṇa, son of Surya, god of the Sun.

And who will Julia go to now?

My stomach whorls like a spindle and I am lost in its dread revolution, tangled up in the swirl of meaningless mind waves, the blurted discharge of neuronal impulses. I swirl with Julia and Draupadī, Karṇa, Kuntī and my mother. Moments drift in unconsciousness: one minute? five minutes? I've no idea. A man by the name of Kamal Khan has been found washed up on the West Sands, obviously in the water a few days, bloated, holed, kebabed through the ear-holes by an eel; so the papers say. I feel I will be ill for days. I trudge back to my flat, lie down on my bed and prepare to forget.

19

I stay in bed until the next afternoon, wallowing in the whole sorry mess and forgetting nothing. A strange interval, but that was then. Now I'm fine, mind steady more or less, and a spring in my step. It's not as if I haven't been here before.

I've had some lunch; the remains of a stew which Séamus must have cooked up yesterday. It wasn't bad at all. One of his mother's secrets perhaps, from the back of the shebeen.

He is now typing on his portable. *Tap tap tap tap* he goes. I regard the curve of his great back as he bends low over the keys. Not good for his eyes being so close.

'Have you seen this?' I ask. No reply, so I wave it at him, a slim red book, my grandfather's *Colloquial Hindustani for Jute Mills*, his boss Hindi.

'I have,' he grunts without looking up.

'Can you imagine what it must have cost him to learn this stuff, how it must have bruised his soul to be doing it?'

Séamus says nothing, carries on typing.

Pacing back and forth, I read out some phrases. '*Aisá karo jaisá ham tumko boltá hai:* Do as I tell you. *Do ádmi kal márdálá gayá:* Two men died yesterday. *Wuh usko ek bará intá se már dálá:* He killed him with a big brick.'

Again, no commentary emerges from the wee man. 'Doesn't it strike you as odd,' I continue undeterred, 'that he's in Bengal, but he's learning Hindi instead of Bengali?'

Séamus remains in his own stooped world. Then, breaking his silence, he murmurs a private mantra. Although I suspect this can't be meant for consumption by a wider public than himself, I am sufficiently intrigued to listen carefully (doing my best to capture in words the incomprehensible sound stream rising from the Irishman's larynx.) 'Commendatore Bacibaci Beninobenone, Monsieur Pierrepaul Petitépatant, the Grandjoker Vladinmire Pokethankertscheff, the Archduke Leopold Rudolph von Schwanzenbad-Hodenthaler, Countess Marha Virága Kisászony Putrápesthi, Hiram Y Bomboost, Count Athanatos Karamelopulos.' His verbal flow, though without intelligible content, has a poetic beauty to it, capturing the ripple and rush of a trout stream in Scotland such as might be experienced by a man, a fisherman perhaps or someone propped on an elbow, book in hand but not reading, when the first midges emerge from their afternoon siesta. As I continue to listen—'Ali Baba Backsheesh Rahat Lokum Effendi, Señor Hidalgo Caballero Don Pecadillo y Palabras y Paternoster de la Malora de la Malaria, Hokopoko Harakiri, Hi Hung Chang, Olaf Kobberkeddelsen, Mijnheer Trik van Trumps, Pan Poleaxe Paddyrisky, Goosepond Prhklstr Kratchinabritchisitch, Herr Hurhaus-direktorpräsident Hans Chuechli-Steuerli, Nationalgymnasium-museumsanatoriumandsuspensoriumsordinaryprivatdocentgeneralhistoryspecialprofessordoctor Kriegfried Ueberallgemein'—I realize that I am transcribing from what can only be his native Gaelic. I also realize that my brain, being an egocentric mechanism, unconsciously chooses words which pose no threat to its equilibrium, when, as in a dream, the deeper or truer meaning of what is being revealed is unknown. (My cerebrum, even in its pristine state, has no knowledge of Gaelic, so I believe.)

Respecting the private nature of his recitation, I say nothing until I am sure that Séamus has reached his end. Then, of course, I make no reference to what I've heard, but carry on where I left off. 'It shows what a magnet the jute was, though, doesn't it? Workers flooding in from all over, Orissa, Bihar, UP, lured by the dreams of riches. Same as us Scots.'

'I'm Irish,' says Séamus. He hits a key with a thump and the printer stirs. He is about to say more when he behaves as if struck by revelation. He throws his head in his hands, moaning, 'Though am I now even certain of that? Gob, but it's wearing me down, having to think like you, Stephen. Every word I write, I ask myself, "Does Stephen have the imagination to come up with this?" I'm getting so I can't tell myself apart. There isn't a moment I don't feel the knot in your arse up my own, as if I want to take a dump but can't. It's how you stand it, being yourself, that I don't know.'

I say nothing, appreciating that Séamus is working through his own problems. Knot up my arse. My arse.

The printer has now done its business. He drags out the pages, hands them over and leaves the room. I hear him moving about in the kitchen. A sharp whiff of disinfectant reaches me, accompanied by sounds of water slurping, a sort of tidal ebb and flow. This means only one thing: Séamus has rolled up his sleeves, he's on his hands and knees, he's cleaning the kitchen floor. It's his idea of therapy. 'You should try it Stephen,' he likes to tell me, 'you'll feel a whole lot better for it afterwards.' Right. An image of the wee man comes to me: his tightly packed forearms energetically working the cloth to and fro, an apron around his middle, his hair held in a scarf of paisley pattern. It's a comforting picture of warm domesticity, peopled now by imagined raisin cakes emerging from the oven, hot and homely. I am about to debate with myself how likely it is that he will offer me one, when my reverie is interrupted by five pairs of underpants arriving under their own steam onto the spot of carpet next to my feet. (I recognize them as my own.) A voice accompanies them enquiring as to my progress with the script.

'Can't put it down,' I call back.

20

The single men's mess, early morning, Stephen's room. There's a knock on the door. No answer. His bearer, Noormahamad, enters, puts down the tea he is carrying and starts to tidy. He folds Stephen's trousers over a chair, picks up his socks and places them in a laundry basket. He wipes the bedside table and places the tea tray on it. Stephen's inert body is lying under a mosquito net.

NOORMAHAMAD: Sahib? Chai?

STEPHEN (*murmuring an endearment not addressed to his bearer*): mmwa.

NOORMAHAMAD (*undeterred*): Chai, Sahib.

NOORMAHAMAD (*pushing his face into the protective mesh of the mosquito net and speaking firmly*): Pánch bajá, Sahib, five clock.

Stephen opens his eyes, shakes his head, props himself up for a mouthful of tea, slumps back and observes a gecko darting along the wall. It spears a slumbering moth. The bearer opens the chick blinds.

The single men's communal room looks out over a veranda to the Hooghly but, in spite of a view of water, manages to appear drab and disgruntled like an old gentleman put into a home by relatives. A teak bookcase supports Kipling, Dornford Yates, P.G. Wodehouse, old copies of *Punch* and faded newspapers. In front of the bookcase is a brown sofa which sags in the middle. Beyond that is a billiard table, made in Liverpool. It has worn runnels at the table edge. The locust-green cloth is soggy with damp and spilled whisky. A sideboard, with a rack attached for holding cues and chalk, is against the wall. Wicker chairs form a watching circle. The floor is polished black.

On the other side of the room is a table. Five men sit around it. Before them, a breakfast of toast and eggs. Last night's cigarettes linger. The milk is blue, boiled, watered and drawn from a buffalo.

Browne is holding court. He is the second in command to the manager, McLeish. Fifteen years ago in Dundee he was Rab Broon, a working man of no particular distinction. Now he is Robert Browne, Esquire.

BROWNE (*sniffing with obvious disgust*): Milk, real milk, milk fit to drink, Abdul, comes from a cow. This has been mentioned to you before, has it not?

ABDUL: Yes, Sahib, mentioned many times. Today, only buffalo. Cow all going. Buffalo is much good-healthy.

The cook puffs out his chest and pats it like a man who holds deep within himself the secret of the life-giving properties of buffalo milk.

BROWNE (*sarcastically*): Well, I'm sure you'll enjoy drinking it when we're gone.

Abdul's head sits upright on his neck and then drops minimally to left and right. He watches as the five men leave.

STEPHEN (*on his way out, reassuring*): Cow's milk is what we are used to, that's all. There are no buffalo in Scotland.

Outside the mess, one of the men, Jimmy Pearson, a salesman, gets into a car and drives off. The remaining four walk to the mill. They are joined by eight others, seven of whom have tiptoed out of married bungalows while their wives sleep. One wife does not sleep. She is in the pool, and gives them a cheery wave as they pass. She blows a kiss in the direction of her husband, but on whom it lands no one can be quite sure.

The twelve Scots, their faces in various shades of Dundee pink, cross the watered green of the compound gardens and enter the brown as mud, massive bricked twenty-foot walls and iron arches of the mill. It is dark inside, jute brown, brown as India, and heating up nicely. The men's mouths open, swallow dust and close. Each goes to his work.

The machines parade in lines, a legion of clanking metallic beasts ravenous for jute and being stuffed with it non-stop by brown sweating mill hands, women and men. Pace is everything, the be all and end all. Pace and sweat and dust. Native sardars, like shepherds, patrol with iron-tipped crooks. Stephen walks up and down, down and up, nodding, saying little. He inspects an open bale from which women are shaking handfuls of fibre. At his side, is McLeish, the manager of the factory.

MCLEISH: The two most important words in the English language, Doig: *jaldi jaldi*. Means get an effing move on. A kick up the backside, a boot up the behoochie, that's what this lot needs. You don't kick them, I'll kick you. Fair enough? Need to know where we stand so we don't get to that, eh.

STEPHEN: A boot up the behoochie.

MCLEISH: Aye, a good strong boot. (*He nods in the direction of a group of Indians.*) You see, son, the heathen is like a child and you're his father. Be fair, but be firm. Let him know who's boss because, if you don't, the sacks don't get woven, and if the sacks don't get woven, they don't make their wages, the investors don't get their dividends and no one's happy, not them, not me. Yi ken whut um sayin ti yi, laddie?

STEPHEN: Aye, aken, sir.

The mess, morning. The mill assistants are eating their second breakfast. Flesh and rice have been added to the base of toast, butter and jam. It is still early.

BROWNE: Christ, Abdul, call this breakfast, we are hungry men. (*Browne chews on a piece of fried fish and downs the first of three whisky pegs.*) The secret is, Doig old son, knowing how much is enough. Too much and you are a menace to yourself. Too little and you are a menace to everybody else. Here (*he reaches across a stubby forearm on which black hairs are dotted like flies on fly paper*) join the club, drink up. (*He hands Stephen the whisky and soda that Abdul has just put in front of him.*)

STEPHEN: It's ten o'clock in the morning. (*He continues to sip his tea.*)

Conversation tires the men out. Silence, pierced only by the clink of china and glass, prevails. The air is now dripping with heat. Sweat bubbles out of their pink faces. The sun steams through the jhilmils.

ANGUS: Aye, well, back to work.

Stephen catches his eye and they walk together to the mill. The men and women who were in the mill earlier are there still, and the babies who were lying on bales of jute fast asleep are still asleep. A baby stirs and a mother (nameless, one among many) notices, bends down and rubs oblivion into his gums. The baby goes back to sleep.

ANGUS: It's a mill, Stephen. What do you expect? What would you do, not employ them?

STEPHEN: And when they're addicted?

ANGUS: If they live that long. They fall asleep under a pile of jute tow, they don't wake up. It's the life they're born to. This is India.

STEPHEN: So this is India, and I, who was not born to it, am a Sahib.

ANGUS (*slapping him on the back*): That's right, laddie, and don't you forget it.

* * *

The colours now are greyer, the faces of the men less precise, the focus hazier. We have a sense of time passing as if one morning has become two or perhaps two hundred. Stephen, Angus and the Kerani (the mill bookkeeper) are sitting down to a muddy soup. Browne's footsteps are heard coming up wooden steps and along the mess veranda. He kicks the door open.

BROWNE (*roaring, even before he is through*): A peg, Abdul, *jaldi jaldi.*

THE KERANI (*putting a finger to his mouth and whispering*): His wife. A letter this morning. Always puts him in a bad mood. (*He looks down into his bowl.*)

Browne flings a sack of courgettes, cabbages, plantains and

cucumbers at Abdul, grabs his whisky and soda, and slumps morosely into the sofa. It exhales with a submissive groan and bends down to the floor.

BROWNE: Sardars, Christ. Vegetables! (*He inspects his now empty glass with irritation.*) Abdul. (*He turns round.*) Abdul... dammit, bolshie nigger, never there when you need him...Abdul, what's happened to the bloody ice?

ABDUL: No eyes, Sahib. Eyes all going. Too hot eyes.

KERANI: This heat.

Abdul brings in a cold ham garnished with cucumber slices. Angus carves.

ANGUS (*passing round the plates*): What about you, Browne? Ham?

Browne doesn't answer. He continues to drink whisky.

KERANI: Eat up. We can't leave it all for...(*He looks over his shoulder at Abdul, then turns back to Stephen. He winks.*) The good Mohammedan caught at it. (*He rocks with laughter, imitating as he does so Abdul's teeth sunk into a joint of ham.*) You should have seen his face, Stephen. (*He continues laughing as if the Abdul-ham incident was the funniest thing he has ever witnessed. Tears roll down his cheeks.*) God. (*He wipes himself dry. He suddenly becomes serious.*) This country! Split so many ways it doesn't know whether it's coming or going. One lot doesn't eat pork, except when no one's looking, the other doesn't eat beef. One water tap for the Hindus, another for the Mohammedans. The wrong person's shadow falls on a Hindu's food, that's it, throw it out. Each for his own, that's their problem. No idea what side they're on. (*He shakes his head in disbelief.*)

ANGUS (*spears a slice of ham, holds it above his head and sings winsomely*: 'Oh dear me, the world is ill divided/Them that works the most are aye wi least provided...' (*Stephen accompanies him by drumming the table top with the flat of his hands.*)

BROWNE (*from the sofa, moaning*): Christ, it's only two o'clock, half the bloody day to go.

—Here the scene ends; inconclusively, I can't help thinking. I am about to write a note to Séamus telling him so, when I realize there is nothing to stop me continuing it in his style; or rather in my own, since Séamus swears it has become his. I move to my desk. I begin; or, rather, I carry on. My fingers flow—

Stephen's room, the afternoon lie-down. He is on his back, looking up at a fan whiring noisily and slowly above him. Close up of Stephen's face on which the shadow of the fan blades circulates, like a wheel in motion going nowhere, like time passing.

Stephen is walking. It is four o'clock on another day, in another year. Dust has scrambled deeper into his clothes than even Noormahamad can dig. His hair lies listlessly on his head. A tailorbird chirrups relentlessly, *chuvee-chuvee-chuvee*. Neem blossoms of faded white give off the pungent smell of sweet sick. Flies hover about them in their millions and form the only black cloud in a glaring sky which otherwise stretches unbreakably blue as far as the great beyond. Grass lies limp. Flowers are withered like hope. In front of Stephen's feet, an army of ants advances. The ants are red like the soldiers of the Raj, and march in step.

STEPHEN (*squatting, inspecting their precise columns*): There's McLeish (*he points*), there's Browne, there's the Kerani, there's Angus, and there, lagging behind, God help me, is me. (*He holds his finger above the trailing ant and, on an impulse, squashes it.*)

21

Howrah station, midmorning, a buzzing behind a blurred image, like a stir of bees. In the blur of the hive, there is movement as of bodies crawling over bodies. Slowly the buzz, the blur and the bodies come into focus. We hear voices shouting, crying, arguing, and we see people swarming over a platform. A night train from up-country—one of many—has just pulled in. It exhales after its journey (a pungent white-grey steamy purr of a breath) and continues to breathe out bodies.

From their dress, we realize that the passengers are poor. They look about in bewilderment as if this is the first time they have seen such things as they see now. Two people catch our interest: a mister and missus from up-country, Sunil Kanaujia and his wife, Parvati. They are villagers like the others, good with buffalo and at making dung cakes; yet there is something about this couple that singles them out.

The husband is young, dignified and tired. Around his wrist he wears the sacred thread, the sign that his forbears, before they were tillers of the land, were Brahmin. We notice how he carries himself: clearly a man not accustomed to taking care where his shadow falls. Yet, it is to his wife, half in shot, that the eye is drawn.

Parvati is busying herself gathering up her belongings on the station platform. As she straightens, we see she is a girl on the cusp between childhood and womanhood, about to step over. Her face is fresh, still soft from the world of family, fields, crops, trees, air, river and rocks that she has left behind. Her body is lithe, almost feline, as it is for young women who have just become aware of the power that has magically descended, the power to attract. We see her pleasure in this, as well as her uncertainty. As she moves, she holds a hand in front of her breast to protect it from men's eyes. She keeps her head lowered and attends only to the commands of her husband.

Sunil looks around at the countless heads on the station platform rippling like the sea, a current of humanity propelled by its own unknowable purposes. He hears the clank of pistons, feels the iron and steel and concrete around him and is gripped by despair.

Sunil and Parvati push through the crowd. He has a roll of bedding balanced on his head. In each hand, he carries a box tied with string from which pots descend. He steps over bodies. Parvati follows. He asks directions of a stranger. Hands point, heads shake.

Three hours later, a *durwan*, the keeper of the mill gate, is looking out from behind the smoke of a strangled bidi and scratching his arse.

SUNIL (*to the durwan*): Bochu Sardar told us to come: that there would be work.

The durwan spits and nods at a boy. The boy runs off. Sunil and Parvati wait in silence staring at the ground. Bochu Sardar, big boned, bandy legged, gnawing on a neem stick, hurries up to the new arrivals.

BOCHU (*in a booming voice*): Ah, welcome, you have come. (*He places his hands on the shoulders of Sunil and smiles at his wife. Parvati's head is tilted at a slight angle, her hair gathered at the back, her teeth are bright, her smile easy. She wears a simple pink sari.*)

BOCHU: Well, you will be tired, so much travel. Come back tomorrow. For now, relax. Do you have somewhere to stay? Relatives? A brother in law? No...? Well perhaps I can find you something. I have some modest bustees, one rupee, eight annas a month, very reasonable. But look around. Try others. (*Sunil shakes his head from side to side.*) You'd like to take it? Good, good, you will not be disappointed. The boy will show you.

Thatched huts of mud sit humped in rows. Between the rows, a stagnant stream of sewage stews like thick soup bubbling in the clotted heat. Mosquitoes swarm. Garbage rots. Parvati gathers her sari about her and steps as lightly as she can down this gutter of filth. The boy stops outside one of the huts. Parvati and Sunil push aside the sacking that is over the doorway, stoop and step down onto a mud floor. Inside, there is no window, no light and no air. Only heat. Parvati puts her hand to her long elegant throat. Above her, one end of the roof is sagging as if about to collapse.

BOY (*smiling*): Bustee very good.

SUNIL: Very good, thank you.

The next morning finds Sunil and Parvati waiting outside the mill gates. Around them are men and boys, thin black and brown with sloping shoulders and towels from waist to knee, and tired women in saris, some with babies lying inert across their chests, and stray dogs nosing about in hope of scraps.

Bochu Sardar moves towards the gate, speaking to this man and that, waving some through and some away.

BOCHU (*to Sunil*): Ah, you have come back. Good. And you want to work, yes? Mm, I wonder. I think we can find something though, as you see…(*Bochu points to the men outside the gates milling around. He scratches his head.*) No, don't mind them, take no notice. (*He waves a hand dismissively.*) Bochu Sardar looks after his people. (*He smiles at Parvati.*) A possibility, perhaps, in *winding*. Four rupees, four annas a week, seventeen rupees a month. And for your good wife, *softening*. Two rupees, four annas a week. That's, let me see, for you both, nine rupees, seventeen… twenty-six rupees a month.

Sunil and Parvati turn to each other happily. They bring their hands together in front of their chests and incline their heads toward the sardar.

BOCHU (*apologetically*): Of course I have expenses, I'm sure you appreciate. Usually, when I give jobs, I require thirty rupees down. Two jobs…in this case…(*he shakes his head*) okay, forty. And then two rupees a month from each of you for two years. Now don't worry. If forty is difficult…?

SUNIL: We do not have forty. We have… (*he looks at Parvati*) ten only. This is all that remains from what we borrowed to come here.

BOCHU: Ten? It's not much. (*He pauses.*) Well, all right, you pay ten now, and I will charge interest on the thirty that you owe me at one anna to the rupee per month. It's nothing. Less than two rupees a month.

PARVATI (*despairing*): It is too much. We pay you for the bustee, then we pay you two rupees a month, then we pay you ten rupees, and now we must pay two more rupees. We also have to eat.

Bochu Sardar shrugs his shoulders and turns to leave.

SUNIL: We are most grateful, Sardar Sahib. (*He bows.*) We will work hard and make much money.

22

I am in the Rook with a pint of Bellhaven and a cheese toastie, when Séamus comes in. He pulls up a chair and nods at the barman. 'I like what you're doing with the script by the way,' he says. 'You've got the hang of it all right.' I find myself more pleased by this remark than I might have imagined.

The barman totters over with a black pint. 'You're a decent man, Terry,' says Séamus, sitting back like royalty. 'My pleasure,' comes the tremulous reply. 'Ah, ow, but I'm gasping for it.' Séamus pours half the jar into himself and declares frothily, 'Bloody good it is, the stout they serve in here.' Terry's back, which is to be seen proceeding at the pace of a moribund barnacle to its station behind the bar, twitches in delight.

'I am touched by your comment, Séamus, I am really,' I tell him, 'but don't you think that, from the point of view of what we can know to be true, we may have a problem?'

'The stuff is there all right,' he replies.

'You mean that our guess is as good as the next man's?'

'I mean nothing of that sort whatsoever. I mean that some facts, deeds, conversations, landscapes, betrayals, sacrifices, acts of love, misery and other things too numerous to mention, are inevitable. You don't have to see for yourself to know: if they don't exist, there will be a gap in the explicable like a missing eon; like having a world with coal and oil and gas, but no Carboniferous Period. Truth is the bridge between two incontestable events which threatens the sanctity of neither.'

'That's good,' I reply, 'I like it. The bridge between two incontestable events. But bridges can come in different shapes and sizes.'

'They can,' he says.

'So how do you know which bridge is the right one?'

'You have to listen, Stephen. You have to use your ears.' He

points earwards. 'Do you not recall the words of the Bard himself?' Séamus leans forward confidentially and, like the ham he is, gives me his Kenneth Branagh whisper: '"And those who wish to hear fall silent as Ulysses begins his pitiful lament."' He straightens up, his eyebrows pendulating in the draft of an open door. 'That's the first thing, anyway,' he says, 'the wishing to hear.'
   'Shakespeare?'
   'Homer.'
   'Homer? Are you sure?'
   'It's either him or the other fellow.'
   Whether I wish it or not, I hear the truth of my grandfather getting closer. I feel my body tightening in anticipation.

* * *

Browne walks up the wide pass between the spinning frames. On either side of him, noise floats on jute dust, the whir of countless bobbins like the hum of a vast army of foot soldiers on the march. It is a noise without end and, on most days, it comforts Browne, as if it is a sign that the industrial power of the Empire is also without end, as if it is a personal reminder of the immensity of the Raj. But today it irritates him. The shriek of wheels above his head driving the cables, powering endless lines of machines, cuts into the back of his eyes. In three months his wife will be back. He brings the short switch which he holds in his right hand down hard on the palm of his left.
   Bochu Sardar who carries a much longer stick, a lathi with an iron tip, rolls towards him. Browne finds his bow legs, his cocky swagger, his very existence irritating.
   BROWNE: No more vegetables, Bochu, if you don't mind. If it's courgettes I bloody want, I can get them myself. Christ, they're on sale in the bazaar for a few pice. Who do you think I am, to be bought for nothing?
   BOCHU (*bowing deeply, his palms pressed together at his*

chest): I am at your service, Sahib. Tell me what is it I can provide. The pleasure will be mine.

BROWNE: My wife is coming back in three months.

BOCHU: Ah, very good, Sahib, very good, Sahib is much pleased and I am pleased for Sahib also. Is it a gift for her that you require?

BROWNE: No, I do not, and Sahib is not bloody well pleased. Sahib is very displeased.

BOCHU: Sahib is displeased?

BROWNE: That's what I said. Displeased. Very. Which means we must make hay while the sun shines. (*The sardar looks at him, uncomprehending.*) Oh, for Christ's sake Bochu, next time bring me a woman, not a brace of cabbages.

BOCHU: Yes, Sahib. Indian women not good for Sahib. Not clean.

BROWNE: I don't mean a street woman you idiot, I don't want a woman that's been used five times a night since last Christmas by every drunk in the bazaar. I mean a better sort of woman. A woman with dignity, with poise. A woman of modesty. A woman like... (*his finger sticks out and points*) that.

Bochu follows the finger. A woman's slender form stands partially framed by a steel girder that runs from floor to ceiling. The back of her hand brushes against the hot metal. On one ankle hangs a simple bracelet. Parvati holds herself erect, except that her long neck is turned to the right as if glancing away. And down. Wisps of jute cling to her sari which is of cotton and undecorated.

BOCHU: She is married, Sahib.

BROWNE: Aren't they all?

The mill, Friday, wage day. Sunil is at his winding machine. As Browne walks by, he puts his hands together and bows deeply, even deeper than Bochu, because Sunil does not hold a lathi in his hand. He coughs, and is rewarded with a light tap, hardly noticeable; Browne's switch jumping out from his armpit, doing the business of the Raj, returning in one efficient move. Sunil, knowing that today he will be paid, smiles. In a moment, he will cough again, and spit.

The Kerani's babus are at a long table by the mill gate calling out names from a list, and behind them, walking with his hands clasped behind his back, is the Kerani himself. Durwans patrol this side of the gate and, on the other, tall beaked men from Kabul stand with smiles on their faces and lathis restless in their hands, like tigers looking down on a watering hole where barasingha and sambar fatten. Sunil is pleased that he does not owe money to the Kabulis.

BABU (*shouting*): Kanaujia Sunil.

Sunil, hearing his name, coughs a small amount of blood into his cheeks, does not spit and shuffles forward. His walk is no longer that of a peasant who breathes fresh air. His feet no longer caress the ground like a man caresses the things he loves. His shadow is no longer careless about where it falls.

BABU: One rupee four annas deducted. Yarn breakages.

A cashier pushes the balance of his wages, three rupees, to the edge of the table and, as part of this same movement, a movement of studied dismissiveness, bends his neck and shoulder away from Sunil, looks down to the lines of his ledger and calls out sharply the name of another waiting man. Sunil gathers his money and tucks it into the folds of his dhoti.

BOCHU (*his arm round Sunil's shoulder*): Fines, Sunil, we all suffer. (*Bochu's eyebrows rise heavenward in an expression of a world replete with ill-divisions; us-them, brown-white, rich-poor.*) But I'm afraid I must ask for the money you owe. Let me see; hardly anything as I recall. (*He flicks through squares of paper held in place by a clip. He hums to himself and, with a gesture that invites a wry smile in recognition of the inadequacies of filing systems the world over, finally alights on the one he is looking for.*) Yes, erm, rent eight annas, interest on loan eight annas, and the money you didn't pay me last week, plus interest...' (*he licks the tip of his index finger*), that is two rupees two annas.

SUNIL: But, Sahib, I only have three rupees. For eating. For my wife eating. She earning little-little. (*Sunil coughs again and this time a red flux shoots from his lips and leaves a stain on the ground.*)

BOCHU: And for betel I see. Spend less on that and you'll be fine, your wife will be fine. Now, (*his grip tightens around Sunil's shoulder*) I must insist, two rupees two annas. Please.

SUNIL: Sahib, I cannot. It is too much. More time needed, Sahib.

BOCHU: That's just the problem Sunil, no more time. What can I do? (*Bochu shrugs.*) I gave you more time last week and the week before and the week before. I am a poor man. I cannot afford such generosity. But you are rich, Sunil. You have a beautiful wife and any man with a beautiful wife is rich. I have none. I am poor.

SUNIL: She is beautiful, yes, but still she has to eat.

BOCHU: A beautiful woman can always eat. (*Bochu looks into Sunil's eyes; but the husband's gaze is on the red mud at his feet.*) I know someone, someone who will pay all your debts, and will ask in return only a small thing; just one month with your wife; how quickly the time will pass. All your debts, Sunil, just one month; so much for so little. No, no, not me (*he laughs in self-deprecation*), me I am not worthy, a much greater man than me, a white man, a soft man, a clean man. One month only. Maybe two.

Sunil thrusts two rupees two annas into Bochu's hand and flees taking with him fourteen annas, the price of a week's work, not enough to feed a skeleton.

23

I am passing the flower shop, just walking, when I see a girl's face, a face which is vaguely familiar, looking out. Not at me. Not even at the street and its passers-by. Her eyes are open too wide, her expression too wistful for that. In her dreams, I suppose. Then, after I walk on a few paces, I remember where I've seen her before. She was talking to Julia in the Big Quad that day I met Julia for the second time.

I go in.

Surrounded by plants, she looks at me closely and asks, 'Can I help you?'

I don't know what sort of opening I'm hoping for, but it isn't this. She shows no sign of knowing my connection to Julia. Yet she must. Julia must have talked about me. And if I recognize her, she must recognize me. It throws me and I say the first word that comes out.

'Roses.'

She waves her arm in the direction of twenty different kinds and colours. 'We have roses.'

Not wanting a flower of any kind, I say, 'Just one, please.'

'For girl?'

I nod, why not.

'Is anniversary?'

'No.'

'Peace offering?'

'No.'

'Is for what, then?'

I don't know how to answer. Thinking of Julia, I say, 'Well, it's for something to bring us closer.'

'What colour you have in mind for closer?'

'Red,' I reply tentatively.

'We have these...colour of blood.' She holds one out to me.

'What you think, too much'—she presses a hand against her breast—'emotion perhaps?'

'Maybe.'

'Okay.' She steps dreamily around a four-foot orchid and points. 'So these? See how light plays with flesh of petals making colour like gold, you don't think so?'

'And when there is no sun?'

'Then dull,' she replies flatly.

Still she gives no sign of knowing me.

'Are you a student?' I ask.

'One day perhaps, not now. I come here to read great writers of Scotland, Robbie Stevenson, Sir Walter Scott, Ian Rankin. You know Rankin? *Hanging Garden, Dead Souls*—like Gogol—*Blue and Black*, very good…' She sighs. 'But most of day I am just flower girl…So you want?'

I say—what else can I say?—'Yes. Three of those please.' I point at random.

And since I can't very well throw them away, I take them home. Séamus squints at me curiously. 'Well now, Stevo, unless somebody's been buying you flowers, which I rather doubt, I believe a most welcome change has come over you.' He puts a hand in the air as if to stop me denying it. 'No, no, let me put into words what I believe has been happening here. First, if I read the situation right, you feel this desire to cheer the place up a bit and perhaps also to cheer yourself up at the same time. That is so, is it not? Then, not wanting the wish to lie unfulfilled, you visit the flower shop. Finally, and not at all like yourself, if I may say so, you reach into your pocket and hand over coin of the realm. Truly this is a wonderful thing for someone like yourself to be doing and nothing to be ashamed of at all.' And he comes over, takes my hand in his and allows happy, if inarticulate, gurgling noises to collect in the back of his throat.

24

It is a strange thing how the death of a mother, the impact of her death, starts to affect you long after you're sure it won't. It's like after a blast in the eardrum, that's all you hear, the blast, and then for a while nothing but that black silence, it's all you think you'll ever hear again; until you wake up one morning and there they are, the old noises back again.

I opened the door yesterday afternoon and found McCorquodale standing on the step, blotting out the light. I don't know how long he'd been there. He came in and sat on the sofa as he had the first time. I'd forgotten how innocent his eyes looked, but perhaps that was just a borrowed innocence, eyes next to pink cheeks, cheeks smooth as blossom: like all reflections, not entirely to be trusted. He leant towards me, apparently considering what to say, or how to say it, but I had the feeling he was trying to intimidate me. Being intimidated by an enormous six-foot-six baby: it was disquieting; that, and whatever new revelation he might have brought with him.

'We searched your mother's flat. We found nothing at first.' He paused.

'At first?' I followed his prompt. Advisable to play along.

'A flat, even a small one, has many hiding places,' he replied, 'but we usually get what we come for.'

'And did you?'

'We did. A room is like the human mind. In the public areas, people put everything they want you to see. In the private areas, in for example the spaces between a ceiling and the floor above, or a wall and the wall beyond'—he pointed with both hands, like an air stewardess demonstrating the position of exit routes—'they put everything they don't. The trained eye is rarely deceived.'

'It must be a bit unsettling when a friend invites you round for a drink…wondering about all those hidden things above your head.'

'Unsettling?' He stared at me quite calmly as if he was sizing me up. 'Not really. Some of my colleagues have told me that when they go to a suspect's house and they know they're being lied to, they have the urge to put their fists through the plaster and rip the whole lot down, but I can't say that's something I struggle with, not particularly. Violence never gets you very far, not in my line of work.'

'No,' I said, nodding in agreement, feeling unsettled. 'And did you find anything in the non-visible part of my mother's little flat?' I enquired. Then I added, 'how did you leave it by the way, in what state?' I grew up in that flat. It wasn't much, but I wouldn't like to think of it as rubble now.

'We were careful. We always are. And, since you ask, we did find a place where things had been hidden.'

'What things?'

McCorquodale probed silently, innocent eyes searching for what I knew, or suspected, or wished to hide, or had already hidden in my cameral subconscious. 'Heroin,' he said.

'You found heroin in my mother's flat?'

'There were traces. Forensics are very thorough these days. They don't miss much. It looks as if somebody removed whatever was there.'

'Does that have anything to do with my mother?' I considered what was being laid before me. I scratched around for alternative explanations. 'A dealer could have been using the flat without her knowledge. Or the heroin could have been put there years ago by a previous occupant, or by anybody passing through for that matter.'

'That's possible, sir, but it was her flat.'

I kept silent. It was her flat. Did that make it her heroin? Probably. Secret lives, secret motivations. My God.

'Forensics also found a hair, a long human hair.'

I let him go on.

'A single hair tells us everything. If we could match the DNA to your mother, or rather not match it, we might be able to rule her out of our enquiries. Except, unfortunately, she was cremated.'

McCorquodale settled back as if waiting for some further explanation of my mother's cremation: a matter which had no further explanation. We had to do something with the body.

'Do you mind if I collect some DNA from you, sir,' he said after a while. 'It would save a lot of police time.'

'Certainly, sergeant,' I replied, 'pleased to help.' I was. I thought it might stop Dundee's finest ripping this place to pieces. He drew a swab from an inside pocket, loomed over me like Jupiter as seen from one of its moons, and poked it into my open mouth. 'That's it, done.'

I got up, rubbing under my chin where he'd swabbed me.

It was McCorquodale's visit that set things off. I was annoyed with myself for not asking where exactly he found the heroin. I wanted to be told, which wall, which ceiling. Before I knew it the place was back in my head and I was a boy in pyjamas, hiding behind my barely open bedroom door, peering through the crack. I wasn't looking so much as listening, wanting to hear but not be heard. How dead it was outside my room, a bottomless pool of absence which seemed to swirl noiselessly around the vortex that was the tremor in my stomach. Then I remembered what I was listening for: a cough, a bottle pouring, a sign of life.

This was after my father had gone, long gone by then, leaving behind nothing except his suit and a small photograph which lived, ruthlessly polished, on the window ledge. Memento mori. He is standing by a dark table, in a different flat, perhaps in a house, somewhere with dark furniture anyway. I liked how he was in that photo: gentle, ruddy, like a farmer in his Sunday best, uncomfortable, his collar too tight and him crammed into a suit (mine?) as if he'd never worn one before. He was older than her, I know that. At least twenty years. I wonder how they met, what he saw in her.

Once you start these memories, there's no end to them. Creep, creep, they tiptoe in. My mother and I must have taken a bus into the country and were walking across a field. It was after the harvest, tufts of stubble under my shoes. My mother was happy. Perhaps that's why I remember it, her face with the lights full on. We were swinging our arms as we walked along, laughing, enjoying being out in the autumn sun, I suppose. There were trees on one side. We must have moved towards them, big trees that towered over us. Were we now in shade? Maybe.

I don't know what it was, I don't think it was a gun, perhaps a farmer had hit his gate with the end of his tractor. *Bang.* God, it was close. It could have been a gun: it had that blasting noise that blots out everything else. I swung round but didn't notice anything which might have explained it. Then I saw my mother, face to face with some awful thing, some terrible ghost. Her legs were trembling as if she wanted to get away but couldn't, as if she was captured by her own nightmare. I've had those nightmares: weighed down and wading through treacle; you struggle, you cry out, but there's no escaping.

But what comes back to me most graphically, most starkly, is that hand. Her hand. It is clinging to me, flush red, veins standing proud, like Scrooge clinging to his last farthing. For grim death. Yet I know this much (and knew it then), that it wasn't me she was holding, not really. I could have been a fence post, the King of England or five thousand volts of live current for all the difference it made. Anything that gave her a grip.

And now, implanted by McCorquodale, I have to ask: was it sins committed she was clinging to, or sins to come?

25

Séamus, stately in a cape of black bought at bargain price from a shop in Edinburgh specialising in whips, nasal safety pins and other esoterica (which he just happened to be passing, so he said), enters, bearing a key. He holds it aloft, mothlike, and proclaims in his own unfathomable gibberish: gyreOgyreOgyrotundO...or something like it. Since the incantation is undertaken without benefit of jaw movement or separation of verbal components, it is hard to be sure. Besides, I am not listening carefully. I am horizontal, on my back, gazing sightlessly upwards, my lids at rest, my mind latched onto an endless repetition of a meaningless question which loops round and round and keeps on repeating even after I've answered it, and answered it again. This happens to me. I am a bull led round a show ring by its nose.

Suddenly a blow lands centrally (liver? kidney? spleen?). 'Wake up,' issues forth the voice of the high priest, Zadok Séamus the self-appointed, 'the disinterring of your grandfather is a matter of the utmost importance, as you of all people should rightly comprehend.'

He raises himself to his full height. Spreading his arms, he invites the spirits to look kindly on our unworthy endeavours and grant us success at the Box Office (but not an Oscar unless it is felt we truly deserve it). Séamus then thrusts the key into its hole. 'Each box is a birth,' he chants, 'little by little, we bring you back, we are your midwives, we are old Indiana himself.' This seems to satisfy him because he turns to me, a glisten in his watery eyes, and declares, 'Sure is it not a great thing to return a man to life, that's all I'll say.'

This piece of bogus sentimentality now behind him, he waves me forward onto my hands and knees. 'There's the reek of old devils in there Stephen, his and yours, sniff them out, boyo, sniff out those slippery time-wasting sons of bitches.' I insert my head.

There's a smell of something in there all right, but whether it's devils is hard to know. It could be. Devils come in all shapes and sizes. Their smells too, I daresay. I remove my grandfather piece by piece and lay him out on the carpet.

* * *

By flower beds and trees, behind the chatter of wives, we hear the *ping ping* of rifle bullets, the sounds of Sunday. The Auxiliary Force is finishing target practice. A group of European Assistants, twenty or so, carrying rifles and a Lewis gun, appear. We recognize Browne and Angus among them, and glimpse the shaded face of a man who might be Stephen.

BROWNE: God, I was good today. (*He puts the rifle to his shoulder, takes aim at something—we can't see what—and pretends to squeeze the trigger.*) *Ppeea*. Couldn't miss. How about you Angus?

ANGUS (*shrugging*): Same as usual.

BROWNE: Doig? (*Stephen doesn't reply.*)

Sounds change. Now it is of tennis balls. *Poonk...pong... pong...thwick...*(a restrained expletive interrupts)*...poonk... pong...thwack.* The court grass is immaculately mown and watered. *Poonk*. Sweat pours down Stephen's face as he runs back to return a high lob. He misses, and dabs his forehead with a handkerchief. Angus (his opponent) is undisturbed in spite of the sun. He is of a darker complexion and was once a member of the Lochee Tennis Club. The game continues watched by two girls, Mary and Monica, who were last seen on Clive Street attracting the interest of cattle.

STEPHEN: Let's have a swim, Angus, for God's sake. A swim, girls?

MARY: Ooh yes, erm but where will we change? There doesn't seem to be...

STEPHEN: You can change in our rooms. We won't look...

Angus, no looking now, you hear.

ANGUS: No looking yourself.

The girls walk off, skirts swinging. They titter, and glance back over their shoulders.

MARY (*coquettishly*): No looking now, you hear.

Monica sits by the side of the pool, her hair under a cap. Her knees are drawn up, her back arched. She has turned away from the sun, and away from Angus whose fingers are inching like five hungry snakes towards her waist. Mary is next to her, balancing on the water's edge. Below her straw hat, with a garland of flowers above the rim, is a friendly open face, rounded like a peach with pink splashes on the cheeks. She wears a shapely swimming tunic with frilly knee-length knickers just showing below. Her hair falls in curls onto her shoulders. She is holding a parasol above her head like a tightrope walker. She folds it suddenly and spears with its point one of the inching fingers. Angus yelps.

ANGUS: Whut fer yi day thit?

STEPHEN (*laughing*): In you go, Mary hen. (*Mary, also laughing, stays where she is, a bubble of pink and yellow, her bright lights playing in the pool's golden refractions.*)

STEPHEN: Come on, I'll catch you. (*He jumps in, and stands in the water holding his hands out.*)

MARY (*preening*): What if you don't Stephen? How do I know I can trust you?

STEPHEN: Oh, you can trust me alright, um fae Dundee.

He reaches out and pulls her gently towards him. She descends with unexpected weight, like an anchor, and takes Stephen down with her. In the commotion of flailing arms that follows, and the surprising sight of knickers appearing above the waterline upside down, he finds he has grabbed a part of the girl that a young man of limited acquaintance should not. His knees straighten and he rises from the foam with his catch.

MARY (*spluttering and blowing out water*): Ppwwwph.

STEPHEN: Och yi. (*He kisses her firmly on the lips.*)

It is now dark. The four of them walk along a red dirt track that will soon pass through the bazaar around which the native mill workers live. They are taking a shortcut to the station.

MONICA: Even if it is horrid as we expect, it will be such fun, won't it?

MARY (*giggling nervously*): How exciting.

They reach a stagnant stream of sewage sweating undigested in the heat. Rows of bustees stretch in unbroken lines of two in front of them. The air is thick with flies. Smoke from cooking fires is coming out through the sides of the hovels. Angus looks enquiringly at the girls.

MARY (*struggling not to gag*): Yes, of course we want to go on.

The girls pinch their noses as tight as breathing will allow and, looking down them, proceed forward like the memsahibs they are thought to be. The habits of Empire are quickly learnt.

They hear a buzz in the distance, a complicated fabric of noise. As they walk towards it, it unravels into the sounds of laughter, shouting, arguing, bargaining, babies crying, mothers soothing. Traders are selling what is sold in every market: vegetables, fruit, sizzling deep-fried samosas, sugar, tea, kerosene, quilts, blankets, bedsheets, saris, sandals, combs, pots, pans, charpoys, bidis, and, as also with every market, toddy, its meaning shared by Hindustan and Scotland, except here it is available as a grey liquid, served in anonymous open bottles. And for those for whom toddy is not sufficient to dull the pain, there is also the peace that comes from the poppy. The searchers after this peace sit cross-legged and oblivious, or with their heads on a brick.

The girls, flanked by Angus and Stephen and holding tight to each other, stop at stalls, examine a comb here, a mirror there, but buy nothing. Beyond, on the outer edges of what is bought and sold, a group of hungry women in thin-bordered saris with black hair stuffed into knots stand by the side of the path.

ONE OF THE HUNGRY WOMEN (*speaking to them in Hin-*

di): Want some fun, duckies...all of you together if you like... never know unless you try?

Stephen tightens his arm around Mary's shoulder. A native constable in blue and silver, with a red puggerie, is on duty in front of a house. He salutes as they walk past and watches as they make their way to the station.

ANGUS: How was that then, girls? Alright?

MONICA: That was...fun. (*She shivers at the recollection of the bazaar and squeezes herself into him.*)

The train comes, consumes and carries them to Howrah, Calcutta's terminus: red brick, arches, square towers, built to last a thousand years, British to its architectural core, imposing, solid; a reminder to all who pass within that the Empire has what it takes.

They make their way down the platform, arm in arm. They cross the polished Rajasthan marble of the main hall, passing on their left and right the Hindu and Mohammedan and first- and second-class refreshment rooms, a grand staircase leading up, a hairdressing saloon, and an enquiry office with a circular counter. They skirt around ear cleaners, boot menders and polishers, astrologers, coolies collapsed under the weight of cases which do not only belong to white men, and a battalion of vendors offering the tawdry contents of a poor man's dreams. None of this affects them. They take it all as a matter of course; just Howrah station, where India creeps up to the Raj and touches the hem of its trousers.

Outside, a sea of beggars, deformed or mutilated, supplicate as best they can. This also they take as a matter of course. The Empire, over which the sun never sets, has many festering corners and many places where beggars uphold the ancient traditions: the Brahmin with his bowl, the Untouchable with his empty eyes. The couples sweep through this mendicant swamp without making a donation and reach the bridge that crosses the Hooghly. Here, an old man in no greater or less distress than others, holds out his right hand. It is split down the middle like the claw of a lobster.

Stephen digs into his pocket and comes up with two annas. The old man bows.

ANGUS (*grinding his teeth*): I keep telling him, (*he interrupts himself to swat aside fifteen boys who have appeared from nowhere*), *jáo*...give to one, this happens...*jáo. Ek dum.*

MARY (*also swatting with gloved hands*): It only encourages them.

STEPHEN: There but for the grace of God...

Angus summons two rickshaws, each with a stick-like coolie, bare but for a grubby dhoti around his loins, between its shafts. He ushers Monica into one. Stephen and Mary take the other. The coolies pull them across Howrah bridge, which they share with cars, trucks, bullock carts, a party of young women in saris strolling in no hurry wearing bangles on their ankles, an elephant also in no hurry, and a cow that is lying down in the middle of the road chewing lazily a booklet entitled *Dr W C Roy's SPECIFIC FOR INSANITY*. The camera pauses on a portion of the half-eaten text: '"Dr Roy's insanity medicine acted a charm, I'm completely cured," says Srinath Ghosh of Bundelkund. 5 rupees per phial.'

Once over the bridge, they head south, passing the entrances of cinemas. The Empire is showing *Love of Savita*: 'an Indian girl and a Scotch adventurer; as flaming as sunset skies; never before have such crowds jammed this theatre.' The two coolies, panting, turn in tandem into Chitpur Road (avoiding an oncoming tram), strike Bentinck Street at a good clip and, now in the quieter air of Chowringhee, stop at number 18/2, Firpo's.

They take cocktails on the balcony overlooking the Maidan. They feast beneath the same crystal chandeliers that have illuminated greater lights than them, on the same Himalayan-white tablecloths, accompanied by violins and piano as before, as always. And, above them, whirs an electric Sirocco fan, imported, no expense spared and capable of a draft of one million cubic feet of fresh air per minute. So that no one sweats at Firpo's.

On this evening, they share the vast dining room with the Maharaja of an unimportant state, four tea planters down from the hills, sundry burra sahibs of Clive Street, a scattering of the great and the good of the Indian Civil Service who wish they were in Darjeeling, a family of Sikhs who own property in the Punjab, and a Mrs Gayatri Sen, daughter of a zamindar with land in Naipur. Mrs Sen is currently engaged in trade union activity. She has with her a brother and a party of young women, including one on whom Stephen's eye falls.

This woman sits straight-backed and composed. Her complexion is fair, the brown of her cheeks yellow tinted, almost as if her skin has been touched with gold: but she is not, perhaps, a beauty; her forehead is a little too wide, her lips a little too full. Rather the slight tilt of her head, the way her front teeth rest reflectively on her bottom lip and the hint of questions at play beneath the shimmering surface of her eyes suggest a woman of independence, someone who respects her own thoughts before the affirmation of others. She is listening to Mrs Sen.

MRS SEN: ...but what point really, when management is noticing shareholders only. We have to hit them where most pain is felt. (*She points to an area below the table and giggles.*) In their pockets, isn't it. I say this (*here she utters the slogan with which her movement will be forever associated*), ATTACK THE DIVIDENDS. Nothing to do but, don't you think?

The woman, Ranjana, claps her hands in delight and half turns. She catches Stephen's eye and regards it, brown on blue, one world on another.

MARY (*to Stephen*): What are you looking at?

STEPHEN (*turning towards her, thoughtfully*): At a woman. (*He pauses.*) Not to be compared to you though, Mary.

MARY (*digging him playfully in the ribs with her elbow*): I should jolly well think not.

In the Louis XVI ballroom with its sprung wooden dance floor, the four of them examine themselves in an enormous golden mirror that stretches from floor to ceiling the entire breadth of one wall.

The girls primp their hair, Angus straightens his jacket, Stephen regards himself in the dispassionate manner of an artist about to begin his own self-portrait and the band strikes up an eightsome reel. It is as cool in Firpo's as in the Angus hills and the evening tiptoes away on the breath of laughter and high spirits.

Yet for all its gaiety, the important place of congregation this evening is not the dance floor, but the hall outside the ladies room, where the two men now stand waiting, and through which Ranjana walks. She passes Stephen. Eye meets eye for the second time, draws its conclusions and moves on. Ranjana reaches the door of the ladies room, hears the chatter of Mary and Monica on the other side, braces herself and enters another world.

26

The image shimmers, slips, takes on the patched quilt of memory, is coloured sepia and shot through the long lens of history. The panelled door that opened into the ladies loom at Firpos now leads to a well-furnished artist's studio, twenty-something years earlier. A piano stands in a corner. In the middle of the room is a solid table of teak. An ayah is looking after a young baby, while the artist, a middle-aged Indian woman clanking with jewellery from ears to ankles, stands back from her canvas and puffs nervously on a cigarette. She has been painting fruit: round glossy apples, bananas bursting out of their skins, cut pomegranates; but in the apple at the bottom of the bowl, almost invisible, a worm is nibbling through the skin; in the banana, the tip of the nose of a fly can just be observed hatching; and on the cut flesh of the pomegranate, mould. The baby starts to cry.

AYAH (*addressing baby*): Ch ch, Renuka, ssssh.

The mother, in a depressed tuneless voice, hums the first few notes of a Bengali lullaby. This quickly drains away, first into discord and then silence. She lights another cigarette and gets back to work.

AYAH (*continuing to soothe*): Ch ch, Renuka, sssssh.

A year later, same scene. The mother is still painting, but this time the ayah is looking after Renuka, now a toddler, and a young baby. The mother is painting fowl: pheasants, partridge, duck. The game birds are arranged in lines, with blood dripping from their mouths, while a shooting party of white men dressed to boiling point, and the flunkeys of a Maharaja, stare disinterestedly ahead. On another canvas, visible in a corner, chickens and turkeys are presented cooked with heads and feet intact as guests tuck in to the uncarved joints.

The baby begins to cry and Renuka, hearing her, joins in. Their mother puts her hands to her ears and screams silently.

AYAH (*addressing the baby*): Ch ch, Ranjana, ssssh.

The woman's husband, a distinguished-looking man, a judge, comes into the room. He looks over his wife's easel.

HUSBAND/JUDGE: Blood everywhere, my dear, look how it drips...a holiday, it would do you good, somewhere, anywhere, the Himalayas, the south of France, why not?'

MOTHER/ARTIST: Husband, I feel my insides. They are torn. (*She holds her hand to her stomach.*) No more children for me. Two is enough, we should set an example.

HUSBAND/JUDGE: I am Indian, my family is ancient, but none of this matters a bloody damn without a son. And does not a son warm a mother's heart?

Two years later. This time the ayah is looking after two young girls and a baby boy. The mother is painting a Calcutta street scene. Men are pulling rickshaws, selling silver, defecating over an open sewer. All are precisely drawn and all have their eyes shut tight, all except those lying down who look up at the sun or the stars as if they see ghosts or winged creatures or phantasms.

BABY BOY (*holding out his hands imploringly towards his mother*): Ma, ma.

AYAH: Ch ch, Satish, ssssh.

MOTHER/ARTIST (*despairing*): God help us all.

Eighteen years later, the husband/judge, now grey, is having dinner with the Governor General. Although Indian, he is dressed like a pukka Englishman in a jacket run up for him by Ranken and Co. of 4 Old Court House Street, Tailors by Appointment to HM the King, HRH the Prince of Wales, sundry other royals, viceroys, governors, commanders-in-chief, as well as Robe Makers to the Most Exalted Order of the Star of India. Both men, judge and governor, were at Oxford together. They have been discussing Hindu/Muslim relations, Gandhi, nationalism, the recent wave of strikes, the prospects for the Oriel boat, the Mahabhárata, Shakespeare and Tagore.

HUSBAND/JUDGE (*apparently quoting*): ...beyond the window frame, behind the tamarisk, the crescent moon.

GOVERNOR GENERAL: And your girls, dear boy? Renuka is doing well in the law, I hear. Takes after her father, eh.

HUSBAND/JUDGE (*shaking his head*): It could be, we shall see.

GOVERNOR GENERAL: And Ranjana?

HUSBAND/JUDGE (*showing signs of exasperation*): Still no husband. Her mother has tried all types.

GOVERNOR GENERAL (*playfully*): Perhaps too much time spent in the company of the infamous Mrs Sen?

HUSBAND/JUDGE: Ranjana has a good heart. She burns for worthy causes: night schools for jute workers, Hindu Women against Rape and Abduction, medical help for pregnant women in the mills, the Association for the Protection of this that and the other; even the mice in our house she looks after, and if the mouse has a damaged leg, she lavishes on it even more of her love and care.

GOVERNOR GENERAL (*smiling*): Ah, yes, daughters; but it could be worse, could it not? May I let you into a little secret, but not a word to the jute barons of Clive Street. (*He puts a finger to his mouth.*) I harbour a sneaking admiration for her Mrs Sen. (*He leans forward.*) This is the twentieth century after all.

HUSBAND/JUDGE: Even in India?

GOVERNOR GENERAL: Even in India.

Both men laugh.

GOVERNOR GENERAL (*now solemn*): I was so sorry to hear about your son. I can't believe he was mixed up in it.

HUSBAND/JUDGE: Thank you. Nor can I. He was always difficult as a child, it's true. Now he sees this nationalism as a worthy cause, but Satish is no terrorist. He is not a violent boy. And to put a revolver to the temple of the District Magistrate of Midnapur while he was at home playing the piano, a man we all knew and liked, he and his wife had been to dinner, no I can't see Satish doing that, I just can't see it. (*He bends his neck for a moment and then straightens looking at the Governor General.*)

GOVERNOR GENERAL (*reassuringly*): Nor can I. Don't you worry. We've put our best men on the case. They'll get to the bottom of it.

HUSBAND/JUDGE: And the constables outside our house, night and day?

GOVERNOR GENERAL: In case he returns. What else can we do? I'm sure you understand.

Across the faces of the men, the panelled door swings on its hinges and reveals Ranjana—we are back in full colour. She looks behind her, an expression of amusement and incredulity on her face, to where Mary and Monica are chattering unseen. Stephen and Angus watch as she turns and sweeps into the dining room where Mrs Sen, under the breeze of the Sirocco fan, is holding court.

27

Lipsticked, glistening and bathed in the gloss of anticipation, Mary and Monica sally forth from the ladies room. In high excitement, they grab the arms of their partners and drag them into the street. Stephen and Angus enquire of each other, by the use of silent gestures, what is up.

MARY: Before taking us home (*she pauses, her lips suggesting a treat might be in store if...*) we'd love to see where you bachelors go when we're not here. (*Monica nods enthusiastically.*)

ANGUS and STEPHEN (*in unison*): Go?

MARY: You know perfectly well what we mean, so don't tease. Go. For companionship. Don't pretend now, boys, that you never have. We'd like to see, very much. Wouldn't we, Monica?

MONICA: Oh yes, very much. (*This time, it is eyes that promise.*)

ANGUS (*reflectively*): Well, there is a place. I don't know it myself, but I've been told. We could take you there I suppose. If that's what you want. What do you think, Stephen?

STEPHEN: Okay by me, if you girls are sure that—

MARY (*cutting him off*): Come on. It'll be fun.

MONICA: Oh, how exciting.

STEPHEN: Just one thing (*he pauses, not knowing how to express the endless permutations that are occurring to him*), is this a whistle-stop tour, or is it...?

ANGUS (*interrupting quickly*): Don't be so stiff, Stephen. It'll end up as it ends up, isn't that right girls?

MARY (*pretending to be insulted*): We only want to look.

MONICA: Yes, only looking, what do you mean? What sort of girls do you think we are?

With this, both girls let go of the elbows they are holding and set off, arms flapping, down Chowringhee. The two men hurry after.

STEPHEN (*apologetically*): Of course. Only looking.

Karaya Road is a modest street lined with trees and quiet bungalows set in their own grounds. Although routinely suburban in appearance, these are sporting quarters; an area of enticing lights discreetly lit, known as *The Rag*.

ANGUS: French I think, don't you Stephen? The auld alliance.

STEPHEN: Aye, the auld alliance.

Angus opens a gate. A stone path leads to a house that is set back. Angus knocks twice.

MONICA (*nervously*): Ah. (*A tremor passes through her body.*)

An Indian retainer, not more than five feet standing straight but now bent double with age and the nature of his duties, draws back the door. He cranes his neck upwards, drops an ancient syllable with impenetrable sadness and urges them to follow. He reverses (his body shaking with the early onset of Saint Vitus's dance) into a salon of red and gold, which is furnished with mirrors and a painting of a nude whose breasts, like open arms, stretch out in welcome. Before them stands the statuesque figure of Antoinette, skin white as ivory, a filly from the neighbouring French enclave of Chandernagore. A silk robe is drawn loosely at her waist and, on it, two dragons are breathing fire.

ANTOINETTE: Good evening, Mr Angus. Welcome messieurs, dames.

The two girls smile in a frozen sort of way.

ANGUS: A round of drinks, Madame, if you please.

ANTOINETTE (*in mock servility*): As you command. (*She claps her hands.*)

Angus goes over to the piano. He accompanies his own singing.

ANGUS (*his rich tenor ringing out*): Far frae my hame I wander, but still my thoughts return/to my ain folk ower yonder, in the shieling by the burn./I see the cosy ingle, and the mist abune the brae:/and joy and sadness mingle, as I list some auld-warld lay. (*As he sings, he loses himself in recollection of the Scotland he has left behind. He pulls himself together.)* Come on Stephen, girls, give me the chorus.

They don't—are in no position to—take up his invitation. Mary and Monica are standing by the side of the piano and as close to each other as they can squeeze. Mary's free hand is clutching Stephen's while, around them, other hands (French, white, from Chandernagore and belonging to Bella Fifi Roxanne) reach out and catch what they can. One slips down and comes to rest on Stephen's trousers. Angus is left to sing on alone.

ANGUS (*ending*): ...tho' the stormy seas di—*(he holds the final low C)*—v...i...d...e...

He looks around, thumps ten fingers into the piano (suggesting an announcement), nods so that all might be ready and touches suggestively the first bars of *La Marseillaise*. As if stung by a cattle prod, the tarts spring to attention: hands by their sides, shoulders back, lost ships far from home but still flying the flag.

The first words, sung in good, almost operatic, style, come from the Du Barry suite, where a naked couple glimpsed through a half-open door, on a bed with silken sheets, are also standing to attention.

NAKED COUPLE (*treble and baritone*): Allons enfants de la Patrie/Le jour de gloire est arrivé...

CHORUS OF TARTS (*joining in con brio, the sound rising*): Aux armes citoyens/Formez vos bataillons/Marchons marchons/Qu'un sang impur/Abreuve...

Angus plays to the end. Monica and Mary, relaxing into the unexpected camaraderie, join in intermittently when they think they know the words.

ANTOINETTE (*sighing and wiping away a tear*): Bravo, Monsieur, bravo. Alors (*another sigh before getting down to business*), gentlemen, ladies, your pleasure? Do you prefer (*here she pauses in contemplation of delectable alternatives, somewhat in the manner of a Parisian restaurateur presenting le menu, one hand on her hip, the other at the level of her right ear*) one by one, ou ensemble? How you say, an eightsome reel?

A young man sits at a corner table. Stout legs, made black by a mat of hair, sprout out of pale cream shorts. Black hairs poke inflexibly from his chin. A girl, pale and frail as powder, perches on his knee. He is an official of the Raj, off-duty, an assistant superintendent of police from a minor public school. In his right hand, he holds a glass of champagne poured from a half-drunk bottle. He guffaws.

HAIRY-LEGGED POLICEMAN (*raising his drink*): Good one Antoinette, eightsome, not a bad idea, wouldn't mind some of that myself, one more who's counting, eightsome ninesome. (*With his left hand, he slaps the waif on her behind.*) No, make that ten. (*The girl neither flinches nor moves a muscle.*)

Mary and Monica squeeze closer to Angus.

MARY (*whispering*): Can we go? This isn't so nice anymore.

MONICA: And besides, everybody here is white.

ANGUS: They want to leave, Stephen, do you hear that? Leave. And we've only just come.

STEPHEN: Let's go.

ANGUS (*regretfully to Antoinette*): Encore une fois, chérie.

Antoinette bows once from the neck.

HAIRY-LEGGED POLICEMAN (*calling out*): That was quick. Next time, eh?

A streetlight outside the house of pleasure in Karaya Road casts a dim pall.

MARY (*shivering in the sticky fetid air*): Thank you, Stephen.

MONICA (*curiously*): And would you have liked, what did she say, an eightsome? What is that? All of us together? With four girls? Why four? Oh, I see, girls for us too. Blimey. All in the same bed?

STEPHEN: Eight white bodies holding tight between silk sheets: that's the Raj.

ANGUS: Where to now, my beauties?

MONICA: Well, isn't there somewhere Indian?

ANGUS: You mean like that, only Indian?

MONICA: No, Angus, definitely not. One brothel in an evening is quite enough, isn't it Mare?

MARY: It certainly is.

MONICA: No, I mean, where we can see Indian people. Like earlier. That was fun. All we ever come across at work are a few fat Marwaris who are stinking rich and Bengali babus who wouldn't say boo to a goose. We want to go somewhere that isn't, you know, the same old thing, I mean British.

ANGUS: We could try the Burra Bazaar. No white men there. Unless they're lost, of course.

STEPHEN: The Raj keeps it at arm's length: like all the things that scare us half to death.

MARY: It's safe, though, isn't it?

STEPHEN: No safer than you'd want it be.

MARY: Well, let's go. It'll be an adventure.

They head back to Chowringhee, then north along Bentinck Street and Lower Chitpur Road; a retreat along the warp line of British India, its stone grey buildings and white faces. Their two rickshaws creak in tandem, the markings and spray of Empire recede and the shot narrows until all Stephen sees (all we see) are the black stick-thin legs of the coolie as he trots panting towards a ramshackle chaos of narrow lanes and humanity's flood.

The camera lifts and looks down. Seen from above, the Burra Bazaar is a maze of congested, squalid, God-forsaken, rat-infested byways. Its colour is brown; brown brick, brown earth, brown skins, bathwater hot. Flags droop on Jorasanko police station, Burdwan Raja's bazaar, the Roman Catholic church, the synagogue, the Nakhoda Mosque and the Temple of Kali. The air is breathless, sagging and stifled by its own dead weight. The two couples slump in their rickshaws, as if paused.

Suddenly, the flags start to stiffen. Awnings of canvas and corrugated iron ripple and tilt. Washing flaps on the roofs of hovels from which bits of reed and mud shake loose and fall to the ground like feathers. A Northwesterly is heading in.

The four of them, now on foot, come to a street twelve feet wide without pavements. It is blocked by a Calcutta box gharrie that has smashed into the side of a buffalo cart and is gobbing melons into the rubble and earth. The melons roll this way and that, chased by a flock of hungry boys and encouraged by a crowd. The two drivers swear and shake their fists in wavy pursuit. The buffalo bellows.

Stephen stares in intense curiosity as if seeing it all for the first time—the upper salivary lip of the buffalo quivering in slow motion as the wave-noise of its bellow passes through, a Punjabi with silver braid on his waistcoat and black gimlet eyes, the walls of the buildings all about him shooting up, higher, higher and holding hands at the top, diminishing to the size of an ant, the watcher, Stephen himself.

MARY (*restored to vigour and clapping her hands in excitement*): Oh, look, isn't it wonderful? This is what we want: the real India.

STEPHEN (*coming to and calling out*): What are we doing here?

ANGUS: Doing? We're not doing anything. Just looking.

They walk down an alley in single file past a rickshaw wallah asleep on his cart. A few overfed raindrops land heavily on their heads.

MARY: You okay, Monica? Hold onto me.

In an alcove somewhere in a maze of lanes, a man shows them gold rings. In another, a bolt of cloth. In another broomsticks, reed matting, charpoys, samosas, barfi, alu-bhurta, jelebis, a coconut with the top cut off, flowers, pearls, betel leaves and nuts. From a hole in the wall, two men sit facing each other doing business to the tune of lakhs of rupees, hundreds of thousands. An open strongbox is just visible.

They continue to walk. The girls look up, down, sideways, mouths open, shocked, excited, safe not safe, indifferent, concerned. They move from spectacle to spectacle, but always in one direction: deeper in. They don't notice that their purposeless footsteps are leading them to a different quarter, where alleys twist, clogs clap, eyes slant and bald yellow faces with yellow high-boned cheeks and long pigtails stare out at them and smile through gaps in yellow teeth.

MARY (*suddenly aware that something has changed*): Where are we? Are we lost?

ANGUS (*looking around, seeing only the tints and trappings of China*): What do you think, Stephen, are we lost? (*He holds both hands up to the dripping heavens, and proclaims*): 'There's a one-eyed yellow idol to the north of Kathmandu/There's a little marble cross below the town/There's a broken hearted woman tends the grave of Mad Carew/And the Yellow God forever gazes down.' (*He stops, lowering his hands.*) Where the hell are we? Are we still in India?

STEPHEN: You have to travel a long way to leave India.

MONICA: It doesn't look much like India.

MARY: But it still belongs to us, doesn't it? It's still British?

STEPHEN: Look at the map; it's as pink as you and me.

The rain falls more heavily. Then in torrents. Unlit footpaths turn into quagmires.

ANGUS: Let's get out of this.

Stephen leans against a doorway. It gives against his weight.

ANGUS: Go in. They're bound to have something they can sell us.

The door opens onto a corridor that is dimly lit by a Chinese lantern in which a candle gutters. At the end of the corridor is a room with cracked plaster walls and, facing out of it, two pairs of eyes, one European blue, the other belonging to a Chinaman.

STEPHEN (*whispering*): There's nothing here. (*He gestures to the others to go back.*)

Angus and the two girls turn around and leave. Stephen starts to follow but something in what he has seen holds him back. He enters the room of cracked plaster. The two men are lying on their sides head to head. The big toe of the Chinaman is waving backwards and forwards as if beckoning him. In time with the movement of the toe, a fan whirs lazily above.

In front of the men is a tray. On it is an oil lamp, a pair of scissors, a scraper and, in the hand of the blue-eyed man, an eighteen-inch pipe made of bamboo. The man puts the pipe to his lips. Through a noise like the gurgling of a happy baby, he pulls a bowl of smoke to the back of his throat and swallows.

Stephen pauses for a moment, listens to the man and the pipe and the gurgling, and finds he cannot leave. He stands staring at the man's smoking eyes which, regarding him with neither interest nor disinterest, hint in their depths at a promise whose nature he can hardly imagine.

How much time passes in a moment? It could be none, it could be hours. Stephen goes outside and finds that the others have gone.

28

The girl in the flower shop smiles when I come in. 'So, those lilies, she like?'

Still, I don't know if she knows they were intended for Julia. Playing along, I say, 'It's hard to tell. But, this time, will you choose?'

'Me choose? Okay, sure. Tell me about her, where she come from this girl, how she look?'

'She comes from a land of ice and snow and has green eyes.'

'Ah, ice, snow…and green eyes too. Yes, I begin understanding. You like eyes? You like whole package?'

'Yes, I like. I miss. I need. I want her back.'

'Okay, this for sure…' She picks out a rose that is almost black in its redness. 'Rose of sadness, no? Who green ice-girl understand.'

'Will you give her a note from me?' I hold out a small envelope.

She pauses for a moment and then, staring directly into my eyes, says, 'Sure I give her. Why you not ask before instead all this flower crap?' She laughs out loud in delight and after a while I can't help it, I laugh too. Then I kiss her. Those pale cheeks, those bright red puckering lips: what else can I do? She lets me but doesn't stop laughing.

My note says this: 'Julia, since you left, words drop into empty space. Nothing comes back. There is no light in the void.'

29

Context. Nothing comes out of nowhere, nobody pops out of thin air, and since it's a film—at least in Séamus's dreams it is, mine too now I suppose—and since what Séamus likes to call "The Audience" won't appreciate being left in the dark, don't we have to explain the background, plug the gaps?

I find a pad and, beginning in the age before history began, jot down a selection of defining moments.

WHERE THINGS BEGAN: A BRIEF CHRONOLOGY.

1. The birth of meditation, humanity's salve. 2. The battle of Kurukshetra, when the Pandavas and the Kauravas fought each other to the last man standing, the consanguineous struggle to end all consanguineous struggles (except that it didn't of course). 3. The glorious flowering of the Hindu/Buddhist settlement, Ashoka, Chandra-Gupta, Khajuraho. 4. Centuries of Muslim invasion, bloody-beyond-belief butchery and the wiping-out of Buddhism in India. 5. The Mughal Empire, an interlude of Muslim tolerance and the Taj Mahal culminating in bigotry and collapse. 6. The British Raj, that peculiar cocktail of trade, double-dealing, unflinching bloody-mindedness, duty, bureaucracy, racism and the rule of law.

Here, my attention is diverted by an itch in my ear. I give it a rub. I start again.

WHERE THINGS BEGAN: THE 1930S.

India is pregnant with the prospect of independence and scratching around for appropriate tools for the delivery: i.e., how to get rid of the British. Otherwise it's business as usual, meaning the everyday laughably chaotic mixture of terrorists and communists and fakirs, Rolls-Royces and elephants waiting at the same traffic junction watched impassively by a native policeman in shorts, Hindus and Muslims with their hands around each other's throats, dinner still at Firpo's in the declining light of Empire which few there have noticed, and everything and nothing as before. Also the Great Depression, America sneezing and the world catching cold. Not good news if you happen to be working in a jute mill. Less for the world's universal wrapper to wrap.

And now my pen wanders into other histories, closer to home. I find myself writing as follows:

WHERE I BEGAN: COMPLETE ACCOUNT OF ALL KNOWN .ACTS CONCERNING MY MOTHER.

1. Born Calcutta 1930s, daughter of Stephen McLeod and an Indian woman (Ranjana?) 2. Came to Scotland, circumstances unknown. 3. Married James Smith (date?), delivered Stephen, me, March 27, 1968. 4. Drank, peddled drugs, gave nothing away. 5. Developed features recognisable to her son: complaint lines around mouth, fear lines around eyes, cigarette smoke in weave of cardigan, dank hair. 5. Died 1999, lamented by unknown stranger, McIntosh, for reasons hard to imagine. (An ex-lover? A dealer? A released inmate of a lunatic asylum?)

Séamus comes in. I explain my thinking on historical context, while stashing my personal details in my pocket. The paper refuses to crumple quietly. It screams. Séamus screws up his eyes. He then declares himself sympathetic, in principle, to the inclusion of certain facts which explain the background while, in practice, believing it to be contrary to the conventions of the best cinema. 'Tell me this,' he declares, 'do you think the audience give a gasp of wind from your backside about the Mughal Empire?'

'Well, I don't know, some people might, but, even if they don't, couldn't we find a way of feeding things in subtly, so they have a visceral feeling that they know more coming out of the cinema than they did going in?'

'Subtle is the word here, boyo. The discerning application of the teaspoon rather than the bang over the head with the shovel. You don't want to be smashing the paying customer's skull in with the back of your spade, if you get my meaning.'

I consider the image, the eggshell skull cracking, myriad lines across like an old woman's face, and I compare it to the harmless provision of information on the Mughal Empire. 'That's a bit strong,' I say. 'Besides, I wouldn't do that. You know me, Séamus. Violence is the one thing you could never accuse me of. It doesn't run in my family.' As an afterthought, I add, 'I believe, by the way, that my grandfather's attack on the overseer in Dundee was entirely justified and not his usual way of behaving.'

'Ah yes, your family, for a moment there I had forgotten them, your close personal interest and all.'

30

McCorquodale is after my DNA, my past and my present, as much as he can find. Julia shows no signs of coming back. God knows where my grandfather will end up. And I'm in the Rook with Karṇa. His helmeted head is bent over, the pint I've bought him draining away like the whole impermanent world—*jagaty anitye satataṃ pradhāvati*—and I wonder, not for the first time, how he can be so comfortable with his impending death. His is a lesson in acceptance, and it makes me want to reach across the ages and give him something, I don't know what precisely, comfort I suppose, an encouraging pat on the back, a word to let him know that I know what he's going through. Of course, it's all stupid, I'm not so deluded I can't see that. 'Terry,' I call out, 'another pint please. Make that two.'

After pouring them, Terry, the barman, says, 'No Séamus then?' I look behind and to left and right. 'Apparently not,' I reply. Terry lifts his shoulders and turns to make adjustments to his toasting machine.

The pavements are wet when we come out, black-patched grey stone from a lunchtime shower, now over. Moss is growing in the gaps between the slabs. I look up to where Karṇa's earrings should be glittering above me, but he's gone. Left me to it.

As I pause for a moment outside the pub rotating my shoulders, trying to encourage my black trench coat into position, a decrepit, gravy-stained spaniel slinks past, sniffs at a drain and lifts his leg over it. His limp ears, aroused (so I assume) by the tinkling melody of his own falling water, lift, and he barks once. *Aaghk.* He is replaced in my attention by an old woman, woollen stockings at half mast, who grabs my sleeve and asks for the price of a cup of tea. Where can she have been hiding? Flat against the wall? Terry shouts angrily from the doorway; '*Gerraway.*' He comes out. 'Not a fucking thing, you hear, not a fucking thing.' He waves his emaciated arms and the woman totters off, abusing us both. From within, one of the geriatrics sings baritone, *When love absorbs my ardent soul*, molto tremolo; while Terry, still gesticulating, delivers to the street an expansive lecture on the evils of charity in the modern world. A falsetto chorus of pubescent schoolgirls rounds the corner and, under cover of air waves suddenly ruptured, I slip away unnoticed.

It's one of those afternoons: my hands won't pull themselves out of my pockets and my head won't lift off my chin. No Julia. My heart beats, my feet take me wherever they wish and my mind chatters, non-stop and inescapable: chatter, chatter, what I said to her, what she said to me, what I should have said (one), what I should have said (two), silent superior comment regarding the erupting pustule on the side of Terry's nose, the anticipation of a forthcoming sentence ('another pint barman'), a schematic tour of Karṇa's unacknowledged lust for Draupadī (and lessons forthcoming), summary of debate on the pros and cons of carrying an umbrella; this that the other and more, all adding up to nothing at all.

So that's where I am, shuffling along, keeping close to the walls of this old grey town, out of sight, out of everybody's mind but my own when, crossing Market Street, I see her: Julia. She is not alone.

Before I know what I'm doing, I've ducked into a shop doorway. Karṇa whispers, 'What did you expect?' I ignore him, but a sharp arrowhead of pain pierces me, penetrates. Perhaps he isn't with her. Just a stranger who happens to be walking alongside. I peer out cautiously, head only. They've stopped. They are looking at each other, talking. Now they move on, in step. Together.

I follow, keeping my distance, pretending (should they look around) that I'm absorbed with business of my own. I crease my brow as if disturbed by deep thoughts, although there's nothing very deep about what's disturbing me now, the bastard. He's my height, perhaps a little shorter. He has on one of those overcoats trimmed with dead animals, obviously expensive. A hand moves up and secures in place a lock of blond hair. Then he says something from beneath his preening. Julia doesn't hear: she doesn't respond anyway.

You can tell a lot about a person from the way he walks. They're not lovers, I know that. They don't walk like lovers: the distance between them is all wrong, no feel, strangers' distance. He's too lumpen, too uncoordinated, his feet are splayed too wide, he's overweighted in the shoulders. Not her type. And he's trying too hard: Julia won't like that. Is he wearing a tie? He is. God, he's an academic. He looks like an academic. I don't recognize him. Might be new. Or a scientist.

Is she trying to replace me?

They approach the bookshop, pause, look at something in the window, and now they go in, first him then her. She's wearing her short blue rainproof coat with the collar turned up. I can't see her face, but the thought of it makes me ache. I wait in the doorway of a pub. A young man in paint-speckled overalls pushes past and gives me a look, which I return with interest. 'Cheers, mate,' he says. My stomach creaks like a wicker chair in the night.

I press myself into the wooden panelling of this narrow entrance so as to provide minimum inconvenience to customers, while at the same time on the lookout for any sign of movement from the bookshop. In this position, sandwiched but alert, a strange feeling comes over me as if suddenly the physical world is in flux, as if my own personal casket (the body that encases the Self) is leaking and I'm flowing into the world around me, the pub, the painter, the great beyond. Is this enlightenment, the ātman released?

I glance across just in time: they are coming out of the bookshop. They don't seem to have bought anything. I think I notice his hand reaching out and hers pulling away. Hard to tell from this distance. Could be. The sky begins to darken, my stomach rumbles like thunder. Did Terry do something to the beer?

They pick up the pace: Woolworths, the Dunfermline Building

Society, across the road, Joy's cameras, Oxfam, Barnardos, one charity shop after another. I stride after them clutching my guts with both hands. They stop suddenly. I realize I'm too close. I edge back. He's trying it again. His fingers are reaching out. He's got her. Shite. Her head is twisting to look behind. God. Quick. I'm in the betting shop. Safe.

I hear a familiar voice. 'Now don't tell me you're the betting man, Stephen. Who would have thought that?'

'Séamus,' I say pulling myself together, 'what are you doing here?'

His eyebrows lift. 'I am repairing the hole in the McGillicuddy finances. Word has reached me there's a good one leaving the Perth stalls in thirty minutes. Twelve to one.' He leans towards me and whispers confidentially, 'Romancer.'

'Romancer?' I blurt out.

'Stephen, for the love of God, will you keep your voice down. At least until the money's gone on.'

'Sorry.'

'And yourself? Will you be placing a bet?'

'I never bet,' I tell him, 'although it may surprise you to know that I was dragged to the Perth races many times when I was a child. My mother.'

'But you're not the betting man, yourself.'

'No.'

'So this is just a nostalgic visit is it down the highways and byways of Memory Lane?'

'You could say that.' I look at my watch. 'Have to go. An appointment.' I walk to the door trying not to hurry, and peer out left and right—they must have gone round the corner by now. Romancer?

God, they're in full view, on the street, and they're coming this way. They must have turned round. I step smartly backwards and stare at a television as if my fortunes depend on it. My mind has blanked, everything is blurred. My stomach bubbles like a bog and wheezes; God, if it deserts me now...

'That's the kind of appointment to have all right,' Séamus says coming over to stand next to me. 'The one that lets you get on with your day.' He is now looking out of the window. 'By Jaysus, there's Julia,' he calls out. 'She's with a fella.'

'Is she?' I pretend disinterest.

Séamus tilts to the left and waves. My stomach contracts violently. I find myself doubling up as a particularly nasty cramp hits home. 'Hello Stephen, I thought it was you.'

I wheel round. 'Hello, Julia,' I say straightening. Sun flashes of blinding red streak across her green eyes.

'Are you alright? You look a little bit strange.'

'I'm fine. I think I've drunk something that disagrees with me.'

'Oh.'

I must have glanced at her companion, because she says, 'May I introduce my good friend, Alexander.'

The name of the place that binds Julia to me slips out before I can stop it. 'From Provideniye?' I couldn't bear the answer to be yes. Him in on her secrets.

'Isn't one person from Provideniye enough?' she enquires.

'Alexander,' the man announces in a voice that is an octave too high for his body. He sticks out a hand and grabs first my own and then Séamus's, pumping it up and down.

'So hello, Sandy,' says Séamus.

'Sundi?' Alexander murmurs. 'Sundi? Is Scottish name, no?'

'Sure, so it is. As Scottish as your deep-fried coley.'

'Sundi.' He rolls the word around his tongue. 'Sundi. Is good. I like.' His mouth begins to flutter at the edges. He smiles. He repeats the word. 'Sundi.' Séamus smiles back, an encouraging twinkle lodged below the twin shelves of his convoluting eyebrows. 'Sundi,' says Alexander yet again and, for some reason, begins to find the whole thing side-splittingly funny, as if previously the word was picking its way down associations of merely mild amusement but has now broken through into the broad seam of uncontrollable hilarity. His face breaks into a barograph of amused creases. He roars with squeaky laughter. He gives out a series of short barks of the sort you might expect from a dachshund. Once under way, he gathers pace. He heaves, his shoulders shake, pendulous tears begin to trickle down his pink cheeks. He convulses. His knees sag close to the floor as if in preparation for some Cossack dance (he's wrapped his arms around his chest and is hugging himself) while at the same time he continues to chirrup, releasing every now and again the single duo-syllable of his delight: Sundi.

I look around. Oh, God no, it's infectious. Séamus is grinning from ear to ear in apparent raptures. Now he's doing one of his jigs, dancing about and slapping his thighs. Julia looks at me with the lights of love for the pair of them shining in her eyes. The punters on their stools put down their copies of the *Racing Post*. Joy spreads among their tired faces as if what they are witnessing demonstrates beyond doubt the truth they have never doubted through all their setbacks: that even someone like them can win big.

'Gob,' says Séamus finally, 'but I'm gasping for it. Do they go in for drinking at all where it is you come from?' he asks.

Alexander, allowing himself one final staccato yap, clasps a tear-drenched hand round his shoulders and says, 'Please my friend to lead yours truly forward to house of sick reputation for tasting beer.'

'Ah, you'll be wanting the Rook then,' responds Séamus. 'Come comrade Sundi.'

So off they go.

Julia, hanging back, says, 'How have you been, Stephen?'

I want to tell her everything. I want to find out what she's been doing, what she plans to do; but at this fated moment, a vision of my stomach floats before me. It is a soggy marsh, green rushes growing round the edges, gas bubbles surfacing all over it and bursting. The bubbling of the marsh is set to the music of creation, the percussive glottal stops of the Big Bang. I realize I have, at best, one complete sentence left in me. 'Julia,' I begin, composing in my head a deranged paean of love that I can never utter, 'I regret that I am not myself today. Terry has poisoned me.'

'You should go home,' she says.

I run. It begins to rain. I look back. Alexander is putting an arm round Séamus and another round Julia. He works his coat over them all, and I watch the three of them fly away like a fat six-legged moth towards the welcoming bosom of the Rook.

31

Séamus is adamant: no box to be opened before work on previous is complete; each new opening to be conducted with reverence. 'Ritual must be observed,' he says, 'otherwise what is its point?'

'Ritual is meaningless,' I reply.

'Well, in that case, observe the decencies why don't you. Since your grandfather, being a far-seeing sort of a man, has troubled himself to reach down through the years and provide the soothing balm of knowledge that your poor empty body appears to crave, the least you can do is show him the respect he's due.'

I play along. 'Do you think he knew his story would be important to me even though neither I nor my mother were yet born?'

'Born, not born, don't be so chrono-logical,' he replies. 'He had an idea about you all right, that's why he put all this stuff down. It's for you, boyo. It's in the way of a legacy.'

'Well, yes, it is a legacy, I suppose.'

'There you are then. So when we open the boxes, we'll do so in the old way like we did it the last time.'

'Anything you say, Séamus,' I tell him. He just wants an excuse to wear his cape. We both know that.

So, anyway, we finally get around to the fourth box. Séamus, who is bending over to push home the key, gives a soft whistle of approval and says, 'That's a decoration alright.' He is not wrong. Water and strange fish rise up one side, an elephant weighs down the lid, a fakir is being strangled by a lady in a white veil, a butterfly sits on a blade of brown grass, while a wasp with a needle for a nose hovers, red rain falls and an egg cracks into a thousand pieces.

I am squatting alongside, concentrating, trying to read the box as you might read an introduction to a book, but in the back of my head, what has been a blur now takes form. Two figures embrace, a man and a woman. They step out of the shadows. They show me green eyes and a hand around the shoulder. They invade my inner space with their inane laughter, driving out all other awareness. I no longer see the elephant, the strangled fakir, the butterfly with its feet stretched out, the needle-nosed wasp, the falling rain or the thousand bits of shell. I am unable even to ask Séamus the obvious questions: When you were in The Rook with the two of them, what did you, they, talk about? Are they lovers? Is there any hope? The best I can do is shake my head and call out. 'Take off that ridiculous outfit, for Chrissake! We have work to do.'

* * *

Browne, a swagger stick under his arm, is patrolling the aisles of the mill. For no reason that would be obvious to an external watcher, his usual brisk vigour leaves him and his eyes sink backwards into his skull. There they review internally, and not for the first time, clips containing images of the beautiful woman he has been promised, a fantasy in one act.

Browne's mental landscape is sparse but softly lit. It contains his bed and himself lying on it in a state of high excitement. There is a knock at the door. His bearer appears, winks disrespectfully—on this occasion Browne is prepared to overlook it—and ushers in Parvati. Her face gives no sign of emotion although, as she comes towards him, she falters and looks down. Gently, he undoes the clasp on her sari and, keeping hold of an end, walks slowly around her. His walk is soothing, his smile mesmeric, his passion fiery yet controlled. Parvati quivers and wilts as the cloth unwinds layer by layer until only one thin piece covers her. This he tears away. She stands before him, revealed. He reaches out and pulls her, meltingly, towards his consuming presence. As he lowers himself onto her breasts, a sharp metallic noise sounds in his ear. Through the shimmering curtains of his passion, drawn tight as they now are, he recognizes the clank of an empty bobbin striking the side of a machine. He swears and Parvati is gone.

With a peremptory wave of his arm, Browne summons Bochu, who takes up the sort of position a man adopts when dealing with a skittish horse.

BROWNE (*staring*): I am waiting Bochu, I have been waiting for some time, my patience is running thin.

BOCHU: Soon Sahib, soon. (*He bows.*) Tomorrow, day after, latest.

BROWNE (*with menace*): Don't let me down, Bochu. I don't forget sardars who let me down.

BOCHU: No, Sahib, Bochu will not let you down. Tomorrow, day after, latest.

BROWNE: It had better be.

Browne continues his patrol. He stops at a frame and picks up a bobbin. He unravels a length of yarn and snaps it between his fingers.

BROWNE (*to himself*): Christ, look at this. Bloody heathens, not a clue, not the first ruddy clue. You (*he points at a mill hand*), yes you, you dirty little wog, is this yours? Look at it.

His swagger stick cuts a slice through the jute-filled air and comes down on green-painted iron.

MILL HAND: Yes, Sahib, it is my work.

BROWNE: Then go, don't come back tomorrow, off, out of here, scarper.

MILL HAND (*standing his ground*): But Burra Sahib must speak, before I go.

BROWNE: I'll give you Burra Sahib, out, get out. (*He brings his stick down hard on the man's arm.*)

MILL HAND (*showing no pain*): Burra Sahib. I will not go until Burra Sahib say go.

The exchange has not gone unobserved. Browne looks around and sees that he is surrounded by a wall of bare-chested brown men in white dhotis.

BROWNE (*realising the need for caution*): Very well. (*He signals to Bochu.*) Bochu, Burra Sahib, fetch.

The black eyes of the spinners widen. Bare feet shuffle forward. It is the sort of audience that can make a man, however seasoned, suddenly feel alone. And the splash that he hears on the floor is the bead of sweat that has jumped ship.

McLeish arrives, takes in the circumstance, and confers in low tones with Browne.

MCLEISH (*at his most patrician, addressing the mill hand*): Browne Sahib says that your work is not up to standard, and that you have shown disrespect.

MILL HAND (*bowing*): My work is good, Burra Sahib. And now my arm has been injured. (*He produces his arm on which the beginnings of a welt are visible. An angry murmur rustles through the group of men.*)

MCLEISH (*as if deep in thought*): Show me the yarn. (*The offending spindle is brought. McLeish pretends to look at it.*) Browne Sahib is right: the quality is poor. Furthermore, we will not tolerate disrespect. I have no alternative but to dismiss you.

Browne and McLeish walk purposefully forward, the sea of workers around them separating to let them pass, its sides held up by the weight of bitter experience. Then somewhere a man shouts, a tentative, hidden and therefore safe dissatisfaction, hardly more than a cough; yet something about the sound (or perhaps something in McLeish) makes the Burra Sahib break the iron rule. He looks back. The Raj never looks back. To look back is to notice, to regret, to care, to be human, and the Raj, so few against so many, knows better than to do that. Too late. McLeish has turned and anything is possible now. He knows it and the men know it and out of that knowledge comes a bobbin rotating end over end, striking McLeish at the top of the nose and bringing him to his knees. Browne drags him away by the shoulders to the shelter of his office. He slams the door and secures it with a heavy metallic bolt.

The men surrounding the bobbin thrower pause, take a moment to digest what it is that they have witnessed and surge forward. They chant, they demand the reinstatement of the mill hand, they throw pieces of brick. The air is suddenly thick with the rumble and clank of spindles striking against the metallic sides of spinning frames. The crowd grows, becomes a mob, gets feverish with the heady idea of revenge. Weavers brandish four-inch cutting knives. An official of the Calcutta and Districts Union of Jute Workers stands on a chair and raises his arms for silence. He doesn't get it, but he speaks anyway through the hubbub.

UNION OFFICIAL: Comrades, you know what happened, you saw it, how this good man, Suresh Kumar—(*The mill hand stands beside him holding aloft his injured arm*)—was assaulted while attending to his work and was then dismissed for no reason. I tell you, as I tell him, he is not alone. This assault is an assault on all of us, on you, on the Union...(*next words drowned out in a roar*)...this man's dismissal is our dismissal (*more shouting and banging*)...this man's blood is our blood...

News travels. Twelve Scottish assistants gather on a square of grass outside the quarters of the single men. Each has with him a .303 service rifle. Each checks the magazine, the sights, the bolt, the breech.

VOICE OF COMMAND: On the order to fire, put the first volley over their heads. That usually takes the fight out of them. If there is a second round, aim at their legs. Best to nip these things in the bud...

The voice, taken for granted by most, leaves Stephen motionless. His rifle sticks to his sweating palms like thirty pieces of silver. Angus is standing close by, making ready his equipment.

STEPHEN (*shaking*): Are we on the right side, Angus?

ANGUS (*absentmindedly, still intent on his rifle*): What other side is there?

STEPHEN: That side, no side. Not this side anyway. Remember Dundee, remember which side we were on then?

Angus stops what he is doing. He draws Stephen away. Preparations are happening all around them. There are shouts from one assistant to another. The routines of training are kicking in. The two men are not noticed.

ANGUS: Dundee was Dundee, a million years ago. This is here, where you are now, in case you've forgotten.

STEPHEN: Are these men any different to us, as we were then? What do they want except respect, as we did, and enough to feed their families, wouldn't we do the same, didn't we?

ANGUS (*firmly*): It's time to decide, Stephen. Are you with us or against us? Make up your mind. If you're going to go over there, and turn your rifle on your countrymen, me included, then off you go, but first you'd better be sure they want you. Oh, and that you want them. Or are you planning to sit the whole thing out, and let us do your dirty work for you?

Angus is looking down at Stephen. He is the taller man. Stephen returns his gaze with quiet eyes, without movement, which is all that a man who wishes to understand can do.

ANGUS (*putting a hand around the back of his friend's arm*): Listen, we've known each other a long time. I'm telling you, don't do this. I'll tell you something else. I gave up thinking about right sides and wrong sides a long time ago. There is just the side you are on, which happens, at this moment, to be bloody Irvine's, or the Governor's or the King's, none of whom has a clue we exist, and the side you're not on, which is them. (*He points in the direction of the mill.*) You're not on that side, you never will be, so look, just do your duty, Stephen, hold your nose and don't for God's sake start asking yourself how you landed in this heap of shite.

The assistants, carrying rifles at the slope, move off. Stephen goes with them but lags behind, like a reluctant child being dragged to a party which he hopes will be over before he arrives.

UNION OFFICIAL: ...And who is to blame for this tyranny if not ourselves, have we not, by bending low, invited the blows of the sahibs on our head...(*angry denials from the crowd*)...no brothers, now is the time to stand up, to deal out two blows for every one received (*greeted by a great roar*), two blows for every one received.

The mob splits. Some stay to continue the siege of the office, while others charge across the factory floor, tumble through the mill doors and turn like a herd with one mind in the direction of the European bungalows. The men are bursting within themselves as the impotent always are when they glimpse that moment, imagined a million times in a million different ways, when finally they turn the tables: the child striking the parent, the downtrodden the despot.

They rampage towards the European bungalows where we see (from above) what they cannot, that the assistants are waiting for them. They are assembled in two ranks of five, the front rank kneeling, the rank behind standing, rifles at the ready. Stephen is at the back gripping his .303 with the look of a man whose nightmares have come true.

The monsoon rain falls turning everything to mud, while the workers, stupid in their fury, thrash around a corner. Gunfire issues from the ten assistants, the thin unbreakable thread of Empire, its emphatic retort. Bullets climb and fall, but the shock of their noise stops the mill hands dead. Some fall to the ground in fright.

MARRIED ASSISTANT IN THE FRONT RANK (*under his breath, squinting down his sights*): Just you make a move you bloody little heathen and I've got you.

The mill hands do not move, neither those standing nor those on the ground. They stare into the smoking barrels of the rifles and, behind those, at the unflinching assumption of superiority on the faces of the white men. They know that the Raj, however outnumbered, is never beaten: the iron will, the stiff upper lip, the unbending courage of the man on the front line: how else could so few have governed so many for so long?

As for the other half of the mob besieging McLeish and Browne, it too has heard the gunfire, it too hesitates and drifts away. No blood has been spilt. The action is paused. It is not over.

32

Lathis rattle against steel railings. Drenched half-naked men, some with torn shirts, jump up and down waving their fists. Some chant '*Bande Mataram,*' others '*Mazdur ki jai,*' whatever is their preference, the motherland or the brotherhood of workers. The hammer and sickle, red but limp, flaps like a half-dead fish against the trunk of a banyan tree. The sky cries monsoon tears; it has been crying all night.

On bedraggled placards, the face and body of Suresh Kumar (now shrunk to the size of a marmoset) peeps out from behind the one part of his anatomy that has grown in the dark; a monumental forearm of the type favoured by artists of the communist school. Across this forearm runs a trench of open flesh in the shape of a mouth and out of the mouth drops a single word, *Victory*: except that Victory is now sodden and dripping away. This does not deter the strikers. They chant with conviction and, with equal conviction, seek to dissuade any mill hand who arrives at the gates wishing to go to work. Should their arguments not succeed, they employ more vigorous methods.

At the Tollygunge Club in Calcutta, the rain has stopped. Through a hole in the drenched veil, the sky glows like a city of skyscrapers on fire. The moon is orange. The trees and fairways of the course are of the deepest green. James Irvine Junior is standing over a two-foot putt. He lines it up carefully, and misses.

IRVINE (*turning furiously on his caddy*): Keep still when I'm putting. How many times do I have to tell you?

CADDY (*a young boy named Anil*): Yes, Sahib.

Later, inside a Bentley, the Irvines, father and son, are seen drawing furiously on Vafiadis cigarettes as the streets of Calcutta pass by.

IRVINE SENIOR: Mrs Gayatri Sen is behind this, she and her ilk. We'll have to break her, before she breaks us.

IRVINE JUNIOR: You're right, father. But how?

IRVINE SENIOR: It's a rich lady's pastime, this Union business. Agree to nothing, give her nothing. She'll find other entertainments soon enough. Discourage her, that's the way.

IRVINE JUNIOR: Do you want to meet McLeish?

IRVINE SENIOR: You do it. Make sure he understands.

IRVINE JUNIOR: Yes, father.

McLeish sits in the boardroom of the mill, with a bandage covering his right eye and the bridge of his nose. Browne is by his side, and opposite are two ladies from the Union, Mrs Gayatri Sen and Miss Ranjana Devi. Behind the ladies, eighteen mill hands stand uncomfortably as men do who are not used to offices and especially not to the offices of Europeans. The men are wearing clean white shirts that hang loosely over a dhoti or a towel. Their mouths are open displaying gapped teeth. On the walls of the boardroom, like distant emperors keeping a watchful eye on their colonies, are portraits of the late Mr James Irvine and Mr James Irvine Senior (now deemed sufficiently close to his demise to be accorded his own picture).

The usual pleasantries, with which all difficult meetings begin, are coming to an end.

MCLEISH: Why we built Calcutta on a swamp I don't know. It floods after the first pipe bursts.

MRS SEN: The monsoon can be trying.

MCLEISH: At least we still have the horse-drawn gharrie. It never breaks down and, so long as I bring my bearer, I don't even have to get my turn-ups wet. You're a bearer, I say to the little man, time you did some bearing. (*He and Browne laugh.*)

MRS SEN: Ah, so not even the monsoon touches the Burra Sahib. But the Burra Sahib touches the men of my Union.

She nods in the direction of Suresh Kumar, who steps up to the table. He presents his elbow, welt forward. McLeish leans towards it.

MCLEISH: *Tut, tut.* Let me take a closer look. (*After a prod or two, McLeish straightens, looking smug.*) Ppa. So much fuss over so little. Yes, I see a few minor abrasions, but if it's serious injury you wish to discuss, you may be interested in this (*a fat finger dabs at his bandage*). Naturally I won't take it off in front of you ladies. Suffice it to say that the steel bobbin is a dangerous weapon. Some would call it a lethal weapon. But I'm not complaining, you notice, I'm not hunting down the mill hand who threw it, I'm not bothering to get even. Jute is a tough business, Mrs Sen, a passionate business, a world of give-and-take, a man's world, if you'll excuse me, ladies. Unfortunate things happen. Fact of life, what can we do except make the best of it? (*McLeish shrugs.*)

MRS SEN: We excuse you.

RANJANA: But violence against mill hands is not excused.

MRS SEN: There are many who saw what was done, so now there will have to be compensation. Kumar must be able to return to his work, this intimidation must end, and you must apologize Mr Browne. My union demands nothing less.

MCLEISH: Yes, I see. (*His fingers poke pensively into his chin.*) But the fact is, Mrs Sen, we do not recognize the Calcutta and Districts Union of Jute Workers. In fact, I shouldn't really be speaking to you. It's only that I believe in talking. Talking is good. Let me be frank. Clive Street will never recognize your Union. They have views, and who can blame them? They believe it's a front for agitators and communists. Not you, Mrs Sen, or indeed you, Miss Devi, but others—(*his eyes and those of Browne move from one man to the next down the table*)—who just want to stir up grievances where none exist. Have we received any petitions about unfair practices, about rates of pay, about hours of work? We haven't, not one. Not a single petition. This trouble now, other troubles, and not just here but in other mills, Indian mills too, are all whipped up by agitators: communists or nationalists it makes no difference. Look, let's remember why we are here. We are here, all of us, to make gunnies, pay wages, feed the hundreds of thousands of honest men and women who live and work on the shores of the Hooghly. As for politics, best leave that to the politicians.

RANJANA: You tell us there are no grievances because no complaints have been received. But here is Kumar. He has been attacked by a manager and ordered out. This is a grievance, is it not? And are we not complaining on his behalf, demanding his position be given back to him, with full apology?

MCLEISH: The reinstatement of Kumar. Yes, well, it would be nice, let bygones be bygones and all that, but unfortunately, as I'm sure you know, Miss Devi, we have too many employed as it is, we should have been tougher earlier, should have cut back, a single shift perhaps, yes, longer hours for the same pay, but it'll have to come, the market for jute being as it is, we're as much victims as you are. And as for the strikers returning, I have a feeling that it'll be okay, that good sense will prevail, that everyone we want back will be at work before you can say *jaldi jaldi*. (*McLeish retracts his lips, exposing yellowing teeth.*) May we offer you tea, or would you prefer...?

MRS SEN: So that is the way things are. Then I think we will return to Calcutta. I admit some disappointment, Mr McLeish, but no matter. There are laws which apply even to a mill such as this one. These are your own laws, dear sir. They are made in Britain. Like cotton, isn't it? Good day to you both.

Browne and McLeish rise to their feet and escort the two ladies to their car. It pulls away along a tarmac road in the mill compound and heads towards the gates, passing Stephen on the way. He peers into the windows and recognizes a face he's seen somewhere before.

The car drives off, but the eighteen mill hands who were present at the meeting, are still in the boardroom, looking at each other, uncertain what to do next. Presently they file out. When they pass the portraits of the two ancient Irvines, they place their palms together and bow. Irvine or Krishna, gods are gods. They come down the steps, staring backwards in wonder at where they have been, and hardly notice as their feet land on earth that is red as betel or as blood. The feathery leaves of a neem tree whisper overhead. In its branches, a common tailorbird calls *chuvee chuvee chuvee.*

They turn and see Browne standing in front of them. Behind him are twenty-five durwans from the mill. They are big men and bear themselves well, although without being able to disguise entirely early signs of running to fat. They carry lathis tipped at the point with iron.

Browne motions them forward with a lazy hand hinged at the wrist. The eighteen men are motionless, filled now with understanding as to what their future holds and bowing their heads before it. Skulls crack. Teeth gap wider. Shirts lose their whiteness. Rain comes down like rifle shot and rivulets of betel run across the flat earth like the many mouths of the Ganges, of which the Hooghly is one.

Stephen hears the sound of men being beaten and runs forward. He arrives to find bleeding bodies on the ground with durwans hitting them.

STEPHEN (*shouting*): What are you doing? (*He runs to a durwan and grabs his arm before he can strike again.*) Stop, now. All of you.

The durwans stand idly by, leaning on their lathis, gathering their breath. Stephen kneels over one of the fallen men. Browne steps out from underneath the neem tree.

BROWNE (*quietly*): I'd keep out of it Doig, if you know what's good for you.

STEPHEN (*looking up and seeing Browne for the first time*): So you're behind this. I might have known.

BROWNE: Behind what? I don't see anything. Oh, you mean that. (*He points.*) Just a few private scores being settled. It happens all the time; as you and I are both well aware.

STEPHEN: Call them off, Browne, before somebody gets killed.

BROWNE: Well, it does look as if the job is done. (*He surveys the scene with satisfaction.*) Perhaps I should intervene, now you mention it. (*He claps his hands*.) Go home all of you. Enough.

* * *

There's a sketch, which I imagine my grandfather drew shortly afterwards. A cockroach is crawling across the mess's billiard table while the spot ball bears down on it. In one armchair, lounging like the cat who's got the cream, is a fleshy man with an upturned nose. A split speech bubble is moored to his lips. 'Pegs all round,' comes out of one side of his mouth. 'That'll teach those coolies a lesson,' out of the other. In two other armchairs, seen from the back, only the speech bubbles are visible. One says, 'Stephen is at it again, playing with his charcoal.' The other says, 'Abdul, God, where the bloody hell is he, Abdul!'

It is an eloquent statement. Such control. Such contrived blandness. The observer's eye is drawn by the lines of the billiard cue and the converging sides of the table, not to the innocent cockroach, but to a small potted plant growing quietly in a corner minding its own business.

I feel the pain in my grandfather's heart.

33

In his wretched bustee, Sunil lies on the floor, his ribs swelling as if a man with steel-rimmed glasses is inside pumping him up. He is sweating with fever. Parvati is kneeling by his side, wiping his forehead. She lowers her neck to touch his lips with her own. She walks to the fire, stirs the thinnest of soups and brings it over. She props him up on a pillow and feeds him. Suddenly his face yellows and globules of phlegm and blood lift out of his mouth like lava from the mouth of Stromboli.

Through the blurred lens of fever, we now see Parvati as Sunil sees her: the gentleness with which she wipes his face; the curve of her neck; the strands of hair that have come loose and fall. Suddenly, Sunil notices a man's head poking through the entrance to his bustee. He lifts himself up for a better look and vomits once more.

BOCHU: Sorry to disturb…agh nasty. (*Bochu turns away.*) It's not a good time is it. Of course it isn't.

Sunil attempts to stand.

BOCHU: No, no, please, stay where you are, I'm only here about well (*pause*) money. What do you think, should I speak to your wife?

Sunil's feverish eyes go blank.

PARVATI: Go away, get out. He is ill. Can you not see?

BOCHU: Yes, I can, not tip-top is he but, forgive me, I think that makes it even more important that we speak, though it might be better if we do this somewhere else. I don't want to upset him you understand. But, if you prefer, here is okay with me.

Sunil shakes all over, like a dog. Parvati is torn between wanting to comfort her husband and her wish to get Bochu out of the bustee. She steps outside. Bochu follows.

BOCHU: It's just that your husband owes me money. This week it's, let me see, one rupee eight annas.

PARVATI: My husband is sick. Last week we ate so little, and now we have nothing. Please, be merciful Sardar Sahib. When he is well again, we will repay you.

BOCHU: I do hope your husband recovers but I must say he doesn't look at all well. Why doesn't he see a doctor?

Parvati laughs thinly.

BOCHU: No, of course, silly of me…money. (*He scratches his arse thoughtfully*.) But then, if he doesn't see a doctor, I suppose he won't be able to go back to work when this strike is over, and if he doesn't go back to work, you won't be able to afford to live in this bustee. Yes? Am I right?

Parvati freezes.

BOCHU: Look, I don't want to move you out but what else can I do? A debt is a debt, and if I don't collect my debts from you then all the others will say to themselves, that Bochu, what a soft touch he is, no need to pay him; and then I'll be finished, *funtoosh*, there'll be no more kind Bochu to do a favour here and a favour there. Then again (*he interrupts himself with further scratching*) there is one thing, I don't suppose Sunil mentioned it, one way that all your debts can be settled, a way for you to stay in the bustee, buy medicine, help your husband recover…

PARVATI (*wishing to believe*): Yes?

BOCHU: How fortunate Sunil is to have such a wife as you, really, what I wouldn't give. Such beauty, I have noticed it many times, but of course what does that matter, who am I? I'm just a nobody, of no account at all. But a better man than me has also noticed.

Bochu's hand reaches out to touch her lightly on her breast. Parvati flinches.

BOCHU (*laughing*): He's a white sahib, a good man. His wife is coming back soon, and he feels that he and you should, in that limited time, erm (*pause*) enjoy each other's company.

Parvati turns away from him, her face to the wall of the bustee.

BOCHU: Of course, if you prefer, you and Sunil can leave here now. No, no, no, my apologies, no need to be so hasty. Shall we say by tomorrow morning?

PARVATI (*turning, her face a mask, a pale and fixed patina*): Tell this white man I will do as he desires.

* * *

Stephen and the Kerani are playing billiards. It is Stephen's shot. The white and red balls are touching, the spot ball a foot away. He rehearses in his mind's eye a caress of the utmost sensitivity; spot onto white onto red, the kiss so slight that neither knows it has been touched; then an infinite sequence of soft cannons, ivory lips brushing each other imperceptibly, kiss kiss kiss; and after each tiny collision, each ball in the same place as before. Stephen crouches over the table, feels the balance of the cue in his fingers, draws it back and waits for that moment when the tip will begin its slide forward.

The door slams. Stephen straightens. Browne appears, comes closer, waves in cheery fashion in the direction of the billiard table and stretches out a hand for the peg that Abdul has ready.

STEPHEN (*to himself*): Shite. (*He chalks the tip and bangs the red into the bottom pocket. He hands the cue to Angus.*) Take over for me will you.

ANGUS: Are you alright, my friend?

Stephen shakes his head side to side Indian-style and leaves the Mess. He walks to the station, avoiding the usual route and keeping to the side of a small path that will take him beyond the coolie lines. His neck seeks anonymity between his shoulder blades. His hands hide themselves in his pockets.

In Calcutta, he skirts past familiar thoroughfares; they are not what he is looking for this night. He turns away, goes north, crosses over. It is dark. He follows twisted alleys and pressing walls. Washed-up faces wait in doorways; Bengali, Orissan, Biharian, Burmese, Marwari, Greek, Turkish, Armenian, Jew, Parsi. They peer but glean nothing of what guides his footsteps; whether it's chance or fate or something else altogether, perhaps simple curiosity, or hope, or despair, or bizarre calculation. On this night, he is inscrutable, but inscrutability is not his alone. Skins yellow, eyes slant; he reaches Chinatown.

In a room, by a platform, Stephen watches as Hot Fat, a Chinaman who is neither hot nor fat, but delicate like a girl and pallid as death, suggests with a sweep of his blousy sleeve that Stephen stretch himself out.

HOT FAT: Rest Sahib.

The words drop from two perfect lips that might be glossed or might shine simply as a consequence of their setting, a sheen of ghostly skin that seems drained of all blood. The Chinaman bends forward to arrange and then manipulate the contents of a tray. A mole, partly obscured by a pigtail and a whisper of black down, grows out of the base of his neck.

Hot Fat works delicately, with delicate hands, skimming with the point of a needle a tear-drop of dark brown paste from an open jar. He brings the needle to the flame of a lamp, twirling it the way a strong man twirls his moustache, until the paste bubbles like porridge. The Chinaman continues, more paste, more bubbling, more twirling, until he has, on the tip of his needle, a round pellet, or (in the softer language of healing) a pill. This he jabs into a tiny depression in the bottom of a clay bowl which rests along an eighteen-inch bamboo pipe. He lies down, the flicker of a lamp between him and the Scotsman.

Hot Fat puts the mouthpiece of the bamboo between his lips. He warms the bowl over the flame until the opium begins to bubble once more. He breaths in, one long continuous pull, so that the pill gives up its secrets and disappears entirely, transmuted into smoke down the Chinaman's throat. The Chinaman takes a sip of tea.

HOT FAT (*in good English*): Sahib would like to smoke?
STEPHEN: Yes.

When the pipe comes to him, Stephen warms it as he has seen it done. He brings it to his lips. He inhales as if smoking a bidi, and coughs the way all first-time smokers cough.

The next pill is Hot Fat's, taken into the lungs in one long breath. Then Stephen, Hot Fat, Stephen, and so on and so on. Time passes in a haze of comfortable smoke. The two men lie on their sides, heads resting on small pillows, silent.

The leaf of a ginkgo tree, unnoticed before on the facing wall of the room, now absorbs Stephen. It is in the shape of a fan, with edges like the edge of the lobe of a weathered ear, perfect in its imperfections. Now he sees the gingko's bark, cracked and rumpled like rock. Now he sees water trickling down it in tributaries of white and brown and red.

All the while the hands of Hot Fat fashion pill after pill until Stephen, feeling the tug of a life not quite forgotten, stands up, walks to the door and, in the fresh air of morning, vomits up everything he has in his stomach.

HOT FAT: When will I see Sahib again?

STEPHEN: No. Once is enough. (*Hot Fat bows.*)

Stephen climbs the wooden stairs of the mess and collapses on his bed. In his dream-filled consciousness, he is aware of the sound of springs creaking, of whimpering, and of Noormohamed pulling off his socks. He smiles the contented smile a man smiles after his first love affair, and falls asleep.

In Chinatown, next evening, a boy comes up to him.

BOY: Follow me, Sahib.

The opium den seems bigger to him this second time, more smokers, four or five pairs, where before there were none, or if not none, less, certainly less. A space on the platform has been kept empty. Stephen lies down. The eyes of other smokers look towards him but without curiosity or surprise. Hot Fat prepares the first pipe.

The flames of oil lamps and a weak bulb hanging from the ceiling give off a flickering half-light which is absorbed by layers of smoke. This half-lit layer gathers, pungent and heavy, over the reclining bodies like a mist, like the sort of ancient layered mist that lies above lochs in Scotland when there is no sun to burn it off. Stephen smokes as before, alternating pipes with Hot Fat.

The gingko tree leans lazily against the facing wall or perhaps it supports it; Stephen cannot be sure. The dense ridges of its bark now appear like rippled sand with, here and there, pools and eddies left behind by the tide. The bark is pocked with white spots, holed and crinkled with age, seemingly dead but for the life sprouting in its leaves, so smooth, so green, so deep. How remarkable this tree is, how changeable, how mysterious its leaves and branches and trunk, how infinite. Stephen reaches for another pipe. The smoke rubs out his yesterdays and tomorrows. There is only now, this tree, this pipe. Another pipe, ah, another pipe.

And yet, once again, when the call comes, he obeys. A pill swallowed at the door holds him in the fresher air of the world outside. He sits on the steps of the mess and listens to the conversation of bats and the semaphore wing beats of distant insects.

He hears the voice of a young woman who is shaking him gently.

PARVATI: Sahib, sleep. (*Parvati helps him to his bed.*)

34

Durwans bearing iron-tipped sticks patrol the gates, but in a lazy, everyday manner with time to stop and smoke and observe with satisfaction the dejection on the faces of the strikers outside. When a car stops and a window rolls down, it is waved through with no greater obstruction than a half-hearted slogan half-shouted and half-suppressed. The keeper of the gate salutes as the car passes and watches it continue on until it comes to steps which lead to a boardroom where eighteen men once bowed in wonder and respect. The driver opens the rear passenger door. Ranjana gets out. She is taller than her driver. She thanks him.

She stands and takes in the building, the bare red earth, the neem tree and a flock of drongos that are whistling to each other in its branches. She scratches the ground with her foot as if to discover what might have been dug over or swept aside. She finds nothing. The camera closes in. She holds her head at a slight angle. Her eyes also, just perceptibly, slope. The whites are clear, and the irises an absorbing black.

A group of mill workers, standing in shadow under the overhanging branches of the neem tree, look on. The men scratch themselves under their long white shirts or across their bare chests. The women stare at her in dull-eyed wonder as native islanders might stare at a passing liner which they know will never stop.

Ranjana, wearing a sari of green and gold, sits in a chair. Opposite her, across a table, is McLeish with a bandage still over his nose and eye.

RANJANA (*matter of factly*): The eighteen men who were in this room when we last met have been beaten most brutally by your durwans.

MCLEISH (*relaxing into his chair*): Have they? I've heard nothing but I can make enquiries if you like. Are you sure?

RANJANA: I am sure.

MCLEISH: Probably as well not to jump to conclusions just yet. Men, here, express themselves (*he searches for the right word*) physically. Well, I don't need to tell you. Particularly during a strike. This incident, if that's what it was, might have been just that. Or perhaps the men attacked the durwans. Strikers hate the sight of those who have a job.

RANJANA: Does it often happen that unarmed men attack durwans armed with lathis?

MCLEISH: Many strange things happen in India especially when feelings run high. Our Muslim workers have returned to the mill, while the Hindus remain on strike. That sort of thing can lead to trouble.

RANJANA (*struggling to keep her composure*): The beatings, these are big things, but I have been sent from Calcutta by Mrs Sen to talk about another matter, a small thing.

MCLEISH: I am a great believer in talking, Miss Devi. Talking is always the best way.

RANJANA: I have come to ask you to set aside a room where the men can go at night to learn to read and write, the basics of language that is all; and where, in the day, the women can get help with their babies. This is a small thing, a sign that the Burra Sahib concerns himself with the welfare of his coolies.

MCLEISH (*considering*): If I were to do this, would you teach politics? Would you recruit men to your Union?

RANJANA: No politics. No Union. Books and babies only. You have my word.

MCLEISH: Mmm. (*He pauses.*) Very well. (*A startled look comes across his face, as if he's surprised at what he's saying.*) A trial, to see how it goes. There is a hut not far from the coolie lines. You may set yourself up there. That's as much as I can do. And may I take it that I will hear no more stories about men being beaten?

RANJANA (*feeling sick at heart*): No more stories.

Ranjana, in the car, again passes Stephen on the road. This time she stops. She gets out.

RANJANA: I have been told it was you who saved the men from a beating. I am grateful. (*She puts her hands together, fingers pointing up, and bends forward.*)

STEPHEN: I saved them from nothing. They had already been beaten. (*Ranjana shakes her head from side to side, Indian fashion.*) Next time will be worse.

RANJANA: Next time? Mr McLeish does not believe he has done enough?

STEPHEN: Not McLeish, another grievance.

RANJANA: You are speaking in riddles, Mr Doig. Explain please.

STEPHEN: I have heard that while the Muslim men have been at work, one of the strikers, a Hindu, has gone to the Muslim lines and exposed himself in front of the women.

RANJANA: Is it true?

STEPHEN (*shrugging*): Who can say. Does it make any difference? It's a dry fire, it won't take much.

RANJANA: What will happen?

STEPHEN: The rumour will bring itself to the boil. One Hindu will become a hundred and there will be a riot. The Muslims will down tools and take what they see as their revenge. The Hindus will fight back. You will see beatings that will make the events of the other day look like nothing.

RANJANA: I know riots. I have seen them in Calcutta. Streets running with blood, women without husbands, children without fathers, mothers without children, and what for?

STEPHEN: If there's an itch, someone will scratch it.

RANJANA: Does it happen in Scotland, this scratching?

STEPHEN: We have the benefit of a cold climate.

RANJANA: Perhaps you should have stayed.

STEPHEN (*suddenly laughing, his red hair coming loose and falling down on his forehead*): In Dundee? Eh dinna think so. (*He brushes it back with his hand.*)

RANJANA: Goodbye, Mr Doig.

STEPHEN: Stephen, Miss Devi, if you like.

Ranjana does not respond to his invitation. The car begins to pull away. She winds down her window as if about to say something, but doesn't.

* * *

Later, beyond the coolie lines, a riot of the usual sort: Hindus on one side, Muslims on the other. The weapons of choice are sticks, spindles and the short lethal knives used by weavers to sever strands of jute. Men are being beaten over the head, kicked in the ribs and balls, or slashed. Blood is everywhere.

At the home of the Assistant Superintendent of Police, a Yorkshireman by the name of Perkins, steam rises from a plate of roast pork and dumplings, a delicacy which reminds him of his mother and which he has spent the last fourteen years teaching his cook how to prepare. Perkins rubs the palms of his hands together and savours in his nostrils its trenchant aroma. The telephone rings. Perkins reluctantly picks up the receiver and responds to the voice on the other end.

PERKINS: Just finished, thank you, sir. (*His eyes follow the wisps of steam that are rising from his plate. He listens to a lengthy instruction. By the time he speaks again, the steam has died away.*) I'll see to it right away.

TELEPHONE (*booming*): Immediately, Perkins, immediately.

PERKINS (*doing his best to put the loss of his roast pork behind him*): Immediately, sir.

Perkins now stands on open ground before a thin and hungry line of native constables; Hindus, Sikhs, Muslims and perhaps even a Christian or two, who, in the line of duty and a regular wage, have put law and order before religion or their lunch. They have come with what was at hand when they received the call, which isn't much: loincloths, uniform puggeries, police belts and lathis.

PERKINS (*addressing his men in a growl*): Those men over there have taken me from my tiffin. They have taken you from your cooking pots. When I say *charge*, charge and let them have it.

NATIVE CONSTABLES (*raising their lathis*): *Huzoor.*

PERKINS (*shouting*): Let them have it.

The lightly dressed brigade moves forward, one white European in front and a hundred sparsely clad brown policemen on his shoulder. The pace gathers; angry legs thinking of good food wasted begin to eat up the ground; the air fills with the whisper of hustling feet; mud spatters, mouths grunt and eyes narrow with intent. None of this is lost on the brawling mob. Or rather it dawns on them as one—a genuinely communal moment this—that out of a sky bunged up with monsoon and about to sneeze apocalyptically, shit also is about to fall. They stop fighting and blink to make sure that what they observe steaming in their direction really is a force of irate half-naked policemen. They scatter up back alleys, down side streets and over the roofs of bustees. One man falls through. Another trips and ends face down in an open sewer. Some are handcuffed. Some receive summary justice: a tickle in the ribs, a gentle dig in the testicles. The monsoon rain falls with a vengeance.

35

Stephen at the pool, Stephen in his room reading, Stephen walking around the compound, around the fragrant frangipani, around the managers' manicured borders. At dusk, he circumnavigates the mess. He tries to settle in one of the wicker chairs that looks out towards the Hooghly, but can't. He picks up a billiard cue, chalks it energetically and pots a couple of balls. He returns the cue to its rack. He goes outside.

The rain has stopped. He walks. Insects swarm out of the hot swampy earth, breed, multiply, dance in columns, *zzz*, *mmm*, *eecheech* and eat. Beyond the lines now, Stephen hears the air alive with their noises. He smells the sweet incense of India and opium and the casings of cartridges sweating in the sun. Looking about and finding himself quite alone, alone in a country where no one is ever alone, he leans against a tree and gazes up into the heavens, into the drying eyes of a God, or gods or whoever does or does not live there. The camera pauses on his face as he tries to frame a question. No words emerge.

Ranjana too is restless: restlessness has many causes. She is arguing with the judge, her father, who is sitting, bathed, powdered and relaxed, in a deep armchair.

FATHER/JUDGE: It's a simple choice, my dear, a choice between order and not-order; between order and chaos; between order and the howling winds so much desired by communists and their like.

RANJANA: And justice, father? Where is justice in the beating of mill hands? They could have been killed.

FATHER/JUDGE: Yes, that is most regrettable. I don't condone it, the taking of the law into their own hands, not at all. But what if prompt action had not been taken? What if no action had been taken? Would matters have got out of control, would life have been lost? As it was, was it not, in the riot that followed?

RANJANA (*becoming heated*): So all action is under the say-so of that ignorant, bone-headed McLeish and that pig Browne. You appoint them judge and jury.

FATHER/JUDGE: I would hear a case against them, if a case were brought, to see if they had overstepped the line; just as I would hear a case against the man who threw the spindle at McLeish if that case were brought.

RANJANA (*angry*): But who will bring this case? You know such cases will not be brought, how many have ever been brought? And so McLeish rules his kingdom with lathis and a Lewis gun. What law is there in that? There is no law, jungle law isn't it?

Her father thinks of saying something but decides not to. He picks up some papers from a table and reads. Ranjana leaves. A door bangs.

We see her mouthing at the world through the accumulated dust of a train window out of which nothing is visible. We see her walking towards the coolie lines. She notices, ahead of her, a man standing quite still gazing up, his mind elsewhere. She stops. The unlikely sight calms her. She stands in silence until he lowers his eyes.

STEPHEN (*surprised*): Hello. How long have you been here?

RANJANA: A few minutes. Weather forecast or God?

STEPHEN: Excuse me?

RANJANA: A white man leaning against a bodhi tree and staring up into the sky can only mean one of two things: weather forecast or God.

STEPHEN (*laughing*): I think it will rain.

RANJANA: You were right about the riot. I will expect rain. (*She holds her hands out.*)

STEPHEN: Yi winna be disappointed. (*He feels a drop of rain on his face.*) You see. (*They both laugh together.*)

RANJANA: Do you find everything in India predictable? *(She kicks off her shoes.)*

STEPHEN (*Reflecting, mock seriously.*) The white man is predictable, except when he's staring at the sky. The brown man, when he meets the white man, is predictable. The same can't be said for the brown woman. The brown woman is always a surprise.

He leans back against the bodhi tree taking her in; her toes caressing the red earth, the tilt of her head, the humour in her eyes, her sari the colour of brick dust.

RANJANA: Do you know many brown women?

STEPHEN (*laughing*): The only one I know is you and you are definitely a surprise.

RANJANA: Am I? Mmm. And what about the rest of India, the India that is all around us? (*She waves her arms expansively.*) Is that a surprise too?

STEPHEN: It is a mystery.

RANJANA: A mystery? What sort of mystery? A mystery that makes you want to discover more, or a mystery that warns you to keep away?

STEPHEN (*now serious*): Sometimes one, sometimes the other. Something else is out there, I know that, something I need but can't touch. Maybe the white man shouldn't touch. Maybe he shouldn't even try. Who knows where he might end up?

RANJANA: Somewhere else, anyway. There are worse places than somewhere else, are there not?

STEPHEN: There certainly are.

RANJANA (*laughing*): Was Dundee so bad?

STEPHEN: One day perhaps you'll let me tell you.

RANJANA: Perhaps I will.

She makes as if to leave, but Stephen speaks again, a little hurriedly.

STEPHEN: A man died in the riot, a Muslim. Did you know?

RANJANA: Yes. Deaths are reported. (*She sighs.*) It seems India never learns. The same old battles.

STEPHEN: Even before we came along?

RANJANA: Hindus and Muslims have been killing each other since the Muslims first invaded a thousand years ago. Before that there were also battles, but we kept them in the family, so the cuts weren't so sore. Face it Mr Johnny Sahib, things have been going downhill for millennia before you. The Raj can't take all the credit.

STEPHEN (*amused*): That's a relief... Not a great believer in progress, are you?'

RANJANA: Progress? Just look. (*She points in the direction of the hovels of the mill.*) Indians do not believe in progress. They believe in the four yugas, the four great ages and, during each one, Dharma, the moral order of the world, declines by a quarter.

STEPHEN (*curious*): The four yugas? Dharma? And which yuga are we in now?

RANJANA: This is the age of Kali, the age of self-seeking, blindness and blood.

STEPHEN: That sounds like the world I know. What about the others?

RANJANA: The first age is Krita. That is the golden age. Priests are saintly, kings follow the rules of the warrior caste. It doesn't last long. Then comes Tretā, which means three. Virtue is down to three quarters. Then Dvāpara, fifty-fifty, half Dharma and half its opposite. Then Kali.

STEPHEN: So that's where it ends, in self-seeking, blindness and blood. (*He shakes his head.*) How long have we got?

RANJANA: Until it can get no worse, at least a week, could be two.

STEPHEN (*laughing*): That's all right then.

RANJANA: All right for you...I have to go now.

STEPHEN: Now? Where to?

RANJANA: Mr McLeish is letting me use one of his huts. I will prepare it, and when I have done that I will try to help the men to read and the women to look after their families. If any wish to learn.

STEPHEN: Ah, so that is you, the lady with the hut. Can I help?

RANJANA: Another time, we will see.

STEPHEN: Aye, well then, good luck. Goodbye, Miss Devi.

RANJANA: It's Ranjana, if you like.

STEPHEN: Ranjana. (*He tastes the word on his tongue.*) Goodbye, Ranjana.

Stephen returns to the mess where he finds Browne and Angus playing billiards. Jimmy Pearson, the salesman, and the Kerani are gathered around.

BROWNE (*good humouredly*): You know what I'd do with these saboteurs?

ANGUS: Which saboteurs are these? Nationalist saboteurs, Marxist saboteurs or some other kind?

BROWNE: All of them, it makes no difference. I wouldn't shoot them or even hang them. No, I think we need to be more inventive.

ANGUS (*bored*): Oh yes.

BROWNE (*his eyes twinkling*): I'd string them up by their toes. Nothing unusual in that you might say, but here's the clever bit: I'd tie them with a length of frayed jute and let them twirl above a weaving frame. Then when the jute breaks, they'll fall, be woven into a gunny bag and end their days serving some useful purpose. (*He slaps Angus on the back and looks round at his audience.*) Not bad, eh?

ANGUS: Very imaginative. (*Angus gathers himself over the spot and pots the red.*)

BROWNE (*animated*): Good shot, old man. (*He slaps Angus on the back once more.*)

They continue playing. Browne's bonhomie extends to the others. He buys pegs all round. He continues to call out 'good shot' whenever he or Angus scores a point.

BROWNE (*looking at his watch*): Oh, it's that time is it, I'd better be going: a visitor.

On his way out, he turns round and taps the side of his nose.

—The sketch couldn't have taken long. There are two thick parallel lines going up and between them a smudge of charcoal. Parvati is climbing the stairs. The door of Browne's room is open.

36

Séamus has been as good as his word. I've been going over the scripts and, okay, maybe you'd have an inkling here and there, but most of the time I can't be sure who's written what. It's a little weird, having somebody copy you like that. Unless, God, here's a thought, unless I'm now writing like Séamus. Suppose he's not copying me, I'm copying him. And I haven't even noticed.

I carry this thought with me, turning it over, trying to come to terms. The only good thing I can think of is that he is at least a professional (best-known work: *Ant and Aardvark*), though if I had to choose someone to morph into, I'd aim a little higher up the literary ladder; I don't know, Vyāsa, Joyce, it's not as if there's a shortage.

We're in St Andrews, Séamus and I, not walking anywhere in particular, so I think it's a good moment to address myself to the occupied space somewhere beneath my left shoulder. I convey my opinion about the seamlessness of the scripts, how you can't tell my writing from his. I go round and round for a bit, and then I get to it: 'Am I you or are you me?'

Séamus stops in his tracks. 'Jaysus,' he says, giving me one of his looks, 'are you standing there, cool as you like, insinuating that the great literary trick of total personality plagiarism has been pulled off by you. Gob, but the bloody cheek of it. And after all the struggles I've been through.'

I placate. 'No, I didn't mean to insinuate anything. I was just asking... What sort of struggles?'

'Struggles like you wouldn't believe, the mother of all struggles, trying not once but time after time to get into that great dark place of yours that you call your head. The moment came, and what a low moment it was, when I felt the effort was beyond me, beyond any mortal man come to that. I was all for giving up, and I would have given up too even though I've set my heart on delivering this text for the acclaim of Hollywood or other filmmakers, but just when I reached my lowest ebb, a magic thread came to me, a way of finding my way in and more to the point of getting out again when the job was done.'

'You kept this very quiet.'

'I was fighting a private battle, Stephen, and I didn't want to alarm my commissioning editor.'

'Who's that?'

'You, who else would it be? You asked me to work on the script. You set out the terms.'

'Oh, I see, me... You say you found a magic thread? Where did you find it, what was its nature, what was it for, when did all this take place?'

'The thread was as follows. I found a portal through which I could pass inside. You had not the least idea. You thought—that is, if you thought anything at all—I was just writing, or reading, or not doing a thing except sitting on my backside. But the truth is I was concentrating entirely on your breathing. In and out you went, and for every single breath you took into yourself, I took the same. It got so I could feel the air passing down your windpipe and into your chest, and then going round a bit—there are a few obstructions down there by the way, you might want to have yourself checked over one of these days—and then coming all the way back out with that controlled exhale I've seen you working on. The thing is that the more I borrowed your lungs, the more I became the air itself inside you and the simpler it was to imagine the internal mechanism which spews out those words of yours. Once I was down in your dank interior, all I had to do then was let the twisted rhythms come to me. Reflect for a moment will you on the sacrifices I've been making, on the kind of places I've had to visit, and then you won't go telling me it's you that's becoming me.'

At this point, I feel myself assailed by two conflicting emotions: relief that I haven't transposed into a leprechaun; and a nauseous feeling that I'm a washing machine and Séamus, eyes wide open like the holes in a pair of dirty underpants, is going round and round inside me taking notes. Bleach, for God's sake. Clean me up. I want to be sick.

'No I won't,' I say. 'Thank you putting my mind at rest. I see now that it was just an irrational fear that came over me.'

Séamus isn't listening. He's had his moment of indignation and moved on. 'Isn't that Julia?' he says.

'Where?' Then I see her myself, at the other end of Market Street. Immediately—that is to say before the intervention of thought—I am running. She is looking into a window. Alone.

* * *

So, I'm running. Well, more like fast walking with long strides. I want to reach her and not be in a sweat. As long as I've got her in my sights, I'm okay. She's still looking into the window: it's a coffee place. What's her interest in that? A notice perhaps: yoga, Spanish classes, a friend on the other side of the glass?

'Oh, hello Julia, I thought it was you.'

'You are not fit, Stephen,' she says looking at me in her usual way, straight in the eye. I don't know if she's pleased to see me but not showing it, or not pleased.

'No, I suppose I'm not.' I pause. 'We could have some coffee if you like. I'd like to anyway.'

'Okay,' she says. 'Here?'

We go in. Antiseptic chrome and white. Music, miscellaneous. No sign of anyone she knows, thank God.

'So, how have you been?' Now I'm finally with her, just the two of us, that's all I can think of.

'Good.'

The thought bouncing in my brain won't be suppressed a moment longer. 'And Alexander?'

'Alexander is good too.' She delivers these words with a smile in her eyes, but what I feel is the terrible weight of everything she isn't telling me: how he understands her, how she thinks she is starting to love him; how last night, or was it the night before, they...

'That's good,' I reply. What was I playing at, asking about Alexander? I might as well have issued invitations. Now I have him sitting at the table with us, making three. And if we count in Séamus, who's no doubt down among my internal organs keeping watch, four. A party, for Chrissake.

'Thank you for your note.'

'She gave it to you then?'

'Yes...she thinks you're funny.'

'The girl in the flower shop?'

'Anna, yes. You made her laugh.'

'Oh, well.' To change the subject, I say, 'I'm making progress on my grandfather's history.'

'I'd like to hear about it. Are you ready to tell me?'

'Soon. I'm getting there. I'm putting it all together in my head.'

'Don't take too long.' She seems disappointed.

'I won't, I promise.' She is far away now, I can see it in her face, further away than before. I grab at something, anything, that will bring her back. 'I'm sorry about my mother's funeral. I should have invited you. I don't know why I didn't.'

'You like secrets, that's why.'

'I suppose I do, but I'm starting to like them less.'

'Prove it,' she says. 'Tell me one.'

'Tell you one? Can it be true or false, fact or fiction?'

She is smiling now.

'Either or both, as long as it is from the heart.'

'Detective Sergeant McCorquodale of the Dundee CID thinks my mother might have been dealing drugs.' Out it comes, before I can think to stop it, and I feel soiled, just saying the words. Dirty.

'Tell me about this McCorquodale.' That's her response, all quite matter of fact, no horror in it at all, no shrinking back, no guilt by association. It astonishes me, so I tell her what Mc-

Corquodale told me, the case against. When I've finished, she says, 'Some hidden things come out, some don't. Destroying the plaster is only the start.' She leans forward over the table and kisses me. It's no more than on the cheek, but it's the last thing I'm expecting.

And if that wasn't enough, she adds: 'Alexander has gone home...to his wife and little girl.' God, I feel good. I look up and see the laughing lights in her eyes and suddenly there's only her and me at the table. Séamus and Alexander have disappeared: in a pub somewhere, sinking pints I shouldn't wonder.

We start talking about my grandfather, just bits and pieces. I don't tell her about the opium. One revelation on that score is enough for today. We talk about his drawings instead. Nice and neutral. In fact, better than that because it allows his talent to rub off on me. Talented by association. Then, as I'm describing a sketch he did of Ranjana, and throwing in a word or two about the role I expect her to play in my life, half my head fills up with another drawing. It's his best: complicated, elusive, full of deep meaning, resonant with revelation. The only problem is I don't think I've ever seen it until now. The picture exists in the outer reaches. Out there. But what is it exactly? Is it a picture he could have done, or am I inventing it for him? Who is the artist? From whom does it come, from him or me, or from both of us together, an amalgam of blood? And what good is it anyway unless I can bring it back, make something of it, make it flesh? And though I'm just sitting on my chair looking at Julia, in that other half of my head I'm concentrating like crazy, stretching out, straining myself to capture it in the here and now.

Somebody turns up the music. *Coldplay*. I reach out for Julia's hand. Withdrawn. Taken away. As if to brush something off her jeans. I force myself to breathe out. Séamus revolves once in my stomach and flops down watchfully. The soak cycle. I want to grab her: hand, arm, anything. My mother: how I remember her grabbing and holding nothing. Now me. Ah, Julia, how to meet you in spirit, how to touch as angels touch, how to obtain the secrets of the women of Provideniye which you will never reveal.

'Time to go, Stephen,' she says. 'It's been good to see you again. I like our chance encounters.'

She gets up. I help her on with her jacket. Then I turn her and kiss her on the mouth in case I never get to kiss her again. In that moment I feel her lips tighten, a slight withdrawal, a reflex smoothed but not quite flattened... Smoothed by what? Her desire for an easy exit? Her not wishing to be cruel? Please God, let it not be that. Not neutrality. Not condescension.

37

Parvati wears a silk sari and bangles which may or may not be of gold. She sits motionless. Her face reveals nothing. She does not eat. Browne, meanwhile, piles toast and marmalade onto his plate of fried eggs. He pauses in his mastication only to look around the table at the others—Angus, Stephen, the Kerani, Jimmy Pearson—and to beam out of his stuffed red face.

ANGUS: When does your wife get back? Can't be long now.

BROWNE: She's had to delay a month, something about a problem with the children's school. (*Browne's hand creeps under the table and squeezes silk.*)

ANGUS: Sorry to hear that.

The men depart for the mill.

STEPHEN (*lingering*): Goodbye Parvati. (*He wants to say more, fails to find the words and leaves.*)

Parvati looks around the room at the table with the coloured ivory balls, the sideboard which holds the cues, the wicker chairs, the black bookcase. She takes down a copy of Kipling, which she cannot read, and turns the pages while, from a doorway, Abdul, the cook, watches her, feeling whatever it is that one kept person feels for another; sympathy, disdain, jealousy, pity.

Parvati leaves, but not for the mill: the woman of the right-hand man of the Burra Sahib does not toil with the common coolies. Looking neither to right nor left of her, nor trying to catch anyone's eye, she goes to the bazaar. At the first stall, she buys fresh vegetables, paying for them with a newly minted coin. She hurries home. She boils up a healing broth. As it cooks, she cleans the bustee and wipes sweat from Sunil's cold forehead.

Come the dark, Parvati bends over her husband. In one hand, she holds a piece of hessian for a final dab of his cheeks and the removal of fluid around the mouth. In the other, hidden behind her back, are silk and bangles which will be needed later.

PARVATI: I have to go. (*Sunil reaches up and holds the top of her arm. He doesn't touch what she's hiding.*) I am working now on the night shift. The pay is better.

SUNIL (*weakly*): That is good.

PARVATI: Three rupees a week.

Parvati tiptoes out with tears in her eyes, as she will tiptoe out the next night, and the night after, and the night after that.

* * *

Using the main gate on Chowringhee Road, Stephen and Ranjana enter the Indian Museum, a massive mausoleum. Stephen hands his umbrella to an attendant in exchange for a token.

RANJANA (*taking the token from him and weighing it in her hand*): This is why the British are so hard to be rid of. Brass, isn't it? Not some scrap of worthless paper that blows away on any gust of wind. (*Her hand flaps at the air.*) It is such solid stuff, what else can it be for if not to show us poor Indians that the Raj is built to last a thousand years.

STEPHEN: Don't Indians know better by now?

RANJANA: Yes, they know, but when they are seeing umbrella tokens that weigh as much as their own leg, when the faces of the pukka sahibs in their suits are as stony as…as stone, when there's nothing else but stone people and stone buildings, and all those stonewalling pompous nose-in-air politicos; it makes them think to each other, what hope is there that we can wear them down?

STEPHEN: Yes, what hope is there?

They mount a short flight of steps, pass the tree Kalpadruma (also of stone but which makes wishes come true), and come to an Ashoka column crowned with four lions.

STEPHEN (*reading the inscription*): Erected by Ashoka in the third century BC. (*He studies the lions with the eye of an artist.*) Look at the detail, the way the lions seem to be smiling. (*He is astonished.*) Someone carved those more than two thousand years ago...

RANJANA: India goes back a long way. Tell me, Stephen, what was happening in Dundee, third century BC?

STEPHEN (*wondering*): I don't know. No carvings like that anyway. I think my ancestors spent most of the day chasing pigs. (*He grunts twice; a poor imitation.*)

RANJANA: You have such strange pigs in Scotland?

STEPHEN (*laughing*): Well, they don't all sound like me.

RANJANA: Thank goodness.

STEPHEN: Who was Ashoka?

RANJANA: Ashoka ruled most of India... He was Buddhist. That's all I know. (*She thinks.*) Oh, and not to forget his pillars like this one. All over, Ashoka pillars advising the people on many subjects, non-violence and good behaviour included: only conquest by Dharma is true conquest; only Dharma gives delight.

STEPHEN: What is Dharma?

RANJANA (*touching him gently*): You have first to find it for yourself and not before then you can know what it is.

STEPHEN: Like an elephant?

RANJANA (*amused*): Mmm, or the right woman.

Now we are in Chowringhee, to the sound of klaxons and the shouts of itinerant hawkers, and then at a small racetrack somewhere in Calcutta. We hear the thunder of hooves: coming round the final bend is a cavalry charge of horses each with two faces (but only the one above is wearing goggles). Two other faces peer out from under an umbrella (one golden brown, one pink, both getting wet).

RANJANA: Are we winning?

STEPHEN (*putting his arm around her waist*): Not yet.

The horses charge across the line. Stephen and Ranjana listen for the announcement.

STEPHEN (*smiling*): Oh well.

RANJANA (*resting her hand on his.*) We should see a film. *Love of Savita* has been playing at the Empire for God knows how many weeks, so perhaps it is even good. I have been informed it concerns the intimate relations between an Indian woman and a Scottish man.

STEPHEN: Do they live happily ever after?

RANJANA: Let me see...(*she pretends to look into the future*)...they do most certainly, but only after much roller-coastering. Her father becomes very angry and says she is bringing shame on his family. Her mother is tearful. This boo-hoo carry-on presents difficulty for Savita, Indian women, young ones especially, loving their mothers so.

STEPHEN: All of them?

RANJANA: A few exceptions, my own being one. She loved paint more than anything. She was artist first, then woman, then wife, and mother about as far behind as our poor horse.

STEPHEN: Yes, a pity about the horse. What happens to the Scotsman?

RANJANA: His friends take him to one side. They squint over their moustaches, they stiffen their upper lips and they speak to him severely. (*Ranjana squints and twirls an imaginary moustache*). 'Look here old man, you're letting the side down, what what. And watch out for the clap. The wogs are riddled with it.'

STEPHEN (*laughing*): Does the Scotsman punch them?

RANJANA: He knocks out two teeth. There is much blood.

STEPHEN: And in the end?

RANJANA: In the end, they run away. The hearts of her parents are broken into so many pieces. His friends stare into the trees when they see him coming. They have a child, a little brown white boy who, when he grows up, will be shunned by the whole world. They don't care. Love conquers everything. It's the cinema.

STEPHEN: Let's see it. At least we'll be out of the weather.

* * *

The rain that has fallen on the racetrack now falls on the reeds of

Parvati's bustee. It stirs up the streams of sewage. Sewage and rainwater are on the move. The jute sacking that is Parvati's door is a sluice and her home a hospital ward of liquid earth with all that fertilizes it floating unabsorbed.

Parvati is doing her best to keep the ground clean. She has a hand shovel. Ranjana is kneeling and giving no indication that she has noticed her surroundings. She adjusts the pillow under Sunil's head. She strokes his shoulder. She spoons food into his mouth.

RANJANA (*feeding him the compassionate lie as lightly as she can manage*): You'll soon be up and about. In no time.

Parvati suddenly leaves the bustee. The monsoon dampens the sound of her vomiting. She returns.

RANJANA (*standing up*): How are you? Have you caught something from Sunil?

PARVATI: No. Not from Sunil.

RANJANA: What is it?

Parvati says nothing. She looks down and her hand inadvertently brushes her stomach.

RANJANA: Oh.

* * *

In a room in Calcutta, in the unfashionable north end of town, north of Park Street, north of Dharamtala Street, north even of Bow Bazar, Stephen and Ranjana lie in bed covered by a thin sheet. They smoke. A blouse lies draped over the back of a chair. Stephen's clothes are on the floor.

STEPHEN: What if your mother could see you now?

RANJANA: She'd tell me to put out the cigarette. 'Fire, Ranjana, are you now wanting to burn your poor mother to death?' Then she'd get out her sketch pad and start drawing.

STEPHEN: I don't blame her for that. You're a bonnie picture all right, what artist wouldn't want you on his canvas.

RANJANA: On canvas only?

STEPHEN (*laughing and peeling back the sheet*): I can think of other places. (*He takes her cigarette and stubs it out.*)

RANJANA: Mama would be pleased. (*She passes her hand through his red hair and brushes his cheek with a kiss. Then coquettishly):* What would they say at the Bengal?

STEPHEN (*kissing her legs, murmuring)*: I'm not a member of the Bengal. (*He moves up her body*) Not even the Turf Club. You?

RANJANA: There's only one club for me. (*She takes his head in her hands. Then, sighing.*) What will happen to us, Stephen? Tell me please, will we come to a bad end?

STEPHEN (*now serious*): Will your parents turn their backs on you? Will we have a child, a little brown white boy? Will he be shunned by the whole world?

RANJANA (*suddenly frightened*): Yes, Stephen, will he?

STEPHEN: It is possible.

RANJANA (*shivering*): And what then, what then? Does love conquer everything, do you think so?

STEPHEN: I don't know. I can't tell.

Stephen gathers Ranjana into his arms, and time passes.

—And as I watch my grandparents sheltering in their mutual embrace, I can't help but wonder. Séamus gives us nothing more than a half-fretful glance, a glance erased by a kiss. Is he right? Was that enough to make them cross the line from which there was no going back? To turn them into outcasts who would be shunned by white and brown alike? Does love conquer all?

Or was it something else altogether? Not love's tug at all but another kind of pull. There are two histories. My grandfather with his despair of the tedium of the Raj, its monochrome ideas, its unflinching verities. My grandmother with her caring heart, her mother distant, her father anglicized, her brother with white blood on his hands. Was it that mix, in whatever precise or magical proportions, which dragged them over?

Séamus doesn't ask. Nor does my grandfather. He leaves only

this: a picture. He is naked, standing in the middle of his room in North Calcutta staring at a sheet of paper, a stub of charcoal in his hand. Ranjana, also naked, is in a chair painting her toenails. Her hair has tumbled forward over her face and, with one hand, she is brushing it away. It's a statement, isn't it? A statement that they were lovers. Not a question. Not a 'Why?' Not a 'What next?'

38

It is now winter, the best time to be in Calcutta. The monsoon is a memory, the sky a cloudless blue and the weather warm like a summer's day in Scotland. The camera observes (*as newsreel*) cricket at the Eden Gardens, paper chases, racing at the track, gallops on the Maidan in the early morning fog, polo, picnics, trips up river, bright eyes and shining lips in the freshness of these glorious days of winter, tennis parties, the merry peal of marriage bells...and observes also a new arrival pushing through the door of the bachelors' mess.

Doris is a woman of late middle age, built like a tug of the sort that manoeuvres large oceangoing vessels down the dangerous waters of the Hooghly. She announces her return to the side of her husband by steaming in and hooting (as tugs do) in a soft but penetrative treble.

DORIS: Rabbie. (*She stops and then repeats the name, the sound building to a seductive crescendo containing the two distinct syllables that are the anchor and mooring of her life.*) Raaabeee.

We hear footsteps coming downstairs.

BROWNE (*morosely*): You're early.

DORIS (*the smile on her face wavering hardly at all*): Aye, eh dinna ken why, sumhin aboot greet tides or winds or sumhin. But it's affy guid ti see yi, Rabbie. (*Browne looks at her with contempt.*)

BROWNE: I've organized a bungalow for you, (*pause*) for us. I'll get my bearer to show you. (*Now shouting.*) Salim, you idle sod, get down here. (*Salim, his bearer, appears.*) Show Memsahib to her quarters and bring my things over.

Later that same evening, Parvati slides quietly up the stairs. She finds that Browne's rooms are empty and begins to tremble. The trembling begins in her fingers and spreads up her arms. It moves across to her chest. Like a jacaranda caught in a sudden breeze, she shakes all over and her delicate flowers, lovely drooping purple bells, scatter and fall.

Stephen in his room hears something and goes to her.

STEPHEN: Parvati. (*He steadies her in his arms.*)

PARVATI: Memsahib come?

STEPHEN: This morning. You don't have to be here anymore. You are free.

PARVATI: Free?

Parvati walks home through the bazaar, a woman to whom men call out. She looks at her feet and hurries back to her husband.

PARVATI (*to Sunil*): No nightshift tonight. (*She cries silently as Sunil lays a tired hand on hers.*)

But the next evening, when Parvati is standing by the roadside in a thin sari, a stranger comes over and she does not look at her feet. He runs his hand down her hair and across her breast. He speaks coarsely, the rough, persuasive language of commerce; to which Parvati in silence acquiesces.

PARVATI (*to Sunil next morning*): I will bring your medicine.

A single rupee on the earth of the bustee floor catches a shaft of sunlight, and sparkles. Sunil is too weak to speak but in his eyes there is a question.

PARVATI: The nightshift.

Parvati leaves.

Sunil stares at the sagging roof of the bustee. His ribs heave as if about to split apart. He coughs. Blood and bile come up. He coughs again this time continuously until, drawing breath for the last time, his body shudders itself into silence.

In the morning, Parvati returns. As she kneels beside him crying, we see the bump beneath her sari.

Bochu pokes his head around the hessian.

BOCHU (*jovially*): Ah Parvati, you're at home. Good. Thought I'd find you in. Sorry about not being able to give you work in the mill, but the Sahib, well he didn't feel he could. You understand.

But we're not here to talk about that. Just the money you owe. It's time to pay. (*He taps the butt end of his lathi against his calf— once, twice, three times*). *Jaldi jaldi.*

Parvati now stands outside the married quarters occupied by Browne and his wife. On her face is hope, that strange bird which can fly in the face of the prevailing wind, its flapping wings drumming out the hum of everything that knows better: it can even suppose that Browne might do the decent thing, reach into his trousers and bring out rupees. She feels the baby that she is carrying inside her and arranges herself so that Browne will not fail to notice. She knocks on the door. Browne, red-faced, appears. He looks left and right.

PARVATI (*bowing*): Rupya, good Sahib, for your son. (*She displays her pregnancy.*)

BROWNE (*whispering, but angrily*): Do I know you?

PARVATI: It is I, Sahib.

BROWNE: Go away. It could be anybody's, how dare you, I am a married man. Perhaps it is Angus's or Stephen's or any one of the men you have turned to. So get out before I kick you out. Go, coming to my house asking for money, what nerve. What bloody cheek.

He slams the door in her face. It is a plain door, without features, covered only in a thin varnish.

* * *

An Indian girl, with gaps in her teeth and pigtails, is gazing down from an open balcony which runs round the inner circumference of a once substantial dwelling. The balcony is connected by Z-shaped staircases to a courtyard below where a boy in a loincloth (perhaps the girl's brother) is wrestling with another. He has him in an arm-lock and wishes to know if his opponent is ready to submit. He isn't. The victim twists around and they wrestle on.

The courtyard is nothing more than red earth daubed with

washing and broken pots, and overlaid with fire smoke which issues through the bricks of every kitchen in this many-times divided house. As we watch the girl, the courtyard, the boys wrestling, the trails of smoke, we notice one trail among all the sooty trails rising and falling on the swirling air streams and, following it to its source, come to a door three storeys up.

Inside is a cracked stone floor, three chairs and white walls decorated only by the stain of betel (put there by a hundred years of wiped fingers and considered by Stephen too artistic to remove). Ranjana is bent over an oven of a few bricks. She is kindling, with cow dung and kerosene, a small deposit of low-grade coke. On the bricks sit a metal grid and an iron pan. The smoke rises dirtily, hits the ceiling, bounces down, swirls around, washes itself in the running tap of the cistern and dries off in the simmering heat that sits like a low cloud over the three chairs and the bed and bedding of the adjacent room. The smoke flicks ash and floats, its wisps corkscrewing around and down until, drawn by the tug of an open window, it lazily bellies out.

Ranjana, now satisfied that the oven is alight, rearranges a vase of midnight jasmine. She stands back, admires through the smoke the bud that will not open until dark, and moves the vase, a distance of inches, to the right. She notices a sweet of boiled and re-boiled sugary milk and carries it into the adjoining room, a bare bedroom.

She finds Stephen lying on an old string bed staring up at the ceiling and seeing in its myriad cracks the soothing drift of clouds. She puts what she's brought to his lips, brushes them with her fingertips, and watches as he works the sweet onto his teeth. She feels a light touch on her arm encouraging her to lie next to him. She rests on her back, the pair of them laid out like two corpses waiting for the first shower of moist earth. After a while, she rolls over, nuzzles into his shoulder, and lets her hand fall limp and sweet across his chest. She drifts off to sleep, sweating in the arms of her lover.

She sweats and drifts in her dreams and wakes up suddenly. She listens wide-eyed and hears a small sound like a mouse tiptoeing across a wooden board. Pulling back the sheet, her bare feet find the floor and move silently towards the scratching.

RANJANA (*calling softly*): Is that you, Satish?

There is no reply except for what might be a scrape of fingernails on the door. Ranjana opens it and finds, standing outside, a woman swathed from head to foot in thin cloth. Her head is lowered and a white swaddled bundle is in her arms. The woman looks up suddenly. It is Parvati, now gaunt and hollowed about the eyes. She raises the bundle and as Ranjana, out of instinct, accepts it into her arms, it gurgles. Both women smile and bend over for a closer look.

RANJANA (*lifting the cloth that has fallen over the baby's face*): How lovely.

Parvati bows, then falls. Her lips touch Ranjana's ankles.

PARVATI: You look after baby, you keep baby.

RANJANA (*groaning an almost inaudible groan, an ancient groan of knowledge and pain*): But I can't, how can I?

In the silence that follows, she gently encourages Parvati to her feet.

PARVATI (*choking*): Sahib is good man, you keep baby.

Parvati opens her hand revealing a few crushed petals of orange and red. She scatters these over the baby's head and, now sobbing without control, turns suddenly and is gone. Ranjana looks down at what she now holds.

STEPHEN (*calling from the bedroom*): Who was that?

RANJANA (*still looking at the baby*): Parvati.

STEPHEN: Parvati? What did she want?

Ranjana walks over to him. He is resting on one arm watching her come in.

RANJANA: This. (*She shows him.*)

STEPHEN: Ah. What will we do?

RANJANA: We will keep it, don't you think so?

Stephen rolls onto his back. He shuts his eyes.

STEPHEN (*after a long period of silence*): Is it a boy or a girl?

RANJANA: I don't know. (*She looks inside the bundle.*) It's a girl.

39

Karṇa is by the banks of the Ganges preparing himself for the war to come, that war in which brother will not know brother, nor father son. *Na putraḥ pitaraṃ jajñe na pitā putram aurasam, na bhrātā bhrātaraṃ tatra svasrīyam na ca mātulaḥ.*

Kuntī, the mother he never knew, comes to beg him for the life of her other sons: Yudhiṣṭhira the pure, Bhīma the mighty and Arjuna of celestial accomplishment.

But Karṇa in the pain, still, of that first rejection, declares, '*Rādheyo 'ham ādhirathiḥ karṇaḥ*—I am Karṇa, son of Adhiratha the charioteer, and his wife, Rādhā.'

'No,' insists Kuntī, 'you are my son, borne by me, swaddled in divine armour, your father the Sun.'

Karṇa doesn't hold back. 'Ha, you, my mother! You abandoned me. You denied me what was mine, all my inheritance, all I could have been. You behaved to me more like an enemy than a mother. It was Rādhā who found me, who cleaned me, who gave me what a mother should. So I choose her and I choose my friend Duryodhana in the war to come. My blood means nothing to me.'

While I, also motherless, touch my arm; the arm in which I must now acknowledge the blood of those who have become my grandparents, the blood of Browne and Parvati.

My arm is as it was. I feel the warm air in my lungs. It feels the same as the warm air I felt yesterday. I lay my fingers on my chest and search for the little man inside, the person of the measure of a thumb who stands in the middle of myself, he who jumps from body to body, from lifetime to lifetime.

What is that thing we receive from what comes before? Is it the colour of skin? The twist of an ear? The minute formative circumstance of this moment and that? Or the beat-beat of the little man on watch?

What is the substance of this little man?

Me.

40

I am in the Rook, well into the black stuff, when Séamus comes in. He waves to all and sundry like bloody royalty as per usual, and sits down opposite.

'So, you've read the thing?' he asks.

'Yes,' I say, 'I've read it.'

'And did you know before?'

'No.'

'Jays, but it must have been a shock, you lining up Stephen and Ranjana for the position and all. Are you okay with it then?'

'I'm going to have to be.'

Séamus shakes his head, looks at me enquiringly, doesn't speak.

'Does it matter to you?' I ask.

'To me?' He looks genuinely surprised. 'It matters my granny.'

'What about to Julia?'

'Julia?'

'You've seen her, haven't you?'

'I've seen her alright.'

'How did she react when you told her?'

'Told her? Told her what?'

'Told her what? Told her that what flows through me is the blood of the world's biggest shite white bastard and a brown prostitute?'

'Well number one, I didn't tell her, and number two, I think you're being hard on Parvati by the way, who was a good woman undone, a victim of the situation in which the fates conspired to place her. But all that makes no difference at all since I didn't say a fecking thing and, if I did, I don't remember what it was.'

'Did she say anything to you in response to what you didn't say to her?'

'Jaysus God, Stephen, but it's a queer bastard you are. I didn't tell her, okay, and if I did, she didn't say anything back, not that I can remember.'

'Nothing from her, nothing from you?'

'There you are now. You've got hold of the thing at last. And even if some crumb of a word has dropped unnoticed from my poor lips, I doubt she'll be interested, now will she? She understands how it is with you and your family. Private matters, that's all I say. Do you suppose she's forgotten how you went over to Dundee that day, and she not knowing there was a funeral.'

Suddenly, for no reason, tears well up inside me. I put my head down on the table with my arms around so nobody will see, and then they start. I feel their slow descent, I feel my shoulders shake. I watch it all, but can control nothing.

The tears are not about Browne, my blood, Kitty or any of that. I don't even know what they are about unless it's this: that through the cloying mud of the unspoken, the buried and the buffed up, I sense something moving: the squeal of a turning lock, the grind and clank of gates, fresh air through a crack. The strangeness of it makes me laugh. God I am laughing, laughing and crying. Salt water, the genuine surprising stuff, is now pouring down my cheeks, as if a dam has burst.

I don't know for how long all this goes on but I pull myself together finally, breathe a deep satisfied breath, wipe my eyes with the back of my hand, do the same for my cheeks, look out through the mist, see a smile on Séamus's face and mumble some sort of apology.

This, for no obvious reason, is the cue for him to slap his chunky thighs, beat me over the shoulder and call to Terry across the pub. 'Can't a man get a drop to drink round here? Is it the Sahara we're living in now, or what?' and old Terry comes running. He puts the stouts down, ruffles my hair in a kindly paternal sort of way (no joke) and shuffles off. Christ, just because a moment of weakness got the better of me.

Séamus, when he's not buried in his pint, is grinning like the village idiot.

'For God's sake,' I tell him. 'This is a public place.'

He looks me in the eye and says in the best confidential manner he can plaster over his ridiculous face, 'There's a word or two of advice I have for you, boyo.'

'Advice? Now?'

'Sure now, while you're head's not stuck halfway up your arse. Write to Julia. Disgorge the whole lot, your mother, Browne, Stephen, Ranjana, and don't you leave out a thing. It'll do you the power of good.'

'What is there to disgorge? That Kitty was adopted. There's not much in that.'

'Not to me. Not to any man with an ounce of sanity in him, but to you there is. So tell her.'

* * *

'My darling Julia,'

I hope 'darling' is okay—it's the word in my head.

'You said once you'd like to hear about the film script when I'm ready. I'm ready now. The void is filling up. Some light. Some surprises. Séamus is pinning his hopes on more, but then Séamus is only interested in what will sell at the box office.

Anyway, read the script if you want to. I'd like you to know. It matters to me that you do. I've had enough of my own small secrets.

I send you my love and my kisses which start at your feet and rise to your lips, pausing at all stops in between.

God I want you here.

Stephen.'

I put together everything Séamus and I have written. On the way to Julia's flat, I go to the flower shop. A man in a raincoat has his back to me. I wait, thinking that the rain will not last much longer.

Anna laughs. 'So why you here, lover-boy?'

'I have something to give her, but would like your opinion. Who better to understand one beautiful woman than another?'

'Now I am Madame as well as flower girl?'

'Not Madame. Love consultant.'

'Ah, love consultant. Mmm, I like how it sound.'

So I tell her what's in the package more or less: not the details of course, but enough so she understands that I'm putting myself in Julia's hands. She looks at me out of pale blue eyes which I've never noticed before, and says, 'Stephen, here you hit jackpot. If this not win back her, I sleep with you myself. Nice sun tan I like.'

I laugh, she laughs. 'It's a deal,' I tell her.

As I step out of the shop, who is waiting but Séamus.

'I am thinking you might be able to use a delivery boy,' he says, taking my secrets from me.

* * *

Two days. Nothing. I am in bed, naked, lying on my back, drifting in and out of sleep. I have left the door unlatched. In case. I have this feeling. Tonight. I have the feeling all over, of her, soft pad in the night, a touch, a kiss, mist on the lips, moist at the conjunction. I create a space for her, a hole. It has its own energy. It's pull. And will suck her in.

Sometime through the dark I hear footsteps on the concrete stairs. My stomach tenses, my blood beats. I hear the rattle of the letter flap, the sound of something falling. I get up, open the door. She's gone. 'Julia,' I call, but hear only the sound of her feet on the pavement. Getting fainter.

I read her note. 'Come. You know where,' it says.

Yes.

41

God, I'm aching to see her. She came in the night. That's something, isn't it? A call. Unless she's humouring me. Calling or humouring? Calling. I hear her birdsong. Definitely.

It's a bright day, a bit of wind but not too cold. I take my time getting over there. South Street looks good. Old and amiable. I smell Julia in the breeze. She smells of apples. I imagine her, green, firm, bubbles of sap beneath, on the tongue, on her bed, restrained, abundance in waiting, in need of heat. I am on my way.

When she opens the door, she has her shoes on and her coat over her arm.

Dream on, Stephen.

'Why don't we go to the West Sands?' she says.' She gives me a peach, cut down the middle, stone removed. I take half, holding it out to her like a begging bowl or an offering. She takes a bite. Juice trickles down her chin.

We walk side by side. The tide is out. She says, 'So, Stephen, Browne was your grandfather, biologically anyway. How do you feel about that?'

'I don't know. I suppose, deep down, it's more or less what I expected. Anyone better than Browne was only a dream.'

'Why do you say that?'

'Because dreams don't come true, do they? I think I've always known that.'

'Can you live with it?'

'I'm going to have to. And at least it's honest. There's comfort in knowing the truth.'

'There is. But where does it leave you? No more dreams?'

'I dream of you. Especially after dark.'

'You do?' she says, shimmering. 'That's good,' and she takes my hand and puts it on her hip. We walk together. Conjoined. In synch. I feel her hip moving beneath my fingers, her separate existence.

'Your mother never told you about her real parents?'

'Never. Nothing.'

'Perhaps she didn't know.'

'Perhaps not, though for something like that, there's knowing and knowing. She must have had an idea.'

'You think so?'

'Maybe.'

'It wasn't easy for your mother, changing horses midstream. Did she suck her thumb?'

I laugh. 'Probably. She always needed something to hold on to.'

We have lunch in the Rook. God knows why I take her there, except I feel it's sort of appropriate somehow. Terry brings us a couple of his cheese toasties and, as he puts them down, his eyebrows rise approvingly. As if he's my benevolent uncle. He says, 'Hello, Julia,' and jibs backwards, overtly discreet.

Julia says, 'I like this place. I came here with Séamus and Alexander. Do you remember?'

'I remember… What shall we do this afternoon?'

'Do?' she replies, 'Anything. Nothing.'

So that's what happens, nothing and something at the same time. We visit Anna. Julia's idea. 'We should, don't you think?' As we enter the flower shop, Anna gives me a complicit smile. The girls, chattering, sandwich themselves between two enormous orchids.

Julia invites Anna for coffee. I'm not sure what to make of it. We go to a French café that's just opened. Anna orders salad. I ask for chips, not because I'm hungry but to have something to put in my mouth. When they come, I smother them in salt and start eating. The girls carry on like old school friends. Suddenly I feel brown, brown-skinned, dark, different, Indian: perhaps it's the whiteness of them; perhaps it's the language I don't understand; perhaps it's the deductions they want me to make. Now they lean towards each other across the table, nose tips sharing air, pausing with identical intent. What can I do? I breathe. I watch. Getting outside my head: it's the only antidote.

Anna looks at a clock on the wall and sighs. 'I must go selling flowers. The day passing slowly, slowly. No more love consultant for poor Anna.' She stands up. She kisses Julia and whispers something. Then she kisses me. On the lips. Is it an invitation by proxy? Have they discussed it?

We spend the rest of the day walking. Around the town, up on the cliffs, just mooching. It is strange, but the things I notice—the gulls, the rocks, the bubbles of seaweed, the marks in the old stone of the town, a crack in the pavement—I notice with a surprising sharpness as if a polythene wrapper has been removed, as if there are no intervening layers between the essence of the object itself and its image in my mind. I put this down to Julia. I wonder if I am seeing the world as she sees it, with her eyes. I think of asking her but don't know how to frame the question, not in a way that would make any sense.

It starts to rain. I offer to cook supper, get as far as putting a corkscrew into a bottle of wine when the doorbell rings. I don't answer it. It rings again. I look at Julia. The bell rings for the third time. It's not going away. I get up. As I open the door, I see a jug-ear, then a face, doleful like a bloodhound.

McCorquodale wipes the soles of his enormous boots on the doormat, discharging in the process the odour of turned earth. He's been digging, I think, a fact immediately borne out by a clod of mud which he dislodges from the underside. It lands solid on the carpet. 'It's only mud,' he says, bending down and taking the offending turd in his hand. He throws it out onto the landing where it splits in two against the far wall. It watches us reproachfully. 'I'll get rid of it when I go,' he declares. Then he says, 'I hope this is not a bad time for you.'

'It couldn't be worse as a matter of fact. I...'

Julia appears.

'Hello, you must be the detective. Come in.' To me she says, 'I'll take a bath.' She mouths silently, 'Okay?'

'Stay in here if you like,' I reply.

'No need. I can listen through the door.'

McCorquodale enters, sits down and examines his boots to see if further dumps are imminent.

'Don't worry about it,' I say. 'Have you been doing some evening gardening or just digging up bodies?'

'Digging up bodies,' he replies matter of factly.

This astonishes me. 'Bodies? More than one? Here?'

'Only one body today, sir. I was using the term generically to denote the kind or species with which I am engaged, rather than the number.'

McCorquodale has dug up a body and then come to see me. I don't know what to make of it. The connection seems fantastical, unreal, ridiculous. My mind is on Julia; I imagine her kicking off her shoes. I tell myself to be careful.

'There have been others, of course,' he continues, 'mostly Asian, male and from the subcontinent. Are you familiar with the subcontinent, sir? India, Pakistan, Bangladesh, the Pathans, the Kabulis, the Bengalis?'

'My mother was half Indian, sergeant.'

'Born there, was she?' he asks in a way which makes me thinks he already knows the answer. He pulls out a pencil and begins to write. 'Where exactly?'

'Calcutta.'

'Calcutta, mmm. My grandmother's sister, well my mother's aunt lived in Calcutta for a while. She went out to marry an Assistant Superintendent of Police in Rangoon, but something happened on the boat, a romantic interlude or some such, and the ASP must have got wind of it. Policeman have long ears. She ended up in Calcutta. Met a sad end.'

Another intimacy from the orphan McCorquodale. It makes me watchful. More watchful. 'Your natural mother's aunt, or your adopted mother?' I ask.

His lids widen as he considers what is to be deduced from the fact that I have remembered his details. 'My adopted mother,' he replies and then he feeds me, for no reason I can think of, her name: 'Denise.' So now I know—if I choose to believe him—that his mother is called Denise. He has drawn me into his family circle. And of course I begin to wonder whether this great-aunt, fictitious or not, might have met my grandfather, either of them. Or Irvine. Whether our stories might have crossed, past lives and present weirdly intertwining. 'What sort of sad end? Denise's aunt? What was sad about it?'

'I don't know. Denise never told me. Just that it was sad.'

'A single woman in Calcutta. Can't have been easy for her, unless she had connections.' I don't give him the picture that's in my mind, a picture of a brothel in Karaya Road. How unexpected: McCorquodale's aunt a prostitute. I wonder if it bothers him. Perhaps it doesn't. It's not as if they were related by blood.

'Not easy, no.' McCorquodale pauses. 'So, your mother was half Indian, was she? I suppose she knew other Indians around Dundee then?'

'As a rule, sergeant, those of mixed parentage, half-castes if you like, chee-chees as some people called them, kept themselves to themselves. For some reason, my mother thought she was better than the pure-bred Indian. She was rather exaggeratedly proud of what she liked to think of as her Mediterranean skin.'

'I know what you mean, sir. Not knowing where you fit in can be difficult.' McCorquodale writes on his pad. He studies what he has written. 'You're of mixed race too, I suppose. How well do you fit in, would you say?'

'I was born in Scotland, I won a scholarship to Dundee High, I have a doctorate from Oxford; I fit in just fine, thank you.' And as I say this, I am surprised by the idea that perhaps this is no more than the truth, perhaps, on certain days, even the whole truth.

He keeps reading his notes as if he's not listening. 'You said, "as a rule—as a rule those of mixed parentage kept themselves to themselves." Does this mean your mother did or she didn't?'

'My mother went out, if that's what you're getting at,' I reply, 'but I told you it's a long time since I lived at home. I'm not up to date.'

'What about when you were younger? Were there any unusual visitors?'

The man pressing something into my mother's hand appears for the second time, his skin now browner. 'Maybe some Indians did come to see us, I couldn't say, not reliably.'

'Fair enough, sir,' he replies, adding all the while to his scribbles. 'The reason I ask is that her passbook, you know I told you we'd got hold of it, well we found it on a man called Khan, the one who was washed up on the West Sands, Kamal Khan to give him his full name, a character well known to the police.'

'Meaning?' I ask.

'He was a supplier, heroin mainly. His death in suspicious circumstances, with your mother's passbook on him; it connects them.'

'You don't imagine she killed him, do you? She was a sick woman. How did he die anyway? Didn't I read he was dead before he entered the water?'

'Forensics found heroin levels in his blood consistent with an overdose. We think he was given a lethal injection.'

'He might have done it himself.'

'Might have, but we don't think so. If he had, we'd have to account for how he got himself into the sea.'

'You don't think my mother stuck a needle in him, do you? Or do you think I did?'

'No, if your mother was responsible, why would she leave her passbook on the body? As for you, sir, you will be pleased to know that your DNA does not match any found around the hiding place in your mother's flat.'

I say nothing. The sound of running water comes from the bathroom and, beneath it, drowned out, I think I hear Julia singing.

'We've been going through telephone records, sir. Usual procedure. It appears your mother made a number of calls to Khan's mobile and also to an address in Dundee. We're checking it out but, if you can help us with this, we would be grateful.'

'I don't think I can help you, sergeant. I don't know anything about my mother's activities. Never have.' The scent of lather and bubbles slips under the bathroom door and passes in suggestive swirls up my nostrils.

McCorquodale stands as if to leave. 'Oh,' he says, sitting down again, 'there is one other thing. That passbook. Something curious about it. Mainly small payments in for several years. Then, in the last three months, ten thousand, twenty thousand and another twenty thousand. Makes you wonder...'

'What?'

'...Whether she was going into business on her own account. That's just conjecture of course.'

I show him out. In the background, the sound of splashing. Bathwater being topped up. Then a hum, barely audible. As the door closes, I catch sight of McCorquodale on the landing stooping to cradle the bifurcated turd in his hand.

My knuckles, running ahead of themselves, rattle the bathroom door. I wait. What now?

'Come in,' she says.

I do as ordered and find her wrapped in steam, lying stretched out with the points of her toes just reaching the taps. Bubbles surround her neck and lie in clumps on her shoulders, breast, belly, thighs: covering her and not covering her; through the foam, an upturned nipple shimmers.

She notices something on her foot. She bends forward—a moment of revelation—and then she is hidden. She examines whatever it is: some kind of blister, or scratch, or minor blemish. She is absorbed, everything else forgotten or ignored. She twists her knee outwards and manipulates her foot so as to get a better look.

'What is it?' I ask. She doesn't appear to hear. She continues to inspect. She dabs it cautiously with a flannel. She turns to look at me. 'It's nothing.' She lies back and sinks low. Beneath the suds.

'Do you know why your mother was a dealer?' she asks.

'Why?'

'Yes, Stephen, why? Tell me, I'd like to understand.'

God, how she prods me. I catch my breath and go searching. 'It wasn't greed, I'm sure of that. She didn't do it just for the money.'

'No, I imagine the things which drove her went deeper than that.'

Then I smell it again, the old smell in that place way behind the nostrils. 'Fear. Fear was part of it. Fear was in the mix.'

'Fear of what?'

'I don't know. Of something. Of life. Of living.'

'You think she wanted to die?'

'Perhaps. She succeeded anyway.'

Julia lies back in the bath again, looking at the ceiling. 'That's good,' she says. She breathes deeply. She asks if I will bring her a glass of water.

I go into the kitchen.

We did have visitors. The man I remembered wasn't the only one either, though he's the only one I can see. After he'd gone, my mother bent down, looked me in the eyes and said, 'He's a friend, I've known him for years, he's helping us out.' It's how she said it; the earnestness, the palpable lie, the insistence that I believe her. One twist to cover up another, that was Kitty; but not good enough to fool a ten-year-old. I may not have known the details but I knew something wasn't right. Not that if I had known how she made her bit extra here and there, before the £100,000 I mean, it would have made any difference. In a whole churning ocean, a single drop for the better or worse changes nothing.

I pour some water. I hold the glass up to the window and look through it. The water is clear but the street beyond obscure, a blur. Out of all that was my mother, what is passed on? Am I her shade, the abode of her disembodied calculations? Am I her shadow? Or am I not? I tap my chest and waken the little man within. He seems perky enough. I take a mouthful. It tastes cold. I swallow. I look outside at the street where a man in a raincoat is walking. He intrudes on my reality for a moment and passes on. He leaves no trace and will not unless I decide to call him back, invent a history for him, have him answer questions.

Something stirs, a mind wave, a shiver in the neurons; which morphs into a bird, dead because it mistook a pane of glass for the clear blue sky.

I was the shadow of the waxwing slain
By the false azure of the windowpane.

An illusory sky and a dead bird. Reflections, things imagined, wings that melt in the sun. I know without knowing, gut knowledge this—and not for McCorquodale's notebook—that such things also had a hand in my mother's death.

Nabokov's Zembla. What kind of frozen place is that? It reminds me of another, it too in the icebound east. Hearing bathwater draining away, I imagine a girl left behind and a towel around her. I return to the bathroom and knock.

'I'll be out in a minute.'

42

The mill, stuffed as usual, burps up its familiar mixture: the impenetrable, sodden, heat-heavy dust; the bottomless cacophony of iron and steel; the scurry without end of the worker ants; the vigilance of the pink sahibs, some whom we recognize and some we don't.

MARRIED ASSISTANT (*to Stephen*): So you're a father.

OTHER ASSISTANT: Got a darkie now, have you, that was quick. You're some worker you are. (*The two assistants wink behind his back. Browne, who is hovering nearby, looks smug.*)

In a room in North Calcutta, a baby bawls. Heavy steps mount a Z-shaped staircase, traverse a balcony, pass through a doorway and find a wicker chair. We see Stephen lowering himself into it, accepting as he does so a peg from Ranjana. He drinks without speaking, adding nothing to the smoke-filled, howling air. Ranjana brings him curried fish and coconut, horseradish pancake, rice pilau, fried parathas, red hot chili fritters and rasgulla.

RANJANA: Leave the mill, Stephen, it's killing you.

STEPHEN: And do what?

RANJANA: I could go to my father, he knows many people, maybe he could find you something.

STEPHEN: Where would he find me something? In the ICS, in the court, in the army? Those doors were never open to me, and they're certainly not open now. I could be a constable in the police, maybe, if they were desperate. Do you see me as a policeman?

RANJANA: Not a policeman.

STEPHEN: To the pukka sahibs of Calcutta, I am only a menial, of no importance at all. I help to manage a mill, to turn out profit, to drive the wheels that make the Raj go round; which makes me not much better than an Indian. And to the Indians, I'm a white man whose time is running out. Out of place and out of time. Not even your father can fix that.

RANJANA: You could paint. I could sell your pictures in the market. We'll live modestly, we don't need much.

STEPHEN (*laughing*): We'll starve, lassie, and so will she. (*He points at Kitty and finishes his rasgulla.*)

At the mill, Browne and another assistant press in on Stephen.

BROWNE (*holding his nose*): Go easy on that Indian food Doig, you're stinking the place out.

THE ASSISTANT: Don't know how you can stomach that muck myself.

STEPHEN: Have you tried it?

THE ASSISTANT: Good God no. What do you take me for?

STEPHEN: I don't take you for anything. I just wondered if you'd tried the muck that you say you can't stomach.

BROWNE: You don't have to try it. Smelling it is bad enough. *Pppchwa.*

They leave, laughing. Angus comes over to Stephen and puts an arm around his shoulders. The two of them walk together down the lanes between the machines, up and back, up and back, patrolling, patrolling, concrete and steel and brick, noise and dust and heat...and the passing of the years...and a baby growing into a child.

RANJANA (*holding Kitty's hair and attempting to plait it*): Be still, how can I make you beautiful with all this wriggling?

Kitty struggles and kicks her feet on the floor until Ranjana gives up. The child picks up a wooden spoon and beats it against a table leg. Ranjana and Stephen take no notice. She cries. Stephen pours himself another peg.

Rifles fire on both sides of the Hooghly. Angus stands next to Stephen, gun in hand.

ANGUS (*whispering*): Stay close, look as if you mean it, say nothing.

Stephen has the face of a man holding on for dear life.

RANJANA: How was it today?

STEPHEN: It's not just Irvine's now. The strikes are spreading. Titaghur, Naihati, Angus, Lawrence, Ludlow, even the Indian mills Hukumchand, Birla, Agapara...they've all got trouble.

RANJANA: What do they do about it?

STEPHEN: Same as we do. They take rifles from the armoury.

RANJANA (*kissing him on the cheek*): How can you stand it?

STEPHEN: I can't.

Now, one sepia toned, blurred, dreamlike take dissolves into the next:

...Stephen walking towards the entrance of the mill, which turns into a gaping tusk-toothed mouth, which swallows him and spits him out...

...Stephen on a train whose wheels are spinning but going nowhere...

...A girl crying...

...Hot Fat preparing a pill...

...Smoke drifting into Stephen's left ear and out of his right...

...Bodies going somewhere, breaking up into a thousand pieces of blood and gore, but flowing, carrying on...

...Stephen smiling serenely...

...A shoulder jolted back by rifle fire...

The same images—Hot Fat, the tears, the smoke, the bodies, the gaping mouth of the mill—repeat in no particular order until there is a knock on the door of the rooms in North Calcutta. The scene is still shot in sepia and slightly out of focus.

RANJANA (*surprised*): Come in, please. Welcome.

Angus enters. He looks about him, realising then, perhaps for the first time, how Indian Stephen has become. He feels out of place and a little awkward. He sits down.

RANJANA: May I bring you something? (*She notices that Angus is hesitant*). Some tea?

ANGUS: Thank you, tea would be nice.

RANJANA: Milk and sugar?

ANGUS (*relieved*): Yes, two spoons.

RANJANA (*laughing*): It's okay, it wasn't cardamom I was going to offer.

ANGUS (*also now laughing*): Well thank God for that, lassie. (*There is silence for a moment.*) I've come about Stephen. He has that look again. (*He shifts uneasily in his chair.*)

RANJANA: Ah. I was hoping it might be something else.

ANGUS: Where is he now?

RANJANA: He went out. (*She pauses thoughtfully.*) Thank you, Angus. I am pleased he has you for his friend.

ANGUS: I will do what I can.

The images now become more ordered, but just flashes as if still in a dream: strike scenes, riots, a British lady assaulted on a train (she defends herself with an umbrella), Muslims killing Hindus, Hindus killing Muslims, Stephen at the mill, pacing, Stephen at home, pacing, pacing.

STEPHEN (*restless*): I have to go out, I'm sorry.

RANJANA (*firmly*): Stay with us here. Your daughter needs you and I also need you.

STEPHEN: I can't. You don't understand. (*He twitches at the corner of his mouth as he speaks.*)

RANJANA: I do. And so does Angus. He is worried about you. He knows.

STEPHEN: Ah.

Ranjana and Angus are with Stephen now at every opportunity: Angus travels home with him; Ranjana and Kitty meet him outside the mill; Stephen stays in the mess overnight while Angus patrols.

Gradually Stephen's look lightens. He laughs easily at something Angus tells him. He plays with Kitty, swinging her round like a whirling dervish at full tilt, her skirt sticking out like an umbrella. They scream and roar. Family moments follow: Stephen, Ranjana and Kitty in the flat; Angus eating with them; a game of golf with Angus at which Stephen is hopeless but doesn't mind, while Kitty and Ranjana look on.

We see the four of them enjoying a walk in the country. The

landscape stretches out into the far distance. The late afternoon sun is gentle; the cows and the village boys idle and content. It is an eternal picture, and Stephen and his family and his friend stroll with easy absorbing eyes, noticing without comment the stony earth and the gaunt rocks and the imperceptibly darkening sky above them in which nothing moves except a vulture returning home, its white tail-feathers flickering behind the sandy brown of its outstretched wings. All are happy to be where they are and in each other's company. They link arms.

Now, in full colour, a row of weaving machines comes into focus. Browne taps Stephen on the shoulder.

BROWNE (*a lopsided smirk capsizing the right side of his mouth*): They'd like to see you, tomorrow morning, eleven o'clock, Clive Street. It's quite an honour, perhaps you're going up in the world...

Clive Street, the hallowed halls, the marble stairs and the knock on the door. The extremely venerable Mr James Irvine Senior invites Stephen, with a palsied wave, to be seated. He then closes his eyes as if contemplating life's bitter mysteries. Young Mr James Irvine assembles his back, neck and chin into an upright and patrician pose. He sweeps a hand through his now thinning hair.

IRVINE JUNIOR: So Doig, loyalty. What does the word mean? It means simply this, that a man can be counted on, hmm. That we can count on you, that you can count on us. Don't you agree?

STEPHEN: I agree, sir.

IRVINE JUNIOR: Loyalty was the virtue on which my father Mr James Irvine, and his father, the late Mr James Irvine, built this company, isn't that right, father? (*The ancient not-yet-deceased worthy nods in his sleep.*) And it is a virtue, the most important legacy there is, which I intend to carry on. As to your own loyalty, Doig, there have been questions. It has been suggested to me, please don't ask by whom, I'm sure you are aware, that you have been, erm, slipping away, that you don't see the mill as your life, as your commitment, that your loyalties might be elsewhere. Now look don't misunderstand, I make no comment about your living arrangements, your erm, wife, that is a matter for you, and the times being as they are, it would not be for us to say you should or you shouldn't (*Irvine stifles a shudder*) but when it comes to it, when it comes to us or them, we need to know where you stand Doig, do you see, and the fact is we don't. You are not trusted Doig, and an assistant who can't be trusted is not an assistant whom we can continue to employ. Do you have anything to say?

Stephen wonders if he has anything to say. Whole volumes open behind his eyes, eyes now suddenly itching from the dust that has been laid down, year upon year, layer upon layer for longer than he can remember, dust upon dust upon dust.

STEPHEN (*peering across the desk*): No, sir.

IRVINE JUNIOR: Very well then, you will be paid to the end of next month. (*He opens a drawer and hands over bank notes wrapped in jute and tied with string.*)

IRVINE SENIOR (*waking up*): Good luck to you, Doig. I remember your mother. Fine woman. Flaming red hair, am I right?

STEPHEN: Yes sir, thank you sir.

43

Stephen, on the broad pavements of Charnock Place and Dalhousie Square, replays, with commentary, the dialogue of his dismissal.

STEPHEN (*muttering*): Loyalty, pah! to his caste, to the Irvines! (*He continues in the same vein.*) To Browne! To McLeish! (*He swears in incomprehensible Scots.*) At least now I'm rid of the lot of them, free. (*For a moment, he relishes this freedom.*) Free, after all these years. (*He does the first few steps of a jig. These peter out.*) Free. (*He utters the word with infinite sadness. A wry smile stretches across his face.*)

Stephen allows his footsteps to take him nowhere in particular, along wide avenues, past stone palaces of commerce, past libraries, rich hotels and the noisy bells of rickshaw wallahs touting for trade. Then, as if in need of the comfort of enclosed spaces, he reverses direction in search of winding back streets and narrow alleys where nothing bears down except walls. He comes to an intersection of passages, humming to the tune of men making a living and of men with no living at all and no teeth lying in rags.

A BUNDLE OF RAGS (*whispering*): Rupya Sahib. For the love of God, rupees.

Stephen puts a coin on the sheet by the bundle. As he straightens, fifteen children stand in front of him with their hands out. Behind them is Hot Fat. He looks as he has always looked, except now thinner and perhaps paler than before.

HOT FAT (*smiling as he speaks*): Ah Sahib, it has been some time. Is our meeting chance? (*The children disappear.*)

STEPHEN: I am pleased to see you.

HOT FAT: Do you wish to smoke?

STEPHEN: Do I? (*He shrugs.*) One pipe, to remind me of times gone by.

Hot Fat bows and moves away with considered footsteps. Stephen follows.

Stephen takes the pipe and draws on it deeply and with relief. Smoke descends to his thighs. The second pipe penetrates into his ribs massaging the meat beneath. The smoke of the third goes up to his brain and seduces into the silence of a forgotten yesterday the chattering voices of spindles and men. His face becomes calm. His mouth settles in repose. Pipe follows pipe. Stephen reclines like a man who has returned to his lover after an absence of too long and, embracing, understands that he has never left.

When he has had his fill, he gets up. It is a beautiful warm winter's afternoon. He walks to the Maidan. Boys are playing cricket, the wood of their bats creaking as they swing through the air and miss. Young men and young women are holding tight to each other, and Stephen hears—and we hear through him—the crackle of energy padding across their skins like the footfall of tigers. The wings of insects twenty yards away whir like fans; and, further on, the Calcutta races are about to begin.

From three stories up, on the top of the first of the racing enclosures, the view stretches out over lawns and triangular track to the great trees of the Maidan, the spire of the cathedral and the polished white marble of the Victoria Memorial on whose vast central dome sits bronze Victory, her wings outstretched and turning, as she was designed to do, in the prevailing wind.

Below, the upper crust of European and Indian society is at play. Flags flutter. In every corner are potted flowers in the red, white and blue of Empire. The scene is brilliant like the light of winter. The ladies wear dresses of moiré and satin. Their escorts are in spotless white, sometimes in cream, but creases always immaculate. The conversation trills and soars; ah, the races, such fun. Discreetly in attendance are the stewards of the Royal Calcutta Turf Club, distinguished by grey morning coats and top hats.

STEWARD (*tipping his topper to a grey-haired gentleman with soft eyes*): And good day to you, sir.

In the second enclosure, the air is not so rarefied. Off-duty soldiers without commission rub shoulders with Indians who do not own estates or preside over the courts of Calcutta, and with Anglo-Indians, the half-castes, who do their best to avoid contact with either the shoulder or other parts of the anatomy of their co-occupants. From the third enclosure, exclusively for the native inhabitants of the subcontinent, comes a gale of laughter and giggles, the noisy eating of food and the placing of any number of five rupee bets.

Suddenly the crowd holds its breath. The band is playing. Coming down the track is none other than His Excellency the Viceroy, the Vice-regal landau beneath him, a DC of Police on each side and behind and in front the Viceroy's bodyguard, big men, matching mounts, sheepskin on their saddles, lance points catching the sun, white breeches, huge turbans, black thigh boots (altogether an impressive sight with which to dampen the enthusiasm of terrorists or communists waiting to take a potshot).

Stephen is wearing his best suit, the suit he wore to meet the directors on that same morning or on another morning, he can't remember. He is admitted into the first enclosure, the stewards being too busy in the rush to inspect each entrant carefully and to pay particular attention to the distant look in a man's eyes. Once inside, Stephen takes in the atmosphere: not visually but aurally. He pricks his ears. He listens for a moment to the conversation taking place next to him, and then to the one beyond that. Neither holds any interest. Casting his ears farther afield, he picks up the sound of envy coming from the wheezing windpipe of a fat woman discussing bungalows with her husband.

FAT WOMAN: And she has been given a B, a B, her, can you imagine? What were they thinking?

FAT WOMAN'S HUSBAND: I really couldn't say, my dear.

FAT WOMAN: It's outrageous, that's what it is, outrageous, why you're twice the...

Stephen's attention wanders and settles on the shoulders of the elegant Mrs Fotheringham who is wearing the feather of a pheasant in her hat. The feather twitches in a sudden gust.

PHEASANT (*on the wing*): Good weather for the time of year. Stephen hears the bang of a twelve bore.

TWELVE BORE: Pchhw.

PHEASANT (*fluttering to earth*): Is this the end, or only the beginning? Is that Mrs Fotheringham's hat?

Next to Mrs Fotheringham, a big man stands with a cigar jammed between his teeth. He removes the cigar and speaks softly to a man half his weight and several inches taller.

BIG MAN WITH CIGAR: I've heard a whisper about Methuselah. Do you know anything?

TALL THIN MAN (*replying out of the corner of his mouth*): His interests are working the odds.

Stephen makes his way down to the ring. Twelve bookies are calling to the crowds. Dancing Boy and Merry Lad (owned by Mr and Mrs Plumpie Doodawhalla) sixes, Imperial Sunset 7–1, Organza and Methuselah 12–1, Pinksleeves 16–1, 25–1 bar the field, another six. A bell sounds. The horses, led by their Indian grooms, enter the paddock. Stephen moves in as close as he can. With ears cupped, he listens.

MERRY LAD: I've had my eye on you, girl, for some time. How about it?

PINKSLEEVES (*whinnying with pleasure*): You are a merry lad, aren't you.

Still cupped, Stephen hears Dancing Boy humming the songs of his native land.

DANCING BOY (*tunelessly*): Waltzing Mathilda, waltzing Mathilda, who'll...

STEPHEN: Homesick, are you old fellow? I know the feeling. Hard to keep on going, isn't it, right to the last drop.

ORGANZA (*bending low and sneezing into the grass*): That Alfie, he hates me, my own trainer and he hates me. No sugar lumps again today.

STEPHEN (*to himself*): Hmm, Methuselah or Imperial Sunset. I wonder. (*Both horses are chewing determinedly on their bits.*)

Methuselah.

Tiny white men in silks—pink-and-purple checks, green bodies with scarlet sleeves, orange-and-black stripes, the rainbow in any combination—are swung into tiny saddles. They parade, walking in single file past the stands, while native Calcutta cheers on the far side of the whiter than white rails and shouts for its fancies. They set out at a canter, as Stephen slips away to place his bet. A big man with a cigar is behind him in the queue.

STEPHEN: Methuselah?

BOOKMAKER: Twelve to one.

STEPHEN (*with conviction*): Methuselah to win. (*He takes out the bundle given to him by Irvine.*)

BOOKMAKER (*wondering*): Very well sir, good luck. (*He hands him his ticket.*)

The horses are back at the start, jostling. Their smell and steam rise into the air. Old Bill, Methuselah's jockey, lifts his mount's ear and whispers into it.

OLD BILL (*calmly and with confidence*): Steady boy, take your time, easy now.

The gate goes up. The field surges. There is a sudden thunder as hooves, arms, legs, powerful hindquarters and small white raised bottoms disappear into the distance, jockeying for position on the first bend. The race is followed over the loud speaker.

LOUD SPEAKER: Pinksleeves from Merry Lad, Dancing Boy, Organza fourth, Imperial Sunset and Methuselah trail… At the second bend, it's Pinksleeves and Merry Lad, Imperial Sunset and Methuselah making ground, Pinksleeves is moving wide, she's going to the rail, most unusual this, she's seems to be slowing, I hope she's alright, Merry Lad's gone wide with her, he's catching her, he's…oh my word, erm, well good heavens I've never seen anything like it…(*The loudspeaker splutters and falls silent as the nostrils of the two horses are seen to touch, as the jockeys dig and whip to no avail, and as, from Merry Lad, visible even from the far end of the course, comes a sign that his interest in his fellow com-*

petitor is not entirely sporting. The speaker coughs and gathering itself, picks up the commentary after the third bend.)...And it's Methuselah on the shoulder of Imperial Sunset, he's moving up, Methuselah, Methuselah from Imperial Sunset, Methuselah wins it by a head. (*Breathless pause.*) Mr Doodawhalla to the Stewards Enclosure immediately.

Stephen, without fuss or excitement, stuffs wads of rupees into the pockets of his white suit.

BOOKMAKER (*grimly*): Come again sir, give me a chance to win it back.

STEPHEN: It's about time I got lucky.

When he returns to the flat in Calcutta, neither his wife nor daughter are at home. He stretches out on an old sofa, he sleeps, and with each unconscious heartbeat the balm of illusion in his bloodstream thins. He wakes to brown walls and a cracked ceiling. His face is agitated. He looks without interest at one of his sketches which Ranjana has pinned up. He walks into the bedroom. A child's toy is on a chair, a picture book of ancient fables on the floor, broken-backed. He goes outside. Washing is hanging on the balcony: two saris side by side. He runs his hand down both and tears come to his eyes.

44

Wearing whites and a boater, Stephen sits beneath the spreading branches of a banyan tree. By his feet is a carefully ironed white cotton sheet that serves as a tablecloth. Ranjana, facing him, is dressed like a European woman in a long-sleeved frock patterned with flowers, and a soft hat with a brim that rises in a wave at the front and sinks down to her shoulders at the back. Around her neck is a thin line of what might be pearls. Between them is the third member of this almost theatrical pastiche, a Chinaman with a long pigtail, a short jacket with buttons, and trousers that are gathered at the ankles. It is Hot Fat. The three of them have strolled in dusty country and paddled at the edge of a salty lake to the east of the city. They are ready for their lunch.

From a bag designed for holding pheasants and from the concealed pockets of a Chinaman's trousers, emerge green and red chutneys, a compote of white spidery oriental vegetables, a buffalo cheese resembling Caerphilly, a glutinous savoury pudding in which banana figures prominently, a cake of rice grains laced with chili, and shortbread biscuits. Each sits on the edge of the picnic, cross-legged, like Buddha; the Scot dressed as an Englishman out for a day's boating, the Indian woman as The Memsahib (exposing, in character, a bulge of pecan skin where the V-neck of her frock is at its lowest), and the Chinaman appearing as himself, delicate and silent. They eat with their fingers. They drink cold tea. No words are spoken, but there is an easy acceptance of each other of the sort enjoyed by old friends.

The three of them fall asleep under the tree, the lunch things scattered, Ranjana and Stephen side by side. Hot Fat is the first to wake. The sun is smouldering on the horizon, its light waning. Shadows are fading. Trees, swamps, villages of dust and dirt, the weary tramp of oxen and small boys returning to their hovels; all are disappearing into dusk.

The party gathers its belongings and walks to the station. Hot Fat is anxious. He runs ahead. When they arrive he is sweating and cold. They stand silently waiting for a train to take them back to Calcutta. Hot Fat fidgets. He shifts his weight first onto one foot, then to the other. His mouth opens and closes.

HOT FAT: When does train come, Sahib? (*His lips quiver as he speaks. His eyelids flicker. His delicate fingers are screwed into a ball, as if he is inflicting pain on himself by driving his nails into the palms of his hands.*)

STEPHEN: You will soon be in Calcutta.

The skin on Hot Fat's face is now drawn back in an uncontrollable yawn, exposing his yellowing teeth in the way a horse does when it whinnies.

HOT FAT (*stammering*): It is a difficult time, Sahib. So-so-so late. (*All that is visible of his eyes are the whites.*)

The train arrives. It inches wheezing along the platform. Hot Fat runs alongside with his gums bared. He finds a seat in a corner, buries his head in his chest and turns away, presenting only the anguished arch of his back to his companions. From time to time he jumps up and punches his thighs. Stephen and Ranjana comfort him with a touch. At the first station he recognizes, Hot Fat jumps out. He runs down the platform as if pursued by the hounds of hell (or wherever it is that a Chinaman's demons come from.)

RANJANA: How much he needs it.

STEPHEN: Yes.

RANJANA: Will this happen to you?

STEPHEN: It may, though it hasn't yet. I don't know.

RANJANA (*touching his face with the back of her hand*): Is it too late for you, Stephen? Can you try again?

STEPHEN (*shaking his head sadly.*) It is too late.

Ranjana looks at him without recrimination. In her eyes is acknowledgment that the long struggle is over. She leans forward and kisses him.

—I have found a portrait of Hot Fat. I don't know when it was done. Earlier, I suppose. He is looking serene, standing upright, holding a pipe in one hand and staring into the eyes of the viewer (and, probably therefore, of the artist). Was it drawn in Chinatown among the lamps; or did he climb the Z-shaped staircase? Was he given tea by Ranjana? I search for clues among the heavy scrawl of black charcoal below Hot Fat's elbow but find none.

The picture is entitled, 'Happy Days.'

45

History is now, once again, on the move: you only have to look at the billboards.

...EMPIRE AT WAR...

...FAMINE IN BENGAL: TWO MILLION DEAD. The streets of Calcutta are littered...

...PAKISTAN POSSIBLE, QUESTIONS ASKED. P is for Punjab, A for Afghanistan, K for Kashmir, but where is B for Bengal? Calcutta Muslims want to know...

...MUSLIM LEAGUE ANNOUNCES ACTION DAY FOR PAKISTAN, AUGUST 16, 1946. Public holiday in Calcutta...

Before the dawn of that same day of action, August 16, a figure dressed as a coolie with no shirt but a cloth wrapped like rope around his head climbs up a staircase to the third floor, presses himself against a door and taps lightly, once twice. Ranjana undoes the latch. The figure pushes past. She looks left and right along the balcony and closes the door behind him. The two embrace.

RANJANA: Satish. (*To Stephen.*) This is my brother.

The two men acknowledge each other, while Ranjana looks at them both, the terrorist and the addict, with tears tumbling down her cheeks. The men in her life come to this.

RANJANA: Can I bring you something, tea, to eat?

SATISH: I am here to warn you. There are those who still believe that the British are the enemy. It is yesterday's thinking. The British are nothing now, a cracked looking-glass in which only the babu sees himself. But some of my comrades of the old days who should know better notice you and notice him, and they don't like it. Be careful, is all.

RANJANA: I will be killed by Hindus?

SATISH: It is possible. But before the Hindus can kill you, you first have to survive the Muslims. It is their day of action. Look after yourself, sister.

He opens the door, stands upright in its frame for a moment and leaves.

RANJANA (*calling softly*): Goodbye, Satish.

A watery sun limps across the sky. It is perfect weather, not too hot and not raining in spite of the time of year. Stephen and Ranjana stroll together holding Kitty's hands and swinging her between them every now and again. At Machua Bazar Street, they prepare to separate.

KITTY: Come with us, Daddy. It's okay for Daddy to come, isn't it?

RANJANA: Yes, it's okay. Will you, Stephen?

STEPHEN (*his jawbones aching, the craving in his neck and teeth taking hold*): I can't, I'm sorry, I have things to do.

KITTY: But it's a holiday today, isn't it? Why do you have things to do? I thought nobody worked on holidays.

STEPHEN (*now yawning uncontrollably*): Well, sometimes you have to, that's all.

Ranjana sits among a group of upper-caste Hindu women considering maternity, child welfare and crèches for the children of working mothers.

HINDU WOMAN: ...And we must try to involve our sisters in the higher castes, some of whom are not allowed to leave their homes except for marriages and such. Purdah, in this day and age. Such a waste, isn't it. (*Around her, the group expresses approval; couldn't agree more, general muttering, well said Lalita, etc.*)

Kitty, who has been playing outside, comes back in, eats something from a table of food, yawns and falls asleep.

KITTY (*now awake*): Time to go, mummy. (*She tugs her mother's hand.*) I'm bored.

Stephen smokes his fifth pipe of the morning. He is at ease, his face is calm and his body in repose. Above him, fume clouds levitate, up-draughts hang suspended by their own inertia, black thermals waft lazily towards a wider world. His eyes begin to pucker and twitch. He is having a vision: a blaze of red-and-orange stripes with a white blur just visible above; the blaze is moving smoothly like an engine on rails. A voice speaks.

VOICE: Listen up Stephen, rouse yourself will you, I've brought you a horse, and by the way before you drift off again, let me remind you, it's not as if you don't need the money, all this smoke doesn't grow on trees, time for another outing don't you think?

Stephen sees a cheering crowd, other dots of colour strung out behind, legs bogged down in monsoon mud, and a finishing post no more than three lengths ahead.

STEPHEN (*from within his vision*): The winner is, the winner is…?

VOICE: Listen, use your lugs, you've done it before. (*Stephen listens and hears indistinctly through the frayed edges of a multitude of voices a sort of chanting, a blurred two syllabled repetition*): dar kee, dar kee.

STEPHEN (*to himself, surfacing*): Dar kee, is it? Darkie? Where? Not the Turf Club, they don't race during the monsoon. Somewhere else…

Huseyn Suhrawardy, prime minister of Bengal and representative of the slim Muslim majority, stands in front of the imposing monument in honour of the imperial general Sir David Ochterlony, defender of Delhi, conqueror of Nepal. Before them both are hundreds of thousands, Muslims to a man. To cheers and waving, Suhrawardy begins to speak.

SUHRAWARDY: Fellow Muslims (*the crowd hushes, no more than a cough across that acreage of expectancy*), our esteemed colleague Dr Jinnah has called for a day of action to promote the case for our own separate Muslim homeland, (*he pauses*) Pakistan. (*Exultant cheering*). Fellow Muslims (*he repeats the phrase but this time steps up the ladder of intensity*), the Congress party of the Hindus wish to govern the whole of India, they wish to create a new Raj, a Hindu Raj. But I say we will resist. There will be a struggle, but what is there in this life worth having that is without struggle. Fellow Muslims (*now shouting*) the struggle starts here. And don't worry (*he raises his hands for calm*), I have made the necessary arrangements. Do you think (*whispering*) that you are the only ones who have taken the day off? What about the police, don't they also need a break? They are, even as I speak, brewing tea in their stations and placing feet on desks: it is a rest they have well deserved. My friends, Dr Jinnah has called for a day of action. Let it be so.

Ranjana and Kitty approach the Sanskrit College Hostel. Ranjana climbs the stairs, while Kitty lingers below.

KITTY: Can I stay down here and play?

Six swarthy men, of the kind you step aside for, leave the crowd at the Ochterlony monument and walk purposefully. Their eyes are empty.

Stephen reaches a racetrack. Men who know him by reputation nod as he moves close to the ring. They watch him as he surveys the list of ten runners, a list which includes a horse called Dark Destroyer and another, Plumpie's Mudlark, owned of course by the irrepressible Mr Plumpie Doodawhalla.

STEPHEN (*the voice in his head*): Dar kee...that must be Dark Destroyer. Plumpie's Mudlark, I wonder. Was it *darkie* I heard? Could it have been *larkie*? Larkie? Would they call him, Larkie? Not likely: *muddy* or *plumpie* perhaps, and when did Mr Doodhawhalla last have a winner anyway?

Stephen, followed closely by two or three who pretend to have business of their own, whispers into a bookie's ear: Dark Destroyer.

The starter raises his flag, while Kitty lies like a hunting panther among a pile of jute gunnies under the stairs and Ranjana, two floors up, sits cross-legged talking to a friend.

A brass handle turns and the first of the six Muslim men puts his foot across the threshold of the Sanskrit College Hostel.

The flag goes down, hooves dig into the sodden earth and kick up showers of mud, a playful meteorite storm of earth pellets. The pace is fast, perhaps too fast for one and three quarter miles. Two horses have stayed behind the gallopers: Dark Destroyer getting browner and therefore lighter by the moment; and the diminutive Plumpie's Mudlark who is skimming along as if on his morning canter.

At the mile post, both are in joint last. With half a mile to go, Dark Destroyer moves up, the field still bunched in front. At the three furlong post, four horses run wide. Darkie fills the gap. At two furlongs he is leading, but being sucked along behind him is a fresh plump Larkie. Plumpie's Mudlark edges in front, he's into the home straight, nothing can stop him now.

The swarthy men climb a flight of stairs. Kitty, crouched in the long grass of her jute sacks, stays still and silent as the planks of wood above her head creak. The men knock on the first door they come to. It is opened by a small man with glasses.

Ranjana, cross-legged, on the floor above, hears a noise like a starlet fainting onto a carpet. She wonders what it might be. She hears footsteps along a corridor, a door opening and that sound again.

A hog badger in a hole hears the rumble of approaching hooves. He does what hog badgers do: he tunnels, shovelling earth with his back legs and releasing from the end that is tilted upwards a skunk-like odour for which his breed is infamous.

The occupants of other rooms are now alert, like deer pricking up their ears at something not quite as it should be.

Hands grasp the third door. It does not open. They kick it in. Hard-nosed pellets spit and push through the flimsy protection of a layer of white cotton, through skin, spleen, liver, kidney into bone. Blood leaks beneath the door. It crosses the landing and onto the stairs, stairs which have a small gap between each wooden board through which air can move. But in this case it is red drops which move and fall through open space, one by one, onto a gunny sack.

The forefoot belonging to Plumpie's Mudlark enters the hog badger's hole. The horse pecks earthward, inhales, veers instinctively to the side and, in so doing, brings Dark Destroyer down on top of him. Both horses die instantly.

Kitty, the panther, is now a panther of stone, frozen before the steady *tock tock* of a world dripping red.

The six men spread out. Each takes a room. Bullets find their way into bodies standing by open windows ready to jump, cowering on beds, hiding in cupboards. The men drag these bodies out. Being careful not to trip over carcasses or bloody the bottoms of their baggy pantaloons, they climb a second flight.

Stephen leaves the racecourse, his pockets empty, the stitches of his life unravelling. He hears the galloping of hooves.

Ranjana stands on the top stair, facing the six men. She says nothing. Disdain is sketched on her face, a disdain born out of incredulity that such things are possible. Her killers divide into two lines opening a channel for her death-fall between. A moment of silence is split by gun noise, and she tumbles, step by step, *bump bump bump* to the bottom adding, when she comes to rest, her own tributaries to the red sea of blood. Her face presses flat on the floorboards and her eyes look sightlessly down through cracks.

Kitty, below her, looks up. Their eyes meet.

46

What happened to Kitty after the men had gone? How did she get out? How did she get home? I find nothing, nothing to tell me how long she stayed there, how she managed to retrace the steps that she had taken with Ranjana only that morning. Nothing. It seems she never told my grandfather, or if she did, he hasn't passed it on. And she never told me, if by then she any longer knew. So, now, after fifty years, I will speak for her. I will have her creeping upstairs, stepping over bodies and kissing her mother for the last time. A goodbye. At least that.

But perhaps the kiss is too much. Her feet on the stairs, the bodies, that face…too much. No, better to leave her as history left her: frozen by sightless eyes, iced by retreating footsteps; preserved.

My mother. My poor sweet tearless mother.

47

Amṛta plates his body, the immortal substance of the gods makes him invulnerable. War now, and the gods must strip him. Indra, Arjuna's father, who is also a god, comes to Karṇa and says, 'Cut off your earrings and the armour you were born with.' Karṇa replies, 'But to cut them off is death.' Indra says nothing.

The wave washes over me. The babble of voices recedes. Just a distant chorus, the opening and closing of mouths, hands waving, silent symphonies...

Karṇa walks, his back is straight, he is lit up by his divine earrings; yet his feet drag. He turns into an alley. His head droops and falls to his chest. He stops. Mist swirls around him, becomes motionless, parts. From between his ribs steps a young woman. Her eyes and face and tongue are brown like old blood and she is decked in old things and she wears upon her wrists two burnt black bracelets. She places the point of a knife under Karṇa's chest plate and cuts, a gentle sawing motion, the blade moving beneath the skin, a slicing of the quick: nerves, blood vessels, sinews. I feel his pain: not a stab; it is insistent, enduring, but sharp nonetheless, as with any loss. I hear the tearing of flesh, the scrape and pull, but no sound from him, just the beating of celestial drums above and flowers raining down from the heavens. His chest plate falls to the floor. The knife moves across to the armour on his legs and his arms and his back, and to his earrings which drop to earth like two crystals of light burning themselves out. Karṇa bends. He hands his invulnerability to Indra with a smile.

I am startled by a bang, the door of the lecture theatre opened and swinging shut. Julia is inside. She is wearing a short black jacket, an oatmeal scarf and brighter redder lipstick than I ever bought her. 'Stephen,' she says, 'are you well?'

'I'm okay,' I reply.

'You are? Sure?'

'I'm sure. Why? What are you doing here?'

'I fell asleep in the Quad and saw you in my dream.'

'You did? Was I ill?'

'Yes, ill, dying, dead, hard to be sure. So here I am. In case.'

'But you put your lipstick on first, before coming.'

'Lipstick, of course, in case the bastard was still living.'

I laugh. 'The bastard is fine. In fact, never better. Reborn. Here feel my hands, steady as a rock.'

She takes my chee-chee fingers and lays them across her white-white palm. Then she kisses them and looks up. Her eyes are a void of green...bottomless, empty of everything except silence. Unless it isn't silence I'm watching but love. And as I stand there in the silence of my own disbelief, I come to wonder if it is.

She puts her arm through mine and leads me out. She takes me to her flat and lays me on her bed. She lies with her head on my chest and says, 'Stephen, cover me with a blanket, a blanket of your words, like petals, like snow, so I feel warm to you, so I feel your blood beating next to mine.' So I do. I drop words into her ear, caress her with the ancient lament, whisper the story of the gods and their pursuit, how he gives up his armour, how he embraces his death to come. I unfold my ear-words before my lover, leaving nothing out, all the hurt, all the history, his and hers and mine. When I finish, she touches her lips to my cheek and licks a tear that has fallen. Without a word she undresses me, slowly, softly. Through a mist, I watch her layers falling away, her skirt, her blouse, the silk that moves against her skin.

48

Julia, sucking on a bread stick, leans across the restaurant table and whispers, 'The prize, Stephen, the women of Provideniye do not forget.' At which, my throat dries, my blood begins to race. The oldest waiter appears, trailing behind him a whiff of his native Hungary. He recommends goulash. Julia says yes, she'd like that. She licks her lips at the thought of it. I order goulash too, with chips and a bottle of the house red.

'That man with the message for your mother...this restaurant always reminds me.'

'His name was Kamal Khan. He was the one they found washed up on the West Sands, dead. No prizes for him.'

Dead, kebabed, without a Julia of his own to reward him. Or perhaps he had. Perhaps he got what was coming. That's the problem with prizes. No guarantees. Someone ends up with the overdose. I wonder what kind of woman she was, Kamal Khan's mother. God, but you have to get lucky. Kuntī, Ranjana, Parvati, Kitty, Julia. Winners and losers wherever you look.

Julia studies me. 'No prizes for him, you say.' She pauses. I know that pause. 'What do you mean? That if you don't win the prize, you die?'

'From loss to death, the inevitable continuum, each step a bit of yourself sliced off.'

'Are you a loaf of bread, Stephen?'

'We all are. We all get pared back.'

She reflects for a moment and says, 'And a good thing too.'

The goulash arrives. 'Mmm,' says Julia reaching for her knife and fork. Melodies on the accordion, waltz time, one-two-three, one-two-three. I want to take her by the hand and dance, twirl her in the perfect circle, spin her to the music of the spheres, why not, what the hell, we've all got it coming...except in this tight little place it's not my goulash I'd end up in.

I feel a hand on my shoulder. I turn round. McCorquodale, in a leather jacket and jeans. He pulls up a chair. 'May I?' he asks and sits down. Thus, with hardly a word, he enters my private life. Julia looks at him. 'Hello detective,' she says.

'I was eating over there. I'm surprised you didn't notice.' He nods his head in the direction of a corner where a rather academic looking lady is sitting. She takes a pair of glasses and a book out of her handbag and starts to read. 'That's my mother.'

'That's Denise?'

'Yes. Look, I'm sorry to disturb you but there's been a development, so when I saw you sitting here I thought I'd come over. But perhaps you'd prefer to discuss it when there's just the two of us?'

'Now's fine, Sergeant, though it depends on what *it* is.'

'We're dropping the case, the investigation I should say. It's going nowhere.'

'You are?' I take stock. The decision seems strange, wrong almost. I find myself encouraging him to carry on. 'But the traces of heroin, the £100,000, Kamal Khan, the telephone number in Dundee. Isn't that evidence of something?'

'It's evidence of something, but it's not proof. We traced the telephone number to a block in the Hilltown. The landlord was unable to help: says he has no idea who's in his flats most of the time. Whoever left the heroin with your mother—Khan or Khan's murderer, or your mother's murderer for that matter, if she was murdered—is either dead or fled.'

'So what happens now?'

'Now? You might want to clear out her flat. We have no objections. And, since your mother left no will, you, as next of kin, will receive the £100,000.

'But it's drug money isn't it? Can I accept it?'

'It's not for me to say, sir. Its origins are dirty, I think we both suspect that, but then again is anything spotless?'

'Hmm, interesting,' says Julia. 'What do you conclude, sergeant? Is anything spotless?'

'In my opinion, where money is concerned, spotless is hard to find. And the criminals are not the only ones with dirty hands. Some of the richest, most respected families in the country have made their money in ways that were, let's just say, dubious. Am I right, Dr Smith?'

'You are,' I tell him. 'The slave trade, selling alcohol to the destitute, forcing opium down the throats of the Chinese.'

McCorquodale fishes in his back pocket. 'Take this fiver. It looks innocent enough, but who knows what tales it could tell you, where it's been, what it's been involved in, if only it had lips to speak. All I'm saying,' he goes on, 'is that this fiver' (he flaps it a couple of times), 'this fiver hasn't spent its whole life in church.'

'The sins of the fiver,' says Julia.

McCorquodale laughs. 'Yes, the sins of the fiver, but I don't care. I absolve you,' he says to the note crossing it with his thumb, 'so long as you don't do it again.' He wags an enormous finger and returns it to his pocket.

'So I should accept the £100,000, let bygones be bygones?'

'That's up to you, sir. It's something to think about.'

'Have a drink, sergeant, will you?' I pour him a glass. He looks over at Denise and concludes that she's quite happy reading. 'Thank you,' he says, throws his head back and downs it in one. I refill it. Mine and Julia's too.

'Whether you accept it or not, it's your inheritance, Stephen, isn't it? It is what has been passed down to you, for better or worse,' says Julia.

'That's true, but I don't have to bank it, I don't have to eat its food or walk round in the clothes it will provide.'

'So? Will you or won't you?'

'I don't know. I haven't decided. *Dharmasya tattvaṃ nihitaṃ guhāyām*. The secrets of dharma are hidden in a cave.'

'Still, nice to have choices,' she says.

49

There is one last box, smaller than the others, more like a casket of the sort in which a woman might keep her jewellery, except that it is entirely without decoration, bare and pale.

It is locked.

'Give me the key, Séamus,' I say, 'let me be alone with him.'

'I don't have it,' he replies. He looks at me as if wanting to say more, but doesn't.

I fetch a screwdriver and remove the clasp.

* * *

As I begin to write what is the last chapter of my grandfather's history, I feel that my own history is coming to an end, that I am being pushed to the point at which history ends and the present begins. One last heave, and that will be it; those who came before me will be truly dead; dead for the first time.

Kitty is sitting on the floor, staring, alone, among old clothes and the remains of food. The scene is described in one of two papers, or letters I suppose you'd call them, though they weren't posted except into this box. They are in a different hand. Angus's.

She is in the flat in Calcutta. The door is ajar and rattling on a slight breeze. Angus enters quietly. He says something soothing and mundane. 'Hello, it's Angus.' He goes over to her. He kneels down. He puts his hand on the back of her head and holds her gently, a human presence nothing more. Kitty doesn't move. 'Where's your daddy?' he asks. 'May I wait? Do you mind?'

Time stops then, or if it moves at all it does so as if bedding in for a long stay. They sit in silence like two planets in empty space and for who knows how many eternities. From the way he describes it, her staring, him watching her afraid to move away, I believe she is aware of his presence. I believe something moves between them across the void, or at least I hope it does.

When Stephen returns, his face is peaceful: his forehead unwrinkled, his eyes quiet, their lids drooping as if in repose. He speaks softly, 'Ah Angus, old friend, it is good of you to come. How did you hear?'

'Calcutta is not such a big place.'

'No.'

'What will you do now?'

'Now? There is nothing I can do. Look at me, Angus.' He stretches out a shaking arm. 'My doing days are behind me.' He smiles.

'And what about...?'

'Yes, Kitty...I don't know.'

'I am going home, Stephen. It wasn't much of a party, was it? I suppose a few will stay on, but not me. I'm going back to Dundee. I'll buy a bungalow, in Monifieth if the money will stretch. Wullye no come?'

'Ah, Dundee...it's too late for me, Angus, not that I ever had much to hold me there. What I have is here.'

'You mean the smoking?'

'Yes, I mean that.'

'And Kitty?'

'You will take her, won't you Angus?' Stephen grabs him with both hands at the wrist.

Angus considers the rumpled skin, his and Stephen's, and what is being asked. After a while he says, 'Yes, I'll take her, if she'll come.'

'She will come,' says Stephen, giving away my mother for a second time. Unless it is history that betrays her. Perhaps it is. The wrong time, the wrong place, no prizes for her.

'And what of you?'

'I will manage.'

'Without Ranjana? After all that has happened? Will you?'

'Come back before you go, Angus. I have some money, not

much but I would like you to have it. You can give it to Kitty if you prefer. It's not a fortune and it will make no difference to me here, whether I have it or whether I don't. And there are other things in the flat, you'll find them, which might help her to understand.'

'Are you going somewhere?'

'Yes. Away. I've had enough of Calcutta.'

'So this is goodbye.'

'This is goodbye, old friend.'

The two men neither hug, nor kiss, but stand in silence. Each looks into the other's face, the old movies of their lives and time playing again.

'I'll tell her what I can, about Parvati and Ranjana and you Stephen, her mothers and her father.'

'Tell her what you think she should know, but don't make me out better than I am.'

'That'll be hard.'

Through worn teeth, Stephen smiles.

* * *

The ending is written into the beginning, like code. Except the course which a man travels forks here, bends there, is knocked askew by a nudge, a stranger, a bolt from the blue; so that a journey has a thousand beginnings and each beginning an ending. But still, like a great river, it continues: the Bhagirathi (sprung from the pure ice of the Himalayas), the Alaknanda, the Brahmaputra, the Yamuna, the Ghaghara, the Gandak, the Son, the Gomti, the Chambal; all flow into the holy Ganges, mother Ganga, who herself becomes the Padma and also that most unholy of rivers, the Hooghly, which, leaching out through a thousand mouths, stains the Bay of Bengal dirt brown.

My grandfather sits alone in the flat, calmed by smoke, the intervals between pipes shortening, one pipe running into another.

The money he has prepared for Kitty stands note on note in a pile in a drawer, wrapped in brown paper and tied with threads of jute. What else he has, he keeps in his back pocket and takes with him when he visits Hot Fat. There is enough still to keep the jar of opium filled, but now the full jar of today terrifies him with the thought of the empty jar of tomorrow.

The end creeps up like grandmother's footsteps. It is not unexpected, it is not even particularly quiet, but so long as your back is turned and there is no tap on the shoulder, then you can whisper to yourself as you toss and turn in unsleeping dreams, *not yet, not yet*.

What wakes him now on the morning of August 21, 1946, wakes him early. At eight he shares pipes with a sailor from Macao. At twelve, he eats lunch brought to him by a young Chinese girl with gap teeth the colour of honey. At one, he makes his way down to the river where boats ply back and forth in a once familiar world of activity that is to him as detached as landscape. Tiring quickly of fresh air, he returns and smokes through the afternoon. At five, he walks to the Strand. There are bodies still in the street and still clandestine murder (garrotting, the knife in under the ribs), still overturned cars, burnt out rickshaws and, tossed away in careless parabolas, guns.

He spends the evening with Hot Fat, each lying on his side facing the other, saying nothing, watching all that passes across the disappearing mind; the leaves of a gingko falling like autumn tears, the scratch of nails on a windowsill, a crawling face behind a shutter banging open in the dark, another pipe! ah another pipe...

In the early morning, Hot Fat, tilting towards him an empty container, whispers, 'Sahib, it is finished.' My grandfather feels in his pockets. 'I have more. I'll bring it.'

My grandfather lies down on his own bed, and sleeps. He wakes refreshed. He writes a note. It says, 'Angus, here is the money for Kitty. If you receive it, it means I have managed to stop before the bottom. I feel some small pride in this, even now, though God knows I've sunk low enough. Thank you for taking care of things. Yer auld billie, Stephen.'

Then he picks up the gun which he found on the Strand. He pulls back the breechblock, hears that forgotten familiar sound again of metal on metal, and looks down to check that there is still a bullet. There is. He prepares himself to face what awaits, though whether he does this with regret or acceptance, with a prayer, a fond memory to hold onto at the last, or with nothing at all but the catch of his own breath, only he can know.

He puts the muzzle to the side of his face and pulls the trigger. Perhaps he tugs as he pulls. The eruption in his ear is like the world's end. He slumps forward confident that this is his final journey, that he is passing through the veil of red mist which divides this world from the next, the curtain which the battered Self parts with its thumbs before disappearing into the cosmic ocean where Viṣṇu sits secure in the coils of Ananta…except, except… the veil of red mist has a viscous feel to it that is somehow familiar, and are these not his fingers that dab the edges of a hole, isn't this blood, and isn't this a piece of bone, and these, on his cheeks, what can they be, round, soft, hanging…if not…

He walks outside onto the balcony. A neighbour leads him downstairs. She puts him in a rickshaw. In this fashion, he is taken to hospital along the rancid streets and choked alleys of Calcutta with his eyes hanging out, protected from flies and solid objects only by the flapping of his sightless fingers.

* * *

Angus has written a testimonial meant for Kitty, though I don't see how she can have read it. He ends it like this: 'It will be hard for you not to blame him, to say that he abandoned you first for the opium and then for death. I'm sure you will feel this, and with good reason. Let me add only that, in my opinion, he was worth more than all of us. He went through India with his eyes open, and he didn't pretend he hadn't seen what he had. He was never any good at pretending. I am proud to have known him, and proud to think I was his friend.'

According to Angus, Stephen asked to be cremated as if he were an Indian; so no doubt his ashes are now mixed with everything else that's been dumped in the Hooghly.

One thing comes back to me, a phrase of my mother's which she used now and again as a sort of lament when I dropped something or knocked something over. Poor blind mouse, she'd call me.

Poor blind Stephen. Poor blind Kitty.

50

'Is it finished then?' she asks.

'It is finished.'

I tell her everything she hasn't heard.

Julia doesn't speak for a while. Then she says, 'Now there's only you.'

'Yes, only me.'

'How do you feel?'

I observe the weight of my feet on the floor and the stillness behind my eyes. 'I feel as if I want to go back to my mother's flat. Will you come?'

'Of course,' she says.

We take the bus. It rattles over the bridge. The waves on the Tay are choppy, their crests like rows of mothers identical in their anxiety. To the sea, to the sea. It happens in slow motion, at least to me, seeing it as I see it now. On another day, in another mood, another speed; perhaps then I'd think the waves were racing. Hard to tell now if they're even moving at all.

At the bus station, Julia wraps her coat around her against the wind, bending into it. We walk up to the tenement. Open corridors of stone pierce its length like one spear thrust after another. We turn into the half dark, our footsteps echoing under the familiar arch. Familiar to me. At the end is a door. I unbolt it for Julia and we pass through to a patch of grass, a separate plot with a fence on each side: not like when you could run the whole length of the backies with the lines of blousey sheets trying to knock you down. Julia faces the stone wall behind us, its forty-nine windows and, high up, a carved inscription long ago worn away that I never managed to decipher. I follow her eyes as they travel across its old unblinking facade, those markings I know so well, every edge, every crack, every worn-out hole.

Back. The rattle of the bolt. We go up stone steps. Graffiti. A drawing of a rat. We walk along a landing, Julia holding me close. My mother's flat, my flat that once was, a long time ago. I unlock the door. My old bedroom on one side, Kitty's on the other. Kitchen, bathroom, and the sitting room at the end. How empty it looks now my mother's gone.

My uncle must have been in before the police cordoned it off, because things have been taken away. An attempt to clear up, half done. The good table made of dark wood is still there and the photograph by the window of my father. The sofa has had its covers removed. White underneath. There's a wheel off. It looks tired. It always looked tired. Dying. Dead.

I enter her bedroom. In the corner, the hole where she kept it has been exposed. There's not much mess. Neat in his work, McCorquodale. The cupboard drawers are all closed. The duvet is on the bed. Did she die in this bed? Probably not. It looks made. I realize now that I don't know. The exact place and time.

Something prompts me to put my hand on the duvet and turn it down. I find a hot water bottle and a teddy bear. There's no stuffing in its left leg and the seam at the back has been re-stitched with black cotton. I turn to Julia, my eyes filling.

She looks at me. 'You didn't know?'

I shake my head. My mother's smile comes back to me, bright and brittle, a tantalising what-might-have-been sort of smile which faded the moment it caught itself at it, only ever a glimpse, here's the sunlight, here are the green fields, seen them? Okay and goodnight, close the curtains.

I touch her cheek with a kiss.

Fate, history, inheritance, blood: not easy to jump clear.

51

I sit on the floor cross-legged, eyes shut. Lately, I've been meditating more. If I don't do it, I find myself becoming anxious. I don't mean desperate like the need for opium. I don't sweat or anything like that and I can live without it, but I'm better with it, that's all. Quieter in the mind. Less nonsense going round. Your addictions choose you, I suppose, and you hope to get lucky.

Straight-backed, chin slightly tucked, I slide into my little thumb-sized guy and watch my cerebral waves performing their tricks. My breathing slows. My mind relaxes its grip, its surface softens, it beckons and draws me in. It is a black lake, black and flat, not a ripple. Within; silence, stillness and now a rustle like bamboo leaves in a breeze. In the middle of the lake a vortex appears, circling slowly, and the light there is brighter, as if the sun is shining up from below. I circle with it, entranced. A boat comes into view. On its prow is an old boatman wearing a dhoti and a red cloth wrapped round his head. He pushes his pole into the water, breathing out with each push. I watch him pole across the lake and disappear. The lake is flat again, like glass.

All the secrets in the world are here in this lake. Within, and nowhere else. Nothing comes from outside. Watching is enough.

52

Séamus has been making himself scarce recently. In fact, I haven't seen him to talk to since we finished the script. On the odd occasions our paths have crossed, he's had that grim man-on-a-mission look about him. Finally I get him cornered.

'How's it going?' I ask.

He looks shifty, lower to the ground than usual, as if he's taking cover. 'I assume,' he replies, 'you are referring to the progress of the script.'

'Got it in one.'

'Things have not been standing still, you can be sure of that.' A biscuit appears between his thumb and first finger and he takes a bite. 'Fir f'all, there wathe forma puthe whothing in'—he gulps, gull-like, peers from side to side with lifted chin, and continues—'such as will be required by the director and whoever else is to take a look. Then, when I was happy with that, well not happy so much as, well, when I thought it would do at least, I sent the lot of it away to she who got me onto the television people the last time, on account of which I will not hear a word said against her.'

'Why would I say anything against her? Does she hate it?'

'She does not. Not at all. She thinks there's good stuff in there.'

'She does?'

'She does, though she's not sure about the finish of the thing.'

'My grandfather shot himself. You can't get more finished than that.'

'There's finished and there's *finished*,' he says with tangible restraint, as if addressing an imbecile. 'Finished as in the finished article, as in not ending the thing with your grandfather's eyeballs hanging out all over the streets of Calcutta.'

'An unfitting finale for a hero?'

Séamus puts an inch or two of his remaining biscuit into his mouth and chews carefully, dabbing foppishly every now and again with the point of his forefinger non-existent crumbs from a bristly growth that has sprouted on his top lip. Curiously I find the spectacle of the man's preening to be engaging, and it comes almost as a surprise when he answers my question, as if the length of time between question and answer is immaterial, as if a thing can be picked up at any moment regardless of what happens in between. 'Well,' he begins, 'I suppose it's heroic enough according to its own lights, but what she says is that you can't have the heroic unless it is itself a step on the road towards something better. The thing is to send the paying public on its way with tears in its eyes and that feeling in its heart that he didn't die in vain. She is a woman who knows what will get the box office tills ringing.'

'Which is what exactly?'

'Which is by turning the film on its head and putting Kitty right there in the middle. She's to be the focal point, the pivot around which the whole lot of it revolves.'

'My mother?'

'Your mother, may God bless her departed soul.'

'I have never before thought of my mother as the centre of anything, not even of herself.'

'Ah well, what is a film for if not to cast a different light on the way we see the world? Anyway, look, the latest thinking is to begin the thing, not with the gulls wheeling in the mist over old Dundee, but instead with little baby Kitty's first appearance in a bustee somewhere, you know the blood and afterbirth and the floating sewage, all that stuff, with Parvati three quarters dead from her labour and herself, your mother-to-be, screaming her lungs out. That's the beginning and then we jump forward to your grandfather sitting upright in an armchair in a tenement flat in the Hilltown, blind and tapping the carpet in front of him with the end of his stick.'

'You mean, dead Stephen come back to life?'

'Yes, but he doesn't die. He comes close mind you, as you would if you shoot yourself in the head, but he doesn't. He recovers, thanks entirely to the devoted nursing he receives in a home for the convalescent in Calcutta, and there may be a further story in that, you know the nurse and all, but maybe not we'll have to see. Anyway, because of her, and because he's there so long getting what's left of his health back, the opium is cleared out of his system. This means that Angus can bring him and Kitty back to Dundee. It's there that we see Kitty growing up. She's a shy, drawn-in-on-herself sort of a girl, which is not surprising at all, who wouldn't be if you'd been through what she had? In spite of this she finds herself a husband who lasts just long enough to produce yourself, the son and heir, so that you and your grandfather can spend his last sunlit days together talking and fishing on the banks of the Tay, or whatever cosy old thing we can come up with.'

'While she's getting drunk and dealing drugs.'

'Not at all, Stephen,' he says, 'just keep in mind that there's the truth, whatever that may be, and then there's Hollywood, okay. Your mother does not do those things, well not the drugs anyway, at least I don't think she does.'

'What about India and all that made my grandfather what he became?'

'Your grandfather will relate the entire story, with you sitting there on his knee, your little ears pinned back soaking up every word while the film flashes over to the mill, Clive Street, Chinatown, the rooms in North Calcutta, the Sanskrit College hostel, all the old places.'

'So he's telling the story to me.'

'That's it, Stephen; so you can see the truth of how it was for him and how it was for your mother. But the twist here is that while he's telling you he's also trying to make sense of it for himself. It's their journey as much as it's yours.'

'I see.'

'In the last scene, you, your mother and the old fella take a boat down the Hooghly and as you pass the mills we understand from the softening of the lines cut around his old blind eyes that your grandfather has made his peace with all the things that were done to him and that he did to himself. We see your mother taking his wrinkled hand in her own and then reaching out for yours, the three of you, a family at last. Or something to that effect at least. What it's called is *closure*. It's the big thing in Hollywood.'

'Is that so?'

'It is.'

'And are you going to do it?'

'I thought I'd give it a try, why the blazes wouldn't I? Is the old fella going to mind, the further fifty years that I add to his life? Is she?'

'I suppose not, since they're dead.'

'There you are then,' says Séamus. 'Do you have an objection of your own?'

'Me? No, I don't think so.' I consider this for a moment. 'I am happy for them both. No reason not to give them a second chance.'

'That's the blessed thing indeed,' he says.

'Who's going to play Kitty?'

'We haven't got to that yet, though I'm thinking I should cast somebody, in my head that is. It won't do the writing any harm if I have the picture of a living actress in front of me when I'm putting our sweet words into your dead mother's mouth. At least it couldn't hurt, now could it.'

Séamus starts to throw out names—Penelope? Renée? Jennifer? Salma?—as if he knows the girls personally. As he conjures up these beautiful women, each one a good foot taller than himself, his hand crawls up his chest, over his chin, along the stubble of his sprouting moustache and up the rough channel between his ear and his eye. Eventually it reaches his hat, and it's in that moment when I see his fingers surprised by the wool and responding by trying to read it like Braille, that I suddenly realize I have warm feelings for the little fellow; for the statement the pair of them make, him and his ridiculous hat; for the composed manner in which they make it; for the floor that supports them, for the air that swirls above. The feeling borders on love, a sort of love.

53

A cloud lounges lazily in the otherwise cloudless sky while Julia shuffles in my arms and turns onto her back. She looks out over the sleeping crab-filled bay. Gold flickers on the top of the water and the distant sound of the screams of children up to their knees blend into other noises floating on the languid air: the buzz of flies, the beat of a bird's wing, the murmur of lovers, a wave slumping onto sand exhausted as a drunk. A summer day has come suddenly to St Andrews, but we have until two before the school takes over the bandstand, first item (so the notice says), *Mac the Knife*. Two is a long way away.

The cloud of egg white and cream drifts and stations itself between us and the sun. The world darkens and Julia, feeling a moment's cold, curls in towards me. 'So, Karṇa, his death, will you tell me?' she whispers sleepily.

'It came to war, inevitable war, two great armies lined up at Kurukshetra, brother against brother, cousins on either side, the final battle of the age. Karṇa commanded the Kauravas and cut great swathes through the ranks of the enemy.'

'Without his armour and his earrings?'

'Even without those. No warrior was greater than him.'

'But he died.'

'Yes.'

'How did he choose his end? In what way? Can Karṇa tell me?'

'I will do my best.' I cough. Julia expects me to cough: it is the necessary preface. She wriggles a couple of times to make herself comfortable.

'But first—did I mention it?—I have a son. In fact I had seven, but one remains, the one I love the most, Vṛṣasena. In plain view, Arjuna kills him. With four arrows he cuts off his arms and his head. My son falls, headless, armless, like a giant sal tree tumbling from the top of a mountain. As never before, I am scorched with grief, flooded with tears. *Vṛṣasenaṃ hataṃ dṛṣṭvā śokāmarṣasamanvitaḥ muktvā śokodbhavaṃ vāri netrābhyāṃ sahasā Vṛṣa.* My face twitches from side to side like a lunatic distraught. My eyes are red with loss and rage. I ache to be united on this battlefield with that bodiless head, his lips next to my lips, his blood and mine conjoined, a final kiss.

'I seek out Arjuna.

'I shoot ten arrows as one and each sinks into his body. I feel ten of his thump into my chest. Arjuna sends a canopy of arrows into the firmament, and as they turn down towards me, I, smiling, cut them off with arrows of my own and let loose a weapon which covers the earth and the ten points of the compass and the sun itself with its red heat: even my own body flares, and the sound of splintering fills the air as when a forest of bamboo ignites. Arjuna snuffs it out, this weapon of mine, so that clouds form from the quenched flames and the world goes dark. He releases other devices and he pierces me, all my limbs, while I pierce him: we bristle with quills like two porcupines and I laugh, wishing myself in no other place than where I am. My body is soaked in blood, but I am resplendent like the sun my father, I am crimson as the fiery dusk. Arrows issue from my bow by the thousands and, in return, I am pierced and pierced again.

'I reach for an arrow, one alone will succeed where all others have failed. I endow it with all my energy, it speeds from my bow, it blazes and divides the world into two halves: it carves a line in the air of the sort you see on the head of a woman who has parted her hair. It is well aimed, it is unstoppable. It speeds towards the point between the two eyes of Arjuna and will kill him. I stop and watch, forgetting again who it is that the gods favour. I see Kṛṣṇa pressing Arjuna's chariot into the earth so that my arrow passes over, striking only the jewel on his helmet. Ah, Kṛṣṇa, who vowed that, in this battle, he would do no more than drive Arjuna's high-stepping horses. The promises of gods! And now Arjuna's chariot rolls once more across the great plain of Kurukshetra;

and arrows come.

'I hear the soft voice of Death. "Look, Karṇa, your wheel." I look. My chariot is stuck, its wheel sunk deep, devoured by the Earth, as rooted as a sacred tree loaded with flowers. I jump down. I grab the axle with both hands and exert all my strength. I heave, I pull so hard that the ground itself rises up, but still my wheel will not release. It is stuck fast, unmoving, unmovable, and I understand that a stronger hand than mine has me in its grip.

'Arjuna, then, as I stand becalmed, takes from his quiver a weapon, *Anjalika*, measuring in length three cubits and six feet. It is besmeared with blood and flesh, and endued with the force of the thunder of the thousand-eyed Indra, his father. I feel hard pebbles borne on violent winds lashing my bleeding wounds. Dust swirls across my eyes. I hear *Anjalika* whispering...'

A seagull swoops down to the surface of the water, ruffles it and flaps skyward again. I imagine a fish I can't see being sucked slowly, inch by inch, into its stomach, as the bird flies on in search of more.

'That's it, the end,' I say, 'my story is done.'

She turns over and kisses me. 'So what now, Stephen?...Will I tell you the verdict of the women of Provideniye? Has the moment come?'

I lie back, reflecting on the nature of hidden things. 'A kiss is enough. As for your secrets, if they are to be mine, I will discover them for myself.'

She replies, clapping her hands: 'Stephen, you know what, there may be hope, even for you. But, tell me, where will you look?'

'You will guide me, little by little.'

'But the secrets of the women of Provideniye are hard to find. They are buried deep and their hiding place is carefully guarded.'

'I know,' I say. '*Provideniyestrinām tattvaṃ nihitaṃ guhāyām.* The secrets of the women of Provideniye are hidden in a cave. I am hoping you will lead me to the entrance.'

Julia laughs as the sun shines on her face. 'Perhaps, who can say, but right now we are in a public place.'

'So we are.'

We take in the sun and the beach and the birds and the day. Then Julia, letting a handful of sand trickle through her fingers, says: 'So, Stephen, if the story of Karṇa had not started with his mother and her breasts, you see I remember, could there have been other beginnings?'

'It could have begun with a king and a shower of sperm.'

'Yes,' murmurs Julia, 'now that is how to begin a story.'

'The king was walking in the woods. It was spring. The frangipani, the magnolia and the sandalwood were in fragrant blossom. The forest was maddened by the sweet notes of the kokila and was humming with the singing of bees. The king lay down, half sleeping, half aroused by the heady fragrance of the season and thought of his wife, the beautiful Girika. His seed spurted from him and was caught by a hawk. The hawk flew off but was attacked by another hawk: they fought, wings and beaks, and the seed fell into the waters of the Yamuna. There it was swallowed by a fish. Months later a fisherman caught the fish and found inside a tiny baby girl. She grew up beautiful and possessed of all the virtues, though she did smell, as fishes out of water do, of fish.'

Julia rolls away. 'I am pregnant,' she says, 'I am going to have our baby.'

My breath stops. My chest no longer moves. So I, who was once one, am now three. Is this a weight that will drag me to the bottom or the oxygen that will hold me up? Like a drowning, floating man, I grab at what is in reach. 'How do you know?' I ask.

'It has been twelve weeks since my last period. I know.' Tears edge up out of her eyes. 'You do not have to marry me, Stephen, I do not expect that, why should you, we have never talked about marriage. You do not even have to be with me unless you want to. I will bring him up on my own.'

Julia's hair falls in waves across her cheek, her eyes glisten with the moisture in them, her lips are red from the blood that is pumping, old blood and new. She has never looked more beautiful than now, in her pride.

I close my eyes, and through my lids come dots of orange sun and the face of a pink baby, its nose resting on mine, its eyes wide with questions. I see what it sees, and it sees what I see, a blurring of the self, the edges cut away. My lips open and weave in and out through the salt and seaweed air. 'Let's call him Stephen,' I say, 'it's not such a bad name.'

'And if it is a girl?'

'If it's a girl, Parvati.'

'Parvati was a goddess wasn't she? Tell me about her.'

'I'll tell you, but it's a long story.'

'I like long stories, didn't you know?'

'By the way,' I say, 'I've been doing some research. There are no polar bears in Provideniye.'

'Which Provideniye is that, Stephen? Do you imagine only one?'

References

Julia's Icelandic in Chapter 1 is the first stanza of *Hávamál*, one of the poems of the Poetic Edda (MS Codex Regius 2365 4to), a collection of anonymous Old Norse-Icelandic poems.

Stephen's reference to a person the size of a thumb in Chapter 4 is from the Katha Upanishad 4.12.

The boss Hindi in Chapter 19 is from *Colloquial Hindustani for Jute Mills and Workshops*, Mohiuddin Ahmad, published by the author, Calcutta, 1947.

The incomprehensible sound stream rising from Seamus's larynx (also Chapter 19) is from *Ulysses*, James Joyce, (Bodley Head, 1960, pp. 397-398).

GyreOgyreOgyrotundO (Chapter 25) is from The Restored *Finnegans Wake*, James Joyce, (Penguin Classics, 2012, p. 228).

The Sanskrit quotes throughout are from the *Mahabhárata*, the Sanskrit (romanized) version with English translation from the Clay Sanskrit Library, (New York University Press and the JJC Foundation). The one exception is, '*Provideniyestrinām tattvaṃ nihitaṃ guhāyām*' (Chapter 53), which is a concocted amalgam by Vaughan Pilikian.

'*I was the shadow...*' (Chapter 41) is from *Pale Fire*, Vladimir Nabokov, (Penguin, 1973, p. 29).

Other sources

In researching the jute industry and the conditions of its employees, I found the following useful:

Basu, Subho, *Does Class Matter?—Colonial Capital and Workers Resistance in Bengal 1890-1937*, Oxford University Press, 2004.

Chakrabarty, Dipesh, *Rethinking Working-Class History*, Princeton University Press, 1989.

Chattopadhyay and Chaturvedi, How Jute Workers Live, Science and Culture, Vol XII, no. 8, 1947.

Cox, Tony, *Paternal Despotism and Workers Resistance in the Bengal Jute Industry 1920-40*, PhD Thesis, Cambridge, 1999.

Fraser, Eugenie, *A Home by the Hooghly*, Mainstream, 1989.

Ghosh, Parimal, *Colonialism, Class and a History of the Calcutta Jute Millhands 1880-1930*, Sangam Books, 2000.

Gordon, Eleanor, *Women and the Labour Movement in Scotland 1850-1914*, Clarendon Press, 1991.

Harrison, Godfrey, *Bird and Company of Calcutta, a History*, Anna Art Press, 1964.

Karnik, VB, *Strikes in India*, Manaktalas, Bombay, 1967. Ludlow Mfr Assoc, *Jute; an account of its growth and manufacture*, 1928.

Read, Margaret, *The Indian Peasant Uprooted*, Longmans Green, 1931.

Report of the Royal Commission on Labour in India, vol. V and XI, London 1931.

Sen, Samita, *Women and Labour in Late Colonial India: the Bengal Jute Industry*, Cambridge University Press, 1991.

Stewart, Gordon, *Jute and Empire*, Manchester University Press, 1998.

Tomlinson, BR, *Colonial Firms and the Decline of Colonialism in Eastern India 1914-47*, Modern Asian Studies, vol. 15, no. 3, 1981.

Wallace, DR, *The Romance of Jute*, W Thacker & Co, 1927. The Verdant Works (Jute) Museum, Dundee.

Acknowledgements

Grateful thanks to the School of Asian Studies at the University of Edinburgh for letting me sit in on their Mahabhárata tutorials, to Simon Brodbeck, my most generous and expert tutor, who helped me to unravel (as far as unravelling is possible) some of the mysteries of that wonderful text in which Karṇa is, of course, the much derided hero, and to Vaughan Pilikian, a Sanskritist with few equals, whose playful understanding of the language has been of enormous help.

Thanks also to Samita Sen for her generosity in sharing her knowledge of old Calcutta and the jute, to K.K. Sonthalia for revealing some of the secrets of the Naihati jute mill, and to Somnath Muckerpadhahy, Gautam Ukil, Gopal Chaudury, Indevir Juneja and Tony Cox.

Many people have provided me with the little (and not so little) details that make all the difference: Alec and Moya Crawford, Jimmy Ferguson, Trevor Royle, Chris Hardwicke, Charles Jackson, Denise Dyer, David O'Brien, Charles MacGregor, Julian James, Rasa Ruseckiene and Roger McStravick. My thanks to them all.

Special thanks to all those who've helped me wrestle with and, hopefully, resolve some of the conundrums of the early drafts (of which there've been plenty): Christopher Rathbone, Peter de Wolfe, Leticia Eyheragaray, Jennie Rutherford, Richard Walsh, Ashley Stokes, Charles Boyle, Charles Palliser, Julio Martino, Antonia Brown, Richard Walsh, Andy Duff, Natasha, Anna and Andrew. Most particular special thanks to Madeleine who, as always, has been my best and most sympathetic critic.

About the Author

Michael Tobert has, for many years, had a deep interest in India; as a visitor, as a student of its history and as a writer. Besides Karna's Wheel, he has written Travels in an Ambassador – a bumpy ride round Northern India, and The Mating Call of the Racket-tailed Drongo. His other books are Cryptogram and Pilgrims in the Rough.

For more, please visit www.michaeltobertbooks.com

Printed in Great Britain
by Amazon